Beyond Good Teaching

Advancing Mathematics Education for ELLs

Edited by
Sylvia Celedón-Pattichis
University of New Mexico
Albuquerque, New Mexico

and
Nora G. Ramirez
Nora G. Ramirez Consulting
Tempe, Arizona

 NCTM | NATIONAL COUNCIL OF
TEACHERS OF MATHEMATICS

www.nctm.org/more4u
Access code: ELL14118

Copyright © 2012 by
The National Council of Teachers of Mathematics, Inc.
1906 Association Drive, Reston, VA 20191-1502
(703) 620-9840; (800) 235-7566; www.nctm.org
All rights reserved

Library of Congress Cataloging-in-Publication Data

Beyond good teaching : advancing mathematics education for ELLs / edited
by Sylvia Celedón-Pattichis, Nora G. Ramirez.
    p. cm.
 ISBN 978-0-87353-688-2
 1. Mathematics--Study and teaching--Foreign speakers. 2.
Communication in education. I. Celedón-Pattichis, Sylvia. II. Ramirez,
Nora G.
 QA11.2.B494 2012
 510.71'273--dc23

                              2011053460

The National Council of Teachers of Mathematics advocates for high-quality mathematics
teaching and learning for each and every student.

Printed in the United States of America

Contents

Chapter 1

Thoughts, Stories, and *Consejos* (Advice) from ELLs and Their Educators 5

by Sylvia Celedón-Pattichis, University of New Mexico, Albuquerque, New Mexico
Nora G. Ramirez, Nora G. Ramirez Consulting, Tempe, Arizona

Chapter 2

Second Language Development and Implications for the Mathematics Classroom 19

by Nora G. Ramirez, Nora G. Ramirez Consulting, Tempe, Arizona
Sylvia Celedón-Pattichis, University of New Mexico, Albuquerque, New Mexico

Chapter 3

Language and Learning: A Conceptual Design from an Apache Perspective 39

by Rea Goklish, John F. Kennedy K–8 School, Cedar Creek, Arizona

Chapter 4
Elements of an Effective Mathematics Community for ELLs 47

by Sylvia Celedón-Pattichis, University of New Mexico, Albuquerque, New Mexico
Nora G. Ramirez, Nora G. Ramirez Consulting, Tempe, Arizona

Chapter 5
Cases of Practice: Teaching Mathematics to ELLs in Elementary School 55

by Sylvia Celedón-Pattichis, University of New Mexico, Albuquerque, New Mexico
Erin Turner, University of Arizona, Tucson, Arizona

by Cathy Kinzer, New Mexico State University, Las Cruces, New Mexico
Maricela Rincón, Monte Vista Elementary School, Las Cruces, New Mexico
as told by Maricela Rincón

Chapter 7

by Marta Civil, University of North Carolina, Chapel Hill, North Carolina
José María Menéndez, Pima Community College, Tucson, Arizona

Chapter 8

by Richard Kitchen, University of New Mexico, Albuquerque, New Mexico
Laura Burr, University of New Mexico, Albuquerque, New Mexico
Libni B. Castellón, Universidad Pedagógica Nacional Francisco Morazán, Tegucigalpa, Honduras

by Anthony Fernandes, University of North Carolina–Charlotte, Charlotte, North Carolina

by María Martiniello, Educational Testing Service, Princeton, New Jersey

Chapter 9

by Mark Driscoll, EDC, Newton, Massachusetts
Daniel Heck, Horizon Research, Chapel Hill, North Carolina
Kristen Malzahn, Horizon Research, Chapel Hill, North Carolina

Chapter 10

by Julia M. Aguirre, University of Washington–Tacoma, Tacoma, Washington
George C. Bunch, University of California–Santa Cruz, Santa Cruz, California

Chapter 11

The Language Demands of Word Problems for English Language Learners 195

by Luciana C. de Oliveira, Purdue University, West Lafayette, Indiana

Chapter 12

Analyzing Effective Mathematics Lessons for English Learners: A Multiple Mathematical Lens Approach 207

by Julia M. Aguirre, University of Washington–Tacoma, Tacoma, Washington
Erin E. Turner, University of Arizona, Tucson, Arizona
Tonya Gau Bartell, University of Delaware, Newark, Delaware
Corey Drake, Iowa State University, Ames, Iowa
Mary Q. Foote, Queens College, City University of New York, Flushing, New York
Amy Roth McDuffie, Washington State University–Tri-Cities, Richland, Washington

Accompanying Materials at More4U

Chapter 1

Chapter 1 Reflections (graphic organizer)

Senior ELLs' Prezi Presentation (link to Web-based presentation)

Chapter 2

Bridging the Language Barrier in Mathematics (journal article)

Mathematical Notation Comparisons between U.S. and Latin American Countries (chart)

Mathematical Notations and Procedures of Recent Immigrant Students (journal article)

Mathematics Homonyms and Homophones (chart)

Professional Teaching Standards—Discourse (expectations)

Chapter 3

(No accompanying materials at More4U)

Chapter 4

Those Kids! (journal article)

Chapter 5

Case 1

Kinder Study Prediction (worksheet)

Kinder Study Results (table)

ELL as a Competent Problem Solver (video clip)

Storytelling—Partitive Division (video clip)

Case 2

Fractions Lesson (Beginning) (video clip)

Fractions Lesson (Group Work) (video clip)

Decomposing 1 Valerie (video clip)

Decomposing 2 Georgieann (video clip)

Case 3

Number Line Prior Knowledge (video clip)

Chapter 12

Learning Lens (template)

Power and Participation Lens (template)

Task Lens (template)

Teaching Lens (template)

Chapter 13

Lesson in Portuguese (video)

Triangle Lesson (video)

Reflections on Teaching Perimeter (first-person notes)

Fractions on a Number Line (video)

Arrays: A Collaboratively Planned Lesson (first-person account)

TODOS LIVE! Presentations

TODOS Teaching English Learners Mathematics (TELM) Resources:

Introduction to TELM (PowerPoint presentation)

TELM Participant Agenda (template)

TELM Agenda for December 6, 2007 (sample)

TELM Overall Goal and Plan (sample)

Planning a Mathematics Lesson for ELLs (worksheet template)

NCSM Position Paper on Teaching Math to ELLs

Online Resources (list)

Foreword

As the population of English language learners (ELLs) increases in U.S. public schools, so do concerns about the needs of these students in mathematics classrooms. Although language issues are important to consider in *all* mathematics classrooms, issues of language are crucial for students who are learning English. Two issues are *specific* to ELLs. First, the label "English language learner," as currently used in the United States, has many meanings. Too often the label is not based on objective criteria, does not reflect sound classifications, and is not comparable across states or classrooms. Sometimes it is used as a proxy for other demographic labels (for example, in place of "Latino/a" or "Hispanic"), rather than as an accurate descriptor of students who are learning English (Gándara and Contreras 2009). Second, language proficiency is a complex construct that reflects proficiency in multiple contexts, modes, and academic disciplines. Current measures of language proficiency may not accurately reflect an individual's language competence. In particular, we do not have measures or assessments for language proficiency related to competence in mathematics for different ages or for different mathematical topics. These two issues, the use of the label "English language learner" and the complexities of language proficiency, can bring confusion into discussions of mathematics instruction for students who are learning English. Thus, instructional decisions should not be made solely on the basis of the label "English language learner." This label can also be replaced by the label "students who are bilingual" to emphasize *what students know* instead of what they don't know—English.

We might imagine that the solution to the "problem" of mathematics instruction for English language learners involves a quick fix: new manuals for teachers, a new piece of software, a new teaching method, and so on. Unfortunately, such solutions risk reinforcing myths about language, about how we learn a second language, and about how we learn mathematics. It is important that recommendations for teaching practices be based on research, rather than on myths. A commitment to improving mathematics learning for all students—and especially for students who are learning English— requires that recommendations for teaching practice be based on research.

It is difficult to make generalizations about the instructional needs of all students who are learning English. Specific information about students' previous instructional experiences in mathematics is crucial for understanding how bilingual learners communicate in mathematics classrooms. Classroom instruction should be informed by knowledge of students' experiences with mathematics instruction, their language history, and their educational background. In addition to knowing the details of students' experiences, research suggests that high-quality instruction that supports ELLs' achievement has two general characteristics: a view of language as a resource, rather than a deficiency; and an emphasis on academic achievement, not only on learning English (Gándara and Contreras 2009).

Research provides general guidelines for instruction for this student population. Overall, students who are labeled as ELL, who are learning English, or who are bilingual are from non-dominant communities, and they need access to curricula, instruction, and teachers proven to be effective in supporting their academic success. In general, such environments require that curricula provide "abundant and diverse opportunities for speaking, listening, reading, and writing" and that instruction "encourage students to take risks, construct meaning, and seek reinterpretations of knowledge within compatible social contexts" (Garcia and Gonzalez 1995, p. 424). Teachers with documented success with students from non-dominant communities share some characteristics, including (a) a high commitment to students' academic success and to student-home communication, (b) high expectations for all students, (c) the autonomy to change curriculum and instruction to meet the specific needs of students, and (d) a rejection of models of their students as intellectually disadvantaged.

As a first step, mathematics instruction for ELLs should follow the general recommendations for high-quality mathematics instruction and teaching mathematics for understanding. According to a recent review of the research literature in mathematics education (Hiebert and Grouws 2007), teaching that makes a difference in student achievement and promotes conceptual understanding in mathematics has two central features: (1) teachers and students attend explicitly to connections and concepts and (2) teachers give students the time to wrestle with important mathematics. One way for teachers to ensure that their students wrestle with important mathematics is to choose, set, and maintain mathematical tasks at a high level of cognitive demand—for example, by encouraging students to explain their problem solving and reasoning (American Educational Research Association 2006; 2000; Stein, Grover, and Henningsen 1996).

Research that is specific to English language learners offers two fundamental principles for teaching mathematics to ELLs (Moschkovich 2010) that go beyond the first step of teaching for understanding:

1. **Treat students' language as a resource, not a deficit.** Treating students' home language, everyday ways of talking, and emergent mathematical discourse as resources, not obstacles, for doing mathematics will provide more opportunities for English language learners to learn mathematics. By learning to recognize how ELLs express their mathematical ideas as they learn English, teachers can maintain a focus on mathematical reasoning as well as on language development. Instruction can draw on the many resources available in classrooms—such as objects, drawings, graphs, and gestures—as well as home languages, everyday meanings for words or phrases, and experiences outside school.

2. **Address much more than vocabulary and support ELLs' participation in mathematical discussions as they learn English.** Instruction for this population should not emphasize low-level language skills but instead provide opportunities to actively communicate about mathematical ideas. One goal of mathematics instruction for English language learners should be to support all students, regardless of their proficiency in English, in participating in discussions that focus on important mathematical concepts and reasoning, rather than on accurate pronunciation, vocabulary, or low-level linguistic skills.

Implementing these principles can be a challenge, especially without classroom-based examples. This new book addresses the urgent need for such examples to guide and support the practices of teachers in mathematics classrooms with English language learners. The cases provided here show multiple ways that instruction can create opportunities for mathematical reasoning and support ELLs in learning to communicate their reasoning. This volume does not offer recipes for teaching or point to quick fixes. Instead, the cases that it presents can help teachers to develop their own approaches to supporting mathematical reasoning and sense making for students who are learning English.

Judit N. Moschkovich
University of California, Santa Cruz

References

American Educational Research Association. "Do the Math: Cognitive Demand Makes a Difference." *Research Points* 4, no. 2 (2006).

Gándara, Patricia, and Frances Contreras. *The Latino Education Crisis: The Consequences of Failed Social Policies.* Cambridge, Mass.: Harvard University Press, 2009.

Garcia, Eugene E., and Rene Gonzalez. "Issues in Systemic Reform for Culturally and Linguistically Diverse Students." *Teachers College Record* 96 (Spring 1995): 418–31.

Hiebert, James, and Douglas A. Grouws. "The Effects of Classroom Mathematics Teaching on Students' Learning." In *Second Handbook of Research on Mathematics Teaching and Learning,* edited by Frank K. Lester, pp. 371–404. Reston, Va.: National Council of Teachers of Mathematics, 2007.

Moschkovich, Judit N. *Language and Mathematics Education: Multiple Perspectives and Directions for Research.* Charlotte, N.C.: Information Age Publishing, 2010.

Stein, Mary Kay, Barbara Grover, and Marjorie Henningsen. "Building Student Capacity for Mathematical Thinking and Reasoning: An Analysis of Mathematical Tasks Used in Reform Classrooms." *American Educational Research Journal* 33 (Summer 1996): 455–88.

Preface

In keeping with its commitment to equity and meeting the needs of all students, the National Council of Teachers of Mathematics (NCTM) asked us to write a book that would focus specifically on the needs of English language learners (ELLs). We would like to thank NCTM's Educational Materials Committee for recognizing the need for this book, for inviting us to write it, and for giving us the freedom to present a vision. The intent was to develop a resource that would be useful for mathematics teachers, coaches, and professional developers. In our journey to fulfill this task, we drew on the talents and expertise of several people who are committed to the mathematics education of ELLs.

We would like to acknowledge the following authors for sharing their experiences as ELLs or as teachers of ELLs and contributing to different chapters and resources available at www.nctm.org/more4u: the students in Rebecca Merkel's class, Iroquois High School, Jefferson County Public Schools, Louisville, Kentucky; Jae-won Jang; Seung-eun Jang; Eddie Mosqueda; Elsa Medina; Edna Alvarado; Bob McDonald; Matthew Winsor; Erin Salazar; Victoria Enoch; Andrew Hutchinson; Elmano Costa; and the leadership of TODOS: Mathematics for All.

Several people were particularly generous with their time in providing feedback. We would like to give deep thanks to Chris Confer, Kathryn B. Chval, Lena L. Khisty, Melissa Hosten, Bob McDonald, and Matthew Winsor, as well as NCTM publications staff members Myrna Jacobs and Anita Draper.

We especially want to thank Cathy Kinzer, the classroom teachers David Lee Ubinger, Maricela Rincon, Ricardo Rincon, Jana Ward, and the students in these classes. Cathy worked diligently to provide video clips of best practices for teaching mathematics to ELLs. We want to thank the teachers for opening up their classrooms and sharing their practice so that we can make a difference in the mathematics education of ELLs.

Finally, we would like to thank Ernesto Ramirez Jr. for his patience and the laughter he brought to our go-to meetings, as well as the other members of the Ramirez family for their patience and support through the many "Mom is in the hole" hours. Marios, Rebecca, and Antonia Pattichis were always patient and encouraging. Sylvia's parents, Valerio Celedón and Antonia Vela Celedón, always provided the moral and spiritual support needed to complete the book. The Pattichis and Panayides families, as well as Klea Christodoulou, provided much-needed support during the final stages. We also thank our many colleagues, from teachers to researchers, who have dedicated their work to teaching ELLs and who have helped us grow professionally to give us the capacity to complete this task.

Introduction

Although various terms have been used to describe students who are learning English as a second language, such as *limited English proficient students* (LEPs), those of us who view language as a basic human right prefer the designation *English language learners* (ELLs). We view the students' native language and their culture as valuable assets that they bring to the mathematics classroom.

Status of ELLs in the United States

English language learners come from other countries, but they are also born in the United States. The National Clearinghouse for English Language Acquisition (NCELA 2010) documented approximately 5.3 million ELLs in the United States in 2008, with a growth of 53.25 percent from 1997–1998 to 2007–2008. Some states have experienced a higher concentration of ELLs than others. For example, according to Payán and Nettles (2008), although ELLs live throughout the United States, the states with the highest numbers of ELLs are Arizona, Texas, Florida, New York, California, and Illinois. In the past decade, some states have experienced dramatic growth in numbers of ELLs. Alabama, Kentucky, Indiana, Tennessee, North Carolina, South Carolina, and Nebraska have seen growth of 300 percent or higher from 1995 to 2005.

According to the U.S. Census, in 2008 80 percent of the total population spoke English-only in the home, while 20 percent of the population spoke a language other than English at home. Of those who did not speak English-only at home, 62 percent spoke Spanish; 4.4 percent, Chinese; 2.4 percent, French; 2 percent, German; 1.9 percent, Korean; 2.2 percent, Vietnamese; and 2.7 percent, Tagalog. In 2001–2002, ELLs in the United States spoke more than 450 languages (Payán and Nettles 2008). The top five languages with the highest number of speakers were Spanish, with 79.05 percent; Vietnamese, with 1.95 percent; Hmong, with 1.56 percent; Chinese, with 1.02 percent; and Korean, with 0.97 percent.

Collectively, the data point to the need to address the growing population of ELLs in all regions of the United States. Thus, all educators should be knowledgeable about the emotional and cognitive demands of students who are engaged in learning mathematics while learning English. According to the National Council of Teachers of Mathematics (NCTM) (2008), "Changing demographics are reshaping our schools, but approaches to instruction and the time allotted for learning have not always changed quickly enough to keep pace." Thus, this book is intended to address the mathematics instruction of ELLs.

Purpose of the Book

This book emphasizes that effective practices for teaching ELLs go beyond what many call "good teaching." These practices expand what we know about good teaching because they specifically address the language demands of students who are developing skill in listening, speaking, reading, and writing in a second language while learning mathematics. A challenge that teachers constantly face is ensuring that the mathematical tasks that they pose to students are both challenging and accessible to ELLs. To meet this challenge, teachers need a multitude of strategies. As we wrote this book, we constantly asked ourselves the following two questions:

1. How are these strategies different from just teaching mathematics to non-ELL students?
2. How will the work of identifying and understanding these strategies be useful to practitioners, coaches, and professional developers?

Overview of the Book

In chapter 1, we open the book with stories of ELLs and teachers of ELLs. In chapter 2, we describe ELLs at different levels of English proficiency so that teachers can be aware of different needs and can take action to teach language while they teach mathematics. In addition, we present specific "teacher actions" and instructional strategies that can help address particular needs. The cognitive demands on ELLs at advanced levels of mathematics are emphasized in chapter 3. We discuss aspects of creating environments conducive to learning mathematics for ELLs in chapter 4. Chapters 5 and 6 present cases of practice that exemplify the points in chapter 2 for elementary and secondary levels, respectively. Parents' insights on educating ELLs are critical, and we address those in chapter 7. Assessments play an important role in observing and learning about ELLs' mathematics understanding. The three cases presented in chapter 8 address different forms of assessment. A middle school vignette lays the foundation for instructional principles and a framework for designing a mathematics lesson in chapter 9. A planning tool is presented in chapter 10 for mathematics instruction that addresses reading, writing, listening, speaking, and representing. An analysis of the language demands of mathematics word problems is described in chapter 11. A multiple mathematics lens approach is featured in chapter 12 to help teachers analyze their lessons. Chapter 13, the final chapter, shares additional ideas, lessons, and resources that can aid in professional development.

How to Navigate the Book

The design of this book is interactive and requires the reader to move back and forth between the chapters and online resources at www.nctm.org/more4u (the access code appears on the title page of the book). Occasionally, we ask the reader to stop and reflect before reading further in a chapter. At other times, we ask the reader to view video clips of teaching practices for ELLs or to refer to graphic organizers, observation and analysis protocols, links to resources, and other supplementary materials. We also encourage the reader to use this resource in professional development.

References

National Clearinghouse for English Language Acquisition (NCELA). *The Growing Number of English Language Learners*. Washington, D.C.: U.S. Department of Education, 2010. http://www.ncela.gwu.edu/files/uploads/9/growingLEP_0809.pdf.

National Council of Teachers of Mathematics (NCTM). *Teaching Mathematics to English Language Learners*. NCTM Position Statement. Reston, Va.: NCTM, 2008. http://www.nctm.org/about/content.aspx?id=16135.

Payán, Rose M., and Michael T. Nettles. "Current State of English-Language Learners in the U.S. K–12 Student Population." Introduction ETS Research and Assessment. Princeton, N.J.: Educational Testing Service, 2008. http://www.ets.org/Media/Conferences_and_Events/pdf/ELLsympsium/ELL_factsheet.pdf.

U.S. Census Bureau. *Nativity by Language Spoken at Home by Ability to Speak English for the Population 5 Years and Over*. American Community Survey, C16005. Washington, D.C.: U.S. Department of Commerce, 2008. http://factfinder.census.gov.

Thoughts, Stories, and *Consejos* (Advice) from ELLs and Their Educators

by Sylvia Celedón-Pattichis and Nora G. Ramirez

more**4**u
- Chapter 1 Reflections (graphic organizer)
- Senior ELLs' Prezi Presentation (link to Web-based presentation)

We send you on your journey through this book by sharing with you the thoughts and experiences of English language learners (ELLs) and their teachers in K–12 classrooms. The term *English language learners* refers to students who are learning English as a second language. Our intent in sharing these excerpts is to give you some understanding of what ELLs think, feel, observe, and recommend regarding better ways to address their needs. In addition, we share with you the insights of some mathematics teachers about teaching ELLs. We invite you to engage with this chapter interactively, and we have placed a graphic organizer at www.nctm.org/more4u to guide you in reflecting as you read.

Voices of High School English Language Learners

The comments in figure 1.1 are from a Prezi presentation developed by a group of high school ELLs. Prezi is a Web-based presentation application; the Prezi presentation that we are discussing, "A Change Is A Comin," is the work of senior ELLs in Rebecca Merkel's class at Iroquois High School, Jefferson County Public Schools, Louisville, Kentucky. Although the students' comments are not specific to mathematics, their observations, feelings, and recommendations are profound.

What ELLs Observe	How ELLs Respond
Teachers think they are saving us an embarrassment by not calling on us.	But not calling on us makes us feel invisible.
Teachers think they are doing us a favor by always grouping us together.	We like to work together, BUT WE NEED to work with all of our classmates.
Teachers avoid conflicts by ignoring students who tease us.	I can't ignore teasing. Address it.
Teachers give us identical assignments instead of accommodations for our needs.	We need accommodations to help us meet YOUR targets.
Teachers assume that when we don't raise our hands this means we don't need help. They also presume that help means translation.	We need your help—which can mean giving an example, explaining the question, defining the word, etc.

Fig. 1.1. Comments of senior ELLs in a Prezi presentation

The chart in figure 1.2 is taken from the students' presentation, which they introduced with the words, "We want acceptance and tolerance."

Reflection 1.1

Figure 1.1 shows the thoughts of students who have experienced the school life of an ELL.

What are your initial reactions? Are there implications that you can address immediately in your role as an educator?

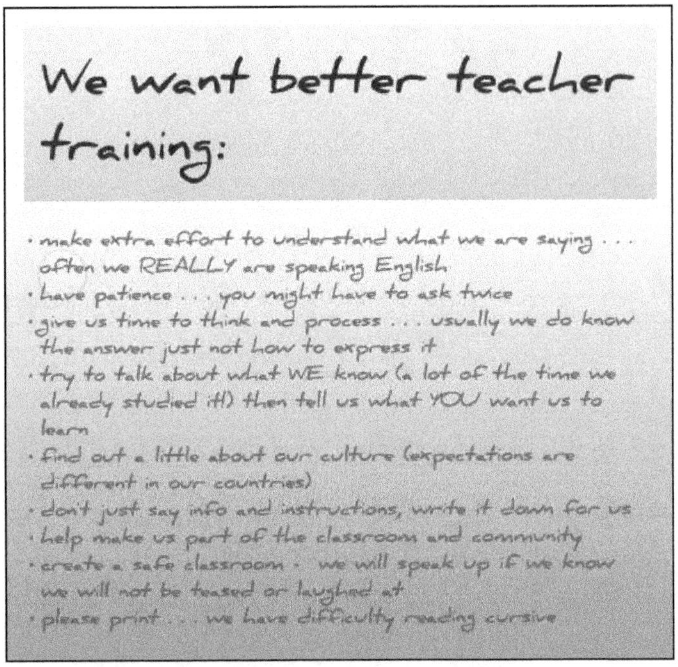
We want better teacher training:
• make extra effort to understand what we are saying . . . often we REALLY are speaking English
• have patience . . . you might have to ask twice
• give us time to think and process . . . usually we do know the answer just not how to express it
• try to talk about what WE know (a lot of the time we already studied it!) then tell us what YOU want us to learn
• find out a little about our culture (expectations are different in our countries)
• don't just say info and instructions, write it down for us
• help make us part of the classroom and community
• create a safe classroom - we will speak up if we know we will not be teased or laughed at
• please print . . . we have difficulty reading cursive

Fig. 1.2. Thoughts of senior ELLs from Rebecca Merkel's class, Iroquois High School, Jefferson County Public Schools, Louisville, Kentucky

Voices of College Students Reflecting on Their K–12 Classroom Experiences

Learning what college students say in looking back on their earlier experiences as ELLs in American classrooms can provide special insight. Consider the following perceptions of two Asian American students.

Reflection 1.2

Our role as teachers includes teaching English, even when our focus is mathematics.

How do you teach ELLs to listen, read, write, and speak in English without neglecting the mathematics but teaching it simultaneously?

Jae-won Jang

When I first came to America, I really did not expect anything to be too different than before. The only things I knew that were going to be different were that I would be seeing Americans walking around and most of them would only speak English. Well, I could never have been more wrong. First of all, one thing that surprised me was how school worked. Because the school year in America and South Korea have different start and end times, I happened to end up going to school during second semester of fifth-grade elementary school when I had just finished fourth grade in South Korea. If that was not strange enough, I also found out that in America, most elementary schools end after fifth grade, unlike in South Korea, which finishes at sixth grade. So those were things that surprised me initially; then, when I started attending school, communication and a difference in culture caused me real problems.

At first I really didn't worry too much about not having knowledge of the English language before coming to the United States because I thought, "Oh, everything will

Reflection 1.3

ELLs new to a school may arrive with a robust knowledge of mathematics.

Have you ever experienced this? If so, what has worked or not worked in your classroom? Based on this fact, what implications are there for you in your position?

work out somehow," but I was careless. Because my English skills were at a kindergarten level, I basically did not speak at all for the first few weeks. During that time, my homeroom teacher tried to communicate with me using a book that had English words translated into Korean, and that worked to some degree, but even so, that did not teach me how to speak nor how to write. The only thing that was beneficial from that experience was I could understand English if it related to an object. Throughout my entire fifth grade, the only class I was able to participate in was mathematics. Since mathematics was something that did not require a lot of English skill, I was able to solve all mathematics problems without any difficulties. While learning mathematics, I also noticed that the stuff kids were learning was what I had already learned when I was in third grade in South Korea. So when I was able to do the problems, the kids were surprised since I knew everything without understanding a single thing that the teacher said. If I remember correctly, there were some projects for other courses that were given throughout the semester, but, of course, I did not do any of those projects due to my lack of English skills. So basically I should have gotten Fs for all of my classes besides mathematics, but the teacher gave me Cs for all of the other courses. I thought the teacher was being thoughtful because of my English skills.

So in the end, throughout my fifth grade, I did not learn anything about English from the teacher; how I was able to learn English, I believe, is through experience. Throughout my fifth grade, none of my teachers ever actually tried to teach me English, and they were satisfied communicating with me using a Korean book of translations. The way I learned English, I suppose, is that I tried to remember what people said in certain situations and then mimic what they were saying without knowing what it actually meant. For example, I remember when I was standing in the lunch line, I saw a kid asking, "Can I have that?" to the lunch lady while pointing to something, and I remembered what he said and thought if I say something like "Can I have that" and then point at the certain object, that would mean I'm asking a person that "I want what I'm pointing at." So I didn't know the alphabet or any grammar, but I remembered sentences and learned English that way. This method of learning became a problem later when I tried to write in elementary school and had to write essays in middle school. For example, this one time in our class was supposed to be quiet time, but this one girl kept talking to me, and I was trying to tell her to be quiet, but I did not know any words for it. Then, I recalled someone was saying something that sounded like "shut up" to another person and the other person became quiet, so I was thinking that if I say something like that, it would make her be quiet. Because it was quiet time, I realized I couldn't speak, so I decided to write it down on paper with the alphabet and show it to her. With my alphabet book open, I wrote something that would match how "shut up" would sound (it was totally a wild guess). So I got to the point where I got "s h ( ) t u p" on paper, but then I didn't know what to put between the *h* and *t*. So I kept debating about which letter is supposed to go between *h* and *t*. During that time I did not know how the alphabet *u* sounded, and remembered seeing a word that had an *i* between *h* and *t*, so I inserted *i* trying to tell her to "shut up," but instead I basically told her to "shit up." This caused a huge misunderstanding. I made her cry, and I ended up getting into huge trouble with teachers, but this method overall gave me what I suppose was my "foundation" of English. So throughout fifth grade, the only course I was able to learn in was mathematics, and the only course I was able to learn through experience was English.

Reflection 1.4

ELLs often need tools to aid them in translations.

Are tools available in your school or classroom? How might you and your students gain access to these tools? Whom should you contact?

Reflection 1.5

According to the old saying, "A picture is worth a thousand words." This is true for all learning but imperative for the learning of ELL.

Do you have pictures and diagrams in your toolbox ready to use when teaching mathematics concepts for understanding? If not, how might you fill this toolbox?

Reflection 1.6

Although it might be difficult or almost impossible to assess all students in their native languages, what might be doable in your setting?

Seung-eun Jang

I was born in Seoul, South Korea. I attended elementary school in Seoul until I was ten years old; then I moved to the United States with my mother. Although I could not speak any English then, the elementary school I attended in the U.S. placed me at a fifth-grade level with students in the same age group.

My schedule consisted of taking the same classes and participating in the same activities as other students, but during the few months of adjustment I also had a tutor who taught me how to speak basic English. I recall that during the first six months of elementary school I carried around a small electronic dictionary, which I referred to often whenever I had conversations with my teacher or fellow students. I also pointed out objects and people, and drew diagrams to communicate and learn English, as well as the school material. My classroom teacher, Mr. Ruiz [pseudonym], also had an English-Korean dictionary, which he frequently used during my few months of adjustment at school. He referred back to the dictionary less often as I became more proficient at speaking English. I feel that Mr. Ruiz's effort to communicate with me helped me in many aspects of learning during my elementary school experience in the U.S. The dictionary I used not only helped me in learning English but also helped me in expressing my thoughts and ideas in mathematics and science, my favorite subjects.

Having confidence in my ability to reason in mathematics and science helped me adjust to a new school setting in the U.S. The learning pace in mathematics and science-related studies was faster in South Korea, so I was able to contribute more in those classes. For example, every week we were assigned to work on a multiplication activity, and I finished first most of the times. If any explanation was needed, I drew diagrams and pictures. Mr. Ruiz once asked the class, "Can anyone tell the class how water boils?" During this period of time, I was able to listen and comprehend English very well, but still had trouble expressing myself by using language. Because I had already learned the concept of boiling water in South Korea, I raised my hand. When Mr. Ruiz called me to answer, I walked up to the class to draw a pot of boiling water and arrows to demonstrate the flow of the heat and the foundational concepts of boiling water.

Learning elementary mathematics in South Korea and the U.S. were similar in some aspects, as both were composed of working and solving problems from a book and required some memorization. Just as it was in South Korea, in U.S. elementary school, I learned the same material and did as much work as other students, since there weren't any higher or lower levels of mathematics class until I was in middle school. Also in both countries, I had the same group of classmates for all of the subjects taken in elementary school.

The main differences were the way teachers taught mathematics in class. In South Korea, the teacher was always standing at the front of the class by the chalkboard, while the students worked independently facing the teacher. In the U.S., Mr. Ruiz was more interactive with his students and arranged the seats differently every once in a while. We also didn't have assigned seating in my U.S. elementary school.

As a learner of mathematics, I felt somewhat hindered in my ability to learn in my U.S. class. Since the learning pace was different, I had already learned the material a year before in elementary school in South Korea. However, I also feel that because of the edge that I had in mathematics, I had more time than I would have had to adjust to a new school as a foreign student. I wish that ESL mathematics classrooms would assess and consider foreign students' knowledge of subjects other than English. The students from foreign countries come from different backgrounds, so their knowledge of subjects such as mathematics and science may be behind or ahead of the rest of the class.

Voices of Adults Reflecting on Their ELL Experiences

The recollections of adults can help us extend our understanding of the experience of learning a new language and a new culture while attending school. Below we offer three adults' reflections.

Sylvia Celedón-Pattichis

I was born in Salineño, Texas, and raised in Miguel Alemán, Tamaulipas, Mexico—two small towns along the border—from birth to age 8. I went to elementary school up to third grade in Mexico. My parents obtained a visa to move to the United States in the mid-1970s. When we moved to California, I was placed in fourth grade; I was very fortunate that I was not placed in a lower grade level because I did not know English. When I first stepped on the school grounds in California, I remember distinctively the different ethnicities represented—Asian, Mexican American, African American, and others. In Mexico, I was used to seeing people who looked like me. I had to adapt to a new culture, a new language, and a new way of thinking about things in California.

My strengths were mathematics and Spanish. When I went to school in Mexico, I was exposed to fractions and problems involving different numbers and operations. In California, we were doing a lot of basic operations, and the mathematics content was not as challenging for me. However, I do recall not comprehending word problems when those were introduced without illustrations. I also remember learning English by listening to the teacher pronounce the words, and then I would repeat the words to myself, using inner speech and saying the words silently. To memorize the spelling of a word in English, I would sound out the word in Spanish. For example, if I saw the word "multiplication," I would say to myself "MUL-TI-PLI-CA-TION" in Spanish. This eventually helped me master the spelling tests we took each Friday in school.

Because I did not speak English, I was immediately assigned the label of "English as a second language" (ESL) student. This label followed me until ninth grade, when my ESL English teacher, Mrs. Barbara Osuna, gave me the opportunity to try a college prep English course. She was a true blessing in my life, and I still thank her for having made such a big difference in my life. Without that opportunity to try higher-level courses in English, my placement as an ESL student would have continued, as is the case for many English language learners in this country. This powerful move of changing my placement to an English college prep course not only afforded me the opportunity to enroll in higher-level mathematics courses and all other content areas, but it also opened doors for me to enroll in a university. By the time I was in ninth grade, I had a better command of English, but I would still make mistakes with verb tenses, especially those involving irregular verbs.

Mr. Sabas Osuna, the husband of Barbara Osuna, taught me pre-algebra in ninth grade and calculus in twelfth grade. He and other mathematics teachers have influenced my career path as a mathematics and bilingual teacher educator. Mr. Osuna *listened* to us and *cared* about us. At the same time, he kept the mathematics content at a very *challenging* level. I remember what was unique about Mr. Osuna's classes was that he would open

Reflection 1.7

Many ELLs don't look, talk, think, or act like the majority population.

What have you done or could you do to ease an ELLs' transition to a different school culture?

Reflection 1.8

As educators we must be aware of our pronunciation.

How might you be more cognizant of this on a daily basis?

Reflection 1.9

ELLs need advocates in schools.

Do you know your ELLs well enough to advocate for them?

Reflection 1.10

A caring teacher is concerned about students both mathematically and personally.

What actions do you take to show that you care about ELLs' development?

Reflection 1.11

Assignments for students need to be both mathematically meaningful and challenging.

How do you ensure that the tasks you assign to ELLs meet these criteria?

Reflection 1.12

The educational system can be difficult to understand or navigate.

What role do you take in forming relationships to guide families in gaining access to college?

Reflection 1.13

ELLs often come to the U.S. because parents want a better life for their children, even though this means leaving loved ones behind.

How do you acknowledge and address parents' interest in what is best for their children?

up the first few minutes of class to discuss any issues that were of concern to us. Many of my classmates were only 14 years old, and we were trying to figure out many things in life. He often offered us *consejos* (advice), and we all listened carefully to his advice. When he was ready to begin his mathematics lesson, we were then ready to listen to him and to engage in doing mathematics. Mr. Osuna asked us questions frequently throughout his mathematics lesson, making sure that we understood the content that was presented and offering examples of different ways or shortcuts to solve problems. He also set up games on Fridays to review the mathematics concepts that we had learned in a given week. His homework usually involved five problems that captured everything he wanted us to know from that day's lesson; these were very challenging problems.

Mr. Osuna's caring was evident throughout my high school years but especially my senior year. During that year, he continually asked me what I was planning to do in the future. I was enrolled in his calculus course, and I was unsure about what I would do. Being the oldest in my family and also having been part of my father's family *conjunto* (musical group), playing an instrument since the age of 9, I felt a responsibility to continue helping the family financially. Mr. Osuna often raised questions about the probability of our *conjunto* making it to the top and how life would be different if I attended a university. My father encouraged me to go to college, but his concern was not being able to afford paying for my college education. Mrs. Osuna, who was a financial aid counselor during my senior year, offered to help with that matter. Mr. Osuna visited my father at home and managed to convince him that it was OK to let me attend the University of Texas at Austin, where I obtained all of my degrees.

My high school years came before the publication of *Curriculum and Evaluation Standards for School Mathematics* (NCTM 1989) and *Principles and Standards for School Mathematics* (NCTM 2000). However, Mr. and Mrs. Osuna, as well as other teachers I had in school, were implementing some of the ideas represented in these Standards, frequently having the students explore why things work or not. So, three important qualities of a good teacher, for me, include caring for, listening to, and challenging students.

Eddie Mosqueda

My road to college was not predetermined by my family background nor any other form of privilege. I was born in Los Angeles, California, and am the son of Mexican-origin immigrants who worked very hard and for long hours for very little compensation. Like many other immigrants, my parents often talked about saving enough money so that one day, my family could return to Mexico to reunite with our extended family. When I was six years old, my parents decided it was time to fulfill their dream, so we relocated there.

In Mexico, I enrolled in school in the first grade. Although I had completed kindergarten in L.A. and was starting to learn English, it was in a Spanish-speaking context that I learned to read and write. My teacher in a small town in Michoacan, Mexico, had very high expectations for me and all of my classmates. In fact, I remember we had to learn our multiplication tables up to twelve times twelve. However, when I was halfway toward completing my second-grade education, my parents decided to return to the U.S. because they found it difficult to maintain financial stability in Mexico.

Upon my return to the U.S., I continued my education in the second grade. I was in an English-only context, so I had little to no understanding of what my teacher was saying. My elementary school had an English as a second language (ESL) pull-out program. So I would leave class to work with a language teacher on learning basic English words

Reflection 1.14

Non-ELLs have privileges that ELLs do not have.

Can you identify some of these privileges? How do you think these privileges affect the trajectory of ELLs' mathematical experiences?

Reflection 1.15

Often ELLs are pulled out of their classes to learn English.

What actions can you take to ensure that students have access to and gain an understanding of the mathematics content that they miss?

Reflection 1.16

What we do as educators can have lasting effects on students.

Do you continually observe and evaluate ELLs' strengths and take actions to give them opportunities that will enhance their mathematical experiences?

for about one hour per day. Although I felt that I was learning English, I often felt lost in class because I had missed out on what my classmates were learning while I was in ESL. Although learning English and content simultaneously was challenging for me in most content areas, I really enjoyed doing mathematics, particularly because the level of mathematics in the second grade focused on mathematics skills I had learned in the first grade in Mexico. As a result of my early arithmetic preparation in Mexico, I always did well in mathematics in the U.S.

Unlike my elementary school, where all of my peers were exposed to the same level of content, the middle school I attended tracked students into general or college-preparatory curriculum. I had been placed in the general track, along with most of the students from my elementary school. Toward the end of my seventh-grade year, my mathematics teacher insisted to the other mathematics teachers that I take the algebra readiness test. Because I earned a high score on the test, I was placed in algebra in the eighth grade, which, by default, moved me to the college-preparatory content courses.

Although academic tracking is a persistent source of inequity that typically disadvantages students with backgrounds similar to my own, I was one of the few Chicano beneficiaries of placement in the college-preparatory track in middle school and in high school, in spite of the fact that over 85 percent of the student population in the schools I attended was composed of Chicanos. Having the good fortune of being on the advantageous side of a mechanism that sorts students by "ability" was one of the primary reasons why I was able to attend college after graduating from high school. I also benefited from an outreach program sponsored through the University of California, Irvine (UCI), that sent undergraduate students to my high school to provide first-generation college students such as myself with information about meeting the prerequisites and guidance throughout the college application process.

As an undergraduate student at UCI, I was determined to make the most out of my opportunity to attain a college education. Although it initially wasn't clear to me what my career goal would be post graduation, my interests began to converge toward the end of my undergraduate years. I had worked every summer as a mentor and tutor with programs designed to prepare students of color for undergraduate majors in mathematics and science. Working in this capacity with undergraduate students allowed me to see how much I enjoyed teaching.

I always had my parents' unconditional support to study and do well in school. However, the high academic aspirations and expectations that my parents held for me were important but not sufficient to guarantee my success in high school. In fact, my family background, including my parents' level of formal education (my mother's fifth-grade and my father's first-grade formal education in Mexico), would indicate that I probably would not graduate from high school. I also credit the "head start" in mathematics that I received in Mexico for my success in school.

Elsa Medina

Have you ever been stressed out when you read the word *merry-go-round* or heard the word *else*? It was during a physics exam that I could not stop thinking about the word *merry-go-round;* I did not know its meaning, and it was on one of the questions. Because of this, I could not understand how to solve the problem. This was at a time when I was still learning English, and I was too embarrassed to ask the teacher about the meaning of the word. I came to the United States at the age of 17. As I was going to school, I had

Reflection 1.17

ELLs at beginning proficiency levels experience high levels of stress.

What linguistically sensitive actions do you take to engage ELLs in learning mathematics?

Reflection 1.18

Oral and written instructions are necessary for ELLs' comprehension and language acquisition.

What steps might you take to ensure that providing instructions both orally and in writing becomes a norm in your classroom?

Reflection 1.19

ELLs need time to process mathematical ideas in two languages.

How many different strategies do you have to give ELLs time to process information?

to sit in many classes where I did not understand a word the teacher was saying. What was worse, in many classes I was very stressed out thinking about the possibility that the teacher might call on me to answer a question. I remember many times I would panic when I heard teachers say the word *else* since my first name is Elsa and in English that word sounded to me very much like they were calling on me. To avoid having to speak in class as much as possible, I would sit in the back of the class and try not to make direct eye contact with the teacher. I never asked questions in class because I could not put a sentence together and also because most of the time I had given up trying to follow the instructor and resorted to taking notes and figuring things out at home with a dictionary or the help of a friend.

These feelings and experiences happened in most of my classes for a long time after coming to this country, but not in mathematics. I loved mathematics and still do. My mathematics classes were a safe haven for me because I could follow most of the lectures without understanding English. I knew when the teacher was solving equations, trying to find the point of intersection between curves, or integrating or differentiating a function, just to name a few, even if I did not understand all the phrases that teachers used as they performed these procedures. Of course, I had a lot of difficulty with word problems during exams, especially if there was no picture to help illustrate the situation. When it came to word problems, I had to resort to guessing what I was asked to do, given the context of what we had been doing, and usually I guessed correctly. I always wished the teachers in my mathematics classes, or in any other class, had written more of their instructions on the board to help me understand what I needed to do and to practice making sense of written instructions in class rather than waiting to see these instructions on exams.

For most people learning a second language, being able to read is easier than being able to speak. When we read, someone has already put the sentence structure in place to present ideas. When we speak, we have an idea that we want to communicate. This idea is probably in our native language and has to be translated, and we have to know how to put words together to make a sentence, to be able to pronounce the words correctly, and to do all of this within seconds. The mental requirement for speaking a new language is much higher than for reading in a new language. For this reason, I feel it would have been more helpful if my teachers had written complete sentences more often when presenting ideas in the classroom. But as I think back, I don't believe that many of my teachers even knew that I could not understand English, so why would they think of writing more to help someone like me? I don't think many knew of the stress levels I had just being in the classroom and the coping mechanisms I used to deal with that stress.

Understanding ELLs' Stories

The high school students from Rebecca Merkel's class have powerful messages for teachers regarding how they feel in class when a teacher makes certain moves. ELL students experience mixed emotions, including frustration, in the beginning stages of developing proficiency in a second language. The ESL seniors note the need for teachers to print rather than write in cursive. This is eye-opening for many of us in relation to the complexity of learning a new language and new content. The already demanding task of learning to read a new language is made even more complex by the need to read it in two different forms, printed and cursive. The type in all the textbooks that are used in schools mimics printed, not cursive, script.

Sylvia's and Eddie's stories both raise the issue of the frequent assignment of ELLs to lower tracks of education. Once students are labeled "English as a second language," or ESL, they often find themselves stuck with, and trapped by, that label for many years. Both stories point to the need to have teachers who advocate for ELLs at all times so that they are provided with more opportunities to learn rigorous mathematics content and to move out of lower levels of education. Jae-won's and Seung-eun's stories inform us about the experiences and challenges of learning English as a second language, the former recounting an experience with a teacher who may not have provided enough support and the latter recounting an experience with a teacher who took an interest in helping the student succeed in class. Seung-eun's teacher, Mr. Ruiz, found ways to position her as a competent student in the class by having her illustrate her thinking at the board with drawings and pictures involving the concept of boiling water during the beginning stages of language development.

Elsa's story clearly shows the challenges of learning English as a second language and the coping mechanisms that Elsa used to survive in this setting. In addition, Jae-won, Seung-eun, Eddie, Sylvia, and Elsa all indicate that they may have been covering mathematics content that they had already learned in other countries, an issue that is evidence of the frequent misplacement of ELLs in the U.S. schooling system. Although all of these students referred to strengths and success in mathematics because the subject matter has less reliance on the English language, current requirements of explaining, writing, defending, and conjecturing in the mathematics classroom pose different challenges for ELLs.

Voices of Teachers

Those who teach ELLs offer another important perspective. Consider the views of the following three teachers. In the first account, note that "sheltering the language" refers to making the language accessible by using various strategies with the intent of helping the student learn the content.

Edna Alvarado

When a researcher asked Edna, a kindergarten teacher in a bilingual school, to make recommendations to teachers who want to engage their ELL students in problem solving, she said, "Definitely with lots of manipulatives, with a lot of extra practice, a lot of visuals. I would do a lot of whole-group explanations before we go to the little groups, so kids can give light to each other, and a kid that is a little more advanced in English than the other ones can help them too. Sometimes you teach in English, and they translate in Spanish by themselves or with partners. If you don't have access to the student's language, then you will need to rely on a lot of practice, a lot of repetition, lots of visuals, and gestures. And definitely you need to shelter the language and discuss the context of problems because if the kids don't understand what you are asking, if they don't understand the vocabulary, then their comprehensible input is like zero. They might imitate what other kids are doing, but they are not developing that problem-solving skill in their brains; they are not developing the concept."

Reflection 1.20

Making meaning of mathematical ideas is critical in a classroom.

What strategies do you use to make content comprehensible?

Reflection 1.21

ELLs need champions—individuals who support their mathematical and language development.

Do you know who the champions are in your school or district? How can you collaborate with these individuals to make a difference for ELLs?

Reflection 1.22

Although teachers might not share the same language as their ELLs, it is important to build trusting relationships with students.

How do you develop these relationships in your classroom?

Reflection 1.23

Engaging ELLs by using multiple modalities that include communication is imperative.

How do you support ELLs as they communicate their mathematical understanding?

Bob McDonald

About seven years ago, a teacher and the principal came to meet with me to ask if I would become the Title I mathematics teacher. This meant that I would need to leave my present team and join the team of teachers who taught English language learners. The seventh- and eighth-grade students would be grouped into two classes, with the level determined by language ability rather than grade. One class would have students at emergent, pre-emergent, and basic levels, as defined by my state; the other class would be composed of students at the intermediate level. The charge from the district and state was to have these students learn English, but my principal wanted them to also learn mathematics so that they would not be too far behind when they left us and went to high school. I live in an English-only state, so the fact that my proficiency in Spanish is minimal was not too much of a concern to the principal. I did not have a bilingual endorsement and had not yet taken the soon-to-be state-required sheltered English instruction classes; those facts could describe the entire math department at my school at that time. My principal felt that I related well with students and that my past experience made me the teacher best suited for the task.

At that time, the school where I taught had about 1400 students in grades 6–8. Over 85 percent of the students were Hispanic and over 90 percent received free or reduced-price lunch. There were few teachers of color on the staff. The newly formed team would consist of two Latina teachers and myself. It was to be an interesting and challenging experience.

The students were a very energetic, close-knit group, and very proud of their Mexican heritage. One of the many challenges I had was to create an environment that would encourage participation by the students, in a language in which they were not proficient, taught by a teacher who looked different from them and did not speak their language. This was an ongoing challenge, since the students needed to see I was "for real" in my concern for them and their education. This continuous process sometimes went well and sometimes was frustrating to myself and to the students.

I learned that lessons that had the students actively involved and using manipulatives were better received and had more student engagement than a "traditional" lesson. I remember one of the first lessons required creating various rectangles that had a common perimeter and examining how the areas would change depending on how the perimeters changed. Getting the students actively involved in groups of four and creating the shapes out of large grid paper worked better than my first attempt at having the students at their desks working alone or in groups of two. I was fortunate to have some good English-Spanish mathematics dictionaries, which were helpful to the students who were proficient in reading in their native language. I also quickly discovered a website that had Spanish-English math cognates.

From my involvement with an NSF-funded urban systemic initiative and a middle school curriculum project, I had a number of good, engaging lessons that called on students to build, record, draw, and explain what we were working on, activities that theoretically take the student from the concrete to the pictorial and abstract levels. But like many middle school students, the ELLs were at varying places in their mathematical development, as evidenced by their proficiency with addition, subtraction, multiplication, and division facts. So my lessons flipped back and forth between skills and applications. I made use of the strategies that I knew about—long wait time, gesturing, and color

Reflection 1.24

Developing presentation skills is an ongoing process for ELLs.

How do you scaffold presentation requirements to facilitate students' growth throughout the year?

Reflection 1.25

ELLs need to use their own language to access mathematical concepts while simultaneously developing facility within the English language.

What tasks do you pose that explicitly address this simultaneous learning?

coding my work on the board to make it stand out more for the students. My efforts to ask probing questions of the students who were stuck were often "lost in translation." I compensated for this by letting one person from the group be a "spy," visiting other groups if they were not making progress. Obviously, because they were teenagers, the talk in groups was not always about mathematics, and my lack of Spanish made it difficult to be certain whether the students were on task. There were times when my requirement that the talk "be about the math" had a negative effect on the environment that I was striving to create.

Toward the end of the first year, the students began to give good presentations of some "big" problems, with all group members having some verbal part in the presentation. Part of the presentations included asking if there were any questions, and there were instances when the students got into some good mathematical discourse.

It was a challenging but rewarding two years. At times I left school happy, knowing I had reached my students; at other times I was frustrated, wondering where and why the day took a detour to rocky ground. As I was unpacking my boxes in a new room for a new five-person ELL team the next year, I found a small whiteboard written on with a permanent marker—a thank-you note in the form of an acrostic poem that touched my heart and brought a few tears to my eyes.

Matthew S. Winsor

Even teachers who speak a second language may still face a daunting task in teaching mathematics effectively to ELL students. I was one of those teachers. From 1995 to 1999, I taught at a high school in Southern California where the student population was 56 percent Hispanic. I spoke Spanish and was hired in part to teach mathematics to ELL students. I taught my classes in English. My school had no materials to use in an ELL class with Spanish speakers, and I could not find a textbook company that offered such materials. I was also not eager to spend enormous amounts of time trying to translate mathematics texts.

As a result, I began a quest to find ways to help ELLs learn mathematics. My initial thesis was that the main barrier for these students was learning mathematics in their new language. I decided to look at research regarding both how one learns a new language and how one learns mathematics, thinking that I could use any similarities between the two bodies of research to come up with a teaching method. After synthesizing the research, I created an approach for teaching ELL mathematics that I called Mathematics as a Second Language (MSL) (Winsor 2007, pp. 372–73). The main components of MSL were vocabulary activities, journals, group work, and projects. One central vocabulary activity was word squares (see Quinn and Molloy [1992]), each made on a 3-by-5 card divided into four quadrants—one for students to write the mathematical term in their own language; a second to write the term in English; the third to write a definition in their own words, which could be in their native language; and the last to include a representation of the concept. Students used their word squares throughout the year and often in the mathematics classes the following year. When students worked in groups, I found that students who were more fluent in English had the opportunity to help peers who were less fluent. While the more fluent students gained a deeper understanding of the mathematics, the less fluent students had the advantage of reviewing the mathematics content with someone who spoke their native language. My students wrote in their journals in the language they were most comfortable with, but they were required to write the mathematical terms in English. I found that this helped students associate the English term with the mathematical concept already in their minds in Spanish. Students' first journal entries were often unsophisticated, relying on nonmathematical terms to express their ideas. As the year progressed, their journal entries became more mathematically precise, and the use of English in their journals increased. Students worked on projects in groups, with the goal of presenting their results orally to the class. When students worked on their projects during class, I would circulate around the classroom and talk to them about their work, questioning them about their ideas and decisions. This gave students the opportunity to express their ideas to me before they presented them to the class.

I recognize that there are many teachers who teach ELL students and may not be aware of the resources available to them. One resource is an ELL student who is fluent enough in English to help other ELL students understand the teacher. Another resource is mathematics glossaries that have mathematics terms in both English and the ELL students' native language. A third resource is instructional assistants who speak the student's language (I met regularly with the bilingual aide, so she was familiar with the goals of MSL and knew how I wanted students to work in my classroom). A fourth, and often underused resource, is foreign language teachers, who have been trained to teach others a new language and can share strategies that can be adapted for a mathematics classroom. Also, learning to speak the language of the students enough to greet them and ask how they are goes a long way toward gaining their confidence. And finally, when you show ELL students that you care about them, they will trust you more and work harder with you (Winsor 2007).

Understanding Teachers' Stories

Matthew and Bob discuss the fact that teaching mathematics effectively to ELLs involves hard work. Both teachers refer to the need to seek resources, such as English-Spanish dictionaries. In addition, these teachers comment on the progress that they noticed from the beginning to the end of the school year regarding their ELLs' ability to give explanations that were mathematically precise. Both of these teachers also comment on the importance of the students' recognizing that they (the teachers) had a genuine interest in the student as an individual.

Edna and Bob recommend the use of manipulatives while students are developing mathematical language to communicate explanations. All three teachers mention the need for group work in the mathematics classroom to allow students time to process mathematical concepts. In addition, all three teachers are aware of the need to focus on teaching language as they taught mathematics content.

Matthew's story points to the need to see "teaching as a scholarly activity, not as a technical activity" (Aguirre and Gutiérrez 2011). In other words, teachers have to conduct research and find resources that will help them understand and teach ELLs. These resources also include collaborating with teachers who are certified to teach bilingual students or ELLs.

This chapter provides personal stories of struggles and successes from ELLs as well as stories from mathematics teachers of ELLs. In addition, both ELLs and teachers of ELLs offer thoughts, stories, and *consejos* to those committed to improving the mathematics education of ELLs. In the next chapter, we discuss stages of second language development to understand issues that are specific to ELLs and provide descriptions of student actions and recommendations for teachers in the mathematics classroom.

References

Aguirre, Julia, and Rochelle Gutiérrez. "Framing and Analyzing (In)equity and Power in Mathematics Methods." Professional development workshop presented at the Fifteenth Annual Conference of the Association of Mathematics Teacher Educators, Irvine, Calif., January 2011.

National Council of Teachers of Mathematics (NCTM). *Curriculum and Evaluation Standards for School Mathematics*. Reston, Va.: NCTM, 1989.

————. *Principles and Standards for School Mathematics*. Reston, Va.: NCTM, 2000.

Quinn, Mary E., and Marilyn Molloy. "'I Learned to Talk Mathematics': Using Cooperative Groups with College Minority Students." In *Cooperative Language Learning: A Teacher's Resource Book*, edited by Carolyn Kessler, pp. 117–28. Englewood Cliffs, N.J.: Prentice Hall, 1992.

Winsor, Matthew S. "Bridging the Language Barrier in Mathematics." *Mathematics Teacher* 101 (December 2007/January 2008): 372–78.

Chapter 2

Second Language Development and Implications for the Mathematics Classroom

by Nora G. Ramirez and Sylvia Celedón-Pattichis

Janice teaches a classroom full of English language learners (ELLs) who all speak the same language but a language that is different from her own. James has five newcomer ELLs who speak different languages. Savannah teaches one ELL, who feels isolated from her peers. If you were one of these teachers, how would you engage each of the ELLs in doing and understanding mathematics in your classroom? To guide educators who find themselves in similar situations, we provide strategies that help teachers so that ELLs can participate effectively in mathematics learning environments. We draw from three bodies of literature—mathematics education, second language development, and mathematics education of ELLs—as well as from practitioners' effective strategies for teaching mathematics to ELLs.

Both research and practice have contributed to the various frameworks that exist for defining stages of second language development. For example, California has a framework that identifies five different levels of language development, whereas Texas uses four levels to describe the stages of language development. The Teaching English to Speakers of Other Languages (TESOL) *PreK–12 English Language Proficiency Standards* (Gottlieb et al. 2006) includes six levels. We use three levels based on the Sheltered Instruction Observation Protocol (SIOP) (Echevarría, Vogt, and Short 2007)—beginning, intermediate, and advanced—to help educators understand and meet the reading, writing, speaking, and listening needs of ELLs.

It is important to note that the levels of language development that we describe in the next sections are guidelines and should not serve to confine ELLs to a particular level. Moreover, teachers must understand that the divisions between language development levels are not well defined and that movement between the levels is usually not linear. Further, these levels of language development are not parallel to similar levels of mathematics learning. In other words, because a student is in the beginning stage of language development, it does not follow that the student has only a basic understanding of mathematical content (Lesser and Winsor 2009). Therefore, teachers should always make instructional decisions on the basis of students' needs—what students do mathematically and how they communicate by using their first and second languages.

As ELLs develop proficiency in English as a second language, teachers should provide support that helps the students develop language that is specific to mathematics, sometimes referred to as *academic language* (Cummins 2000, 2003, 2008). Researchers argue that focusing on academic language alone may promote teaching vocabulary without a context or viewing the students as lacking because of their inability to use academic language (Edelsky 2006; MacSwan and Rolstad 2003). Rather than emphasize academic language, we choose to focus on making mathematical meaning in social contexts, with an emphasis on mathematics discourse. This requires that teachers and students create a mathematics discourse community (MDC) (Willey 2010), in which teachers interact with students and students interact with their peers to develop knowledge of the mathematics while using the language of mathematics. Using Gee's (1996) work, Willey conceptualizes MDCs as communities that "involve ways of being, thinking, and speaking that are unique to a mathematics environment" (Willey 2010, p. 4). "Regular and active participation in the classroom—not only reading and listening but also discussing, explaining, writing, representing, and presenting—is critical to the success of ELLs in mathematics" (Application of Common Core State Standards for English Language Learners 2010, p. 2). Some may think that the problem with academic language is big words, but we argue that it lies in shifting the focus away from understanding the mathematical meaning of concepts, knowing how to use precise mathematical language, and using terminology to explain and connect mathematical concepts. Thus, we move away from using academic language and instead choose to use mathematics discourse as a focus for teaching mathematics to ELLs. We define mathematics discourse as communication that centers on making meaning of mathematical concepts; it is more than just knowing vocabulary. It involves negotiating meanings by listening and responding, describing understanding, making conjectures, presenting solutions, challenging the thinking of others, and connecting mathematical notations and representations.

Guiding Principles for Teaching ELLs in Mathematics

Traditionally, second language development has consisted of listening, speaking, reading, and writing, all of which are directly related to the skills needed to meet the expectations of NCTM's Process Standards for problem solving, reasoning and proof, and communication (NCTM 2000). It is imperative that the remaining Process Standards, for representation and connections, also be a focus in teaching ELLs. Constructing viable arguments, critiquing the reasoning of others, and explaining and justifying mathematical thinking are critical mathematical practices (Common Core State Standards Initiative 2010). As NCTM (2008) states, "It is important for all students, but especially critical for ELL students, to have opportunities to speak, write, read, and listen in mathematics classes, with teachers providing appropriate support and encouragement" (NCTM 2008, p. 1). Having ELLs share their mathematical thinking positions them as *competent problem solvers*, and thus as *contributors of mathematical knowledge*, and places them on a trajectory for increased participation in the learning process (Empson 2003).

When we consider the Common Core State Standards and the NCTM Process Standards, we perceive the need—and accept the opportunity—to articulate some guiding principles that are specific for ELLs to engage in MDCs that foster learning rigorous mathematics. Consider the five principles below:

Guiding Principles for Teaching Mathematics to English Language Learners

1. *Challenging mathematical tasks:* Students at all levels of English language development need challenging mathematical tasks, made accessible through supports that clarify their understanding of the task. Although the tasks may be the same for all levels, the teacher actions required for students to have access to them and to communicate their understanding often differ at each level.

2. *Linguistically sensitive social environment:* Mathematical learning occurs in a linguistically sensitive social environment that takes into consideration linguistic demands and discourse elements (Chval and Chávez 2011/2012; Chval and Khisty 2009) and is characterized by teacher-supported, ongoing, high-quality interactions that include all forms of communication between teachers and students and between students and students.

3. *Support for learning English while learning mathematics:* Facility with the English language is acquired when ELLs learn mathematics through effective instructional practices, including support structures that scaffold students' language development, engage students in MDCs, make mathematics content linguistically comprehensible to them, and assess their progress in reaching predetermined linguistic and mathematical goals.

4. *Mathematical tools and modeling as resources:* Mathematical tools and mathematical modeling provide a resource for ELLs to engage in mathematics and communicate their mathematical understanding and are essential in developing a community that enhances discourse.

5. *Cultural and linguistic differences as intellectual resources:* Students' cultural and linguistic differences in the mathematics community should be viewed as intellectual resources rather than as deficits and should be used in the classroom to connect to prior knowledge and to create a community whose members value one another's ways of engaging in mathematics.

Teacher and ELL Actions Based on Stage of Language Development

To provide educators with useable information for classroom practice, we describe ELLs, specify effective actions of both students and teachers, and share vignettes of classroom interactions. We begin by describing teacher behaviors that are appropriate in any mathematics classroom with ELLs. We provide characteristics of ELLs at each stage of second language development to inform practitioners about the subtle and not-so-subtle differences among students at the various stages. We describe student actions to support educators in identifying, understanding, and responding to ELLs' needs. We then include a list of specific teacher actions to engage students at each stage of language development in learning mathematics while simultaneously developing facility with the English language. We have organized these lists of teacher actions by connecting them to the guiding principles that we have identified for teaching mathematics to English language learners. These teacher actions encompass good teaching strategies, but they do more than that. The suggested instructional techniques are more than good teaching strategies; they are imperative to support ELLs in learning mathematics because they give explicit attention to the linguistic demands of a mathematics classroom.

Finally in this chapter, we present vignettes to invite the reader into a mathematics classroom to highlight explicit behaviors of ELLs and teachers. In addition, we provide specific examples by including links to video clips, vignettes, reflections, and mathematics lessons that exemplify the teacher actions and student actions at each stage of second language development. The reader can navigate these examples by going to the More4U website for this book as well as referring to suggested examples in other chapters. It is our intent that these research-based teaching practices and the linked examples will enable educators to support ELLs at all stages while challenging them intellectually and engaging them fully in the mathematics learning process.

Essential teacher actions with all ELLs

Some actions are imperative for teachers to use consistently with all English language learners in mathematics. The following list enumerates these indispensable teacher actions and indicates in parentheses the relevant guiding principles (e.g., P1: Challenging mathematical tasks). In addition, the cases of practice presented in chapters 5, 6, and 8, the videos and lenses described in chapter 12, and additional materials in more4u provide specific examples of these teacher actions.

An effective teacher of ELLs always does the following:

1. Uses challenging problems and provides access by—
   a. assessing students' prior knowledge to determine ELLs' familiarity with the context of a task rather than assuming that ELLs are familiar with contexts and language that may be commonplace to others;
   b. integrating culturally relevant tasks;
   c. planning for the use of a variety of tools and mathematical models; and
   d. focusing on students' understanding of both the mathematical and everyday language involved in the task by—
      i. using strategies such as "acting it out" and displaying Web-based pictures or videos;
      ii. explicitly addressing unfamiliar contexts and linguistic structures within the task (see chapter 12);
      iii. using manipulatives, diagrams, models, and symbolic notations. (P1: Challenging mathematical tasks; P2: Linguistically sensitive social environment; P3: Support for learning English while learning mathematics; P4: Mathematical tools and modeling as resources; P5: Cultural and linguistic differences as intellectual resources)

2. Makes grouping decisions based on the cognitive demand of the task with awareness that the higher the level of complexity, the more one uses his or her first language to think and reason. (P1: Challenging mathematical tasks; P2: Linguistically sensitive social environment)

3. Carefully sequences activities and tasks to set students on a trajectory that continually develops facility with language while at the same time developing competence with mathematics. (P3: Support for learning English while learning mathematics)

4. Facilitates and guides the mathematical discourse in the classroom so that ELLs have the opportunity to engage in MDCs to develop conceptual understanding, becoming mathematically proficient while simultaneously increasing their language proficiency (National Research Council 2001). (P2: Linguistically sensitive social environment; P3: Support for learning English while learning mathematics; see chapter 12.)

5. Structures opportunities that scaffold the complexity of the language demands in tasks. (P2: Linguistically sensitive social environment; P3: Support for learning English while learning mathematics; see chapters 10, 11, and 12.)

6. Allows processing time, recognizing the difference in the mental requirements for speaking, reading, and writing a new language. (P2: Linguistically sensitive social environment; P3: Support for learning English while learning mathematics)

7. Provides opportunities for students to read and write about their mathematics learning, gives students written feedback that purposefully focuses on mathematical language development, and allows students to revise their writing (Chval and Khisty 2009). (P2: Linguistically sensitive social environment; P3: Support for learning English while learning mathematics)

8. Uses both rich mathematical contexts and sophisticated language to help ELLs advance in their linguistic development and their mathematical learning. (P2: Linguistically sensitive social environment; P3: Support for learning English while learning mathematics; P5: Cultural and linguistic differences as intellectual resources; see case 1 by Celedón-Pattichis and Turner in chapter 5 and case 5 by Chval in chapter 5.)

9. Writes mathematical terms so that they are visible in the classroom; explicitly refers to the terms and their meanings often; and engages students in interacting with the chart by asking them to read, describe, model, and use the terms orally and in writing. (P3: Support for learning English while learning mathematics)

10. Considers the level of the cognitive and linguistic demands of participating in a new learning community and engaging in mathematical tasks, and plans for an appropriate amount of processing time. (P2: Linguistically sensitive social environment; see chapters 10 and 11.)

11. Facilitates the use of tools (e.g, tables, graphs, cubes, calculators, electronic whiteboards) to enhance mathematical discourse and understanding. (P3: Support for learning English while learning mathematics; P4: Mathematical tools and modeling as resources)

12. Consistently makes visual references to mathematical models in the environment while facilitating classroom discourse and interactions. (P3: Support for learning English while learning mathematics; P4: Mathematical tools and modeling as resources)

13. Highlights distinctions between the meaning of terms used in mathematics and the meaning of terms used in everyday life. Emphasizes homonyms as needed to develop mathematical understanding. (P2: Linguistically sensitive social environment)

14. Listens to, cares about, guides, and mentors students while advocating for their human and educational rights. (P2: Linguistically sensitive social environment; P3: Support for learning English while learning mathematics; P5: Cultural and linguistic differences as intellectual resources)

15. Enhances teacher-student interactions by being linguistically sensitive and by learning about the students' and their communities' culture, languages, differences in dialects, and ways of knowing and communicating. (P2: Linguistically sensitive social environment; P5: Cultural and linguistic differences as intellectual resources)

16. Understands the effect that acceptance of the students' language and culture can have on the students' learning. Explicitly models acceptance and interest in the culture and language to ensure that students have a positive academic identity. (P2: Linguistically sensitive social environment; P5: Cultural and linguistic differences as intellectual resources)

17. Models making sense of written instructions during lessons rather than letting students encounter these instructions for the first time on exams. (P3: Support for learning English while learning mathematics)

18. Recognizes that writing in cursive may add to the cognitive demands for some ELLs but not for others. (P3: Support for learning English while learning mathematics)

Three stages of language development

Each stage of language development—beginning, intermediate, and advanced—has its own characteristics (Cummins 2008; Echevarría, Vogt, and Short 2007; Krashen and Terrell 1983; Thomas and Collier 2002), and students demonstrate common behaviors and actions at each stage. Specific teacher actions can scaffold students' progress through particular stages. Below are characteristics, common student actions, and appropriate teacher actions for the beginning, intermediate, and advanced stages of language development. (Previously, we presented teacher actions that are appropriate for *all levels* of English proficiency. Now we identify actions that are especially appropriate for *each stage* of language development, and we categorize them according to the five guiding principles for teaching mathematics to ELLs, although we recognize that some may be appropriate for other categories as well.)

Beginning stage

Characteristics of an ELL

- Experiences this stage for about two years.
- Exhibits periods of silence followed by speech emergence.
- Uses unclear pronunciation that may inhibit communication.
- May or may not be at the beginning stage of mathematical development for his or her grade level.

Common Student Actions

- Is a silent observer while processing mathematical concepts.
- Learns object words first because of the ease of using pictures or examples.
- Continually participates in an internal dialogue, attempting to identify first-language terminology for the second-language terminology that is in use in the classroom.
- Primarily uses first language to keep records of mathematical concepts by using graphic organizers and journals that include words or phrases, examples, and drawings.
- May or may not already know the mathematical concepts or related terminology in his or her first language.
- May use different procedures or notations (see Mathematical Notations and Procedures and Mathematical Notation Comparisons at www.nctm.org/more4u).
- Responds to gestures, pictures, and visuals.
- May appear engaged in classroom activities or display body language to pretend to understand or to reduce the chances of being called on to speak.
- At the beginning, may use few words or give one-word answers to communicate mathematical thinking. Often consults mathematical references (e.g., first-language textbooks, electronic sources, dictionary, journal) to enhance communication of the mathematical concept.
- May use nonverbal representations (e.g., gestures, models, drawings) to show understanding of concepts and communicate mathematical thinking.
- Copies printed text but not necessarily with comprehension of the language or the mathematics.
- Reads few words alone but can participate in choral reading.
- Interacts with peers by observing, gesturing, and responding with few words. Often requires teacher support for interactions.
- May not ask questions because of the difficulty of forming sentences.
- May require an alternative task for reflection that requires less verbal communication, such as questions calling for short answers or illustrations.

Appropriate Teacher Actions

P1: *Challenging mathematical tasks*

All mathematical tasks should challenge students at all stages of language development. The level of content instruction should never be reduced for ELLs. Teacher actions that support P1 at this stage of language development are the same as those described in the section "Essential teacher actions with all ELLs" (see pp. 22–24).

P2: *Linguistically sensitive social environment*

1. Allows silence; in the beginning does not require students to speak in whole group but encourages students to use multimodal approaches to communicate (Chval and Khisty 2009; Morales, Khisty, and Chval 2003).

2. Models pronunciation and usage of conversational and mathematical language, enunciates clearly, and avoids the use of slang or idioms.

3. Recognizes the difficulty that a student may have in understanding terms related to abstract ideas. Uses gestures or diagrams to relay meaning when appropriate.

4. Provides opportunities for students to listen to others and to read sentences.

5. Uses pictures or real-life clues to make distinctions in meaning between terms used in mathematics and terms used in everyday life, emphasizing homonyms (see List of Mathematics Homonyms at www.nctm.org/more4u).

6. Facilitates students' engagement in in-depth mathematical discussions and reflections by placing students who share the same language together to lower the linguistic cognitive demand and give students an opportunity to participate in dialogue.

7. Provides students with opportunities to listen to one another by helping guide the conversation so that English learners have more access (e.g., asking students to repeat information, draw models, or use classroom technology such as document cameras to explain their thinking as they talk).

8. Is aware that simple sentences in the present tense are easily comprehensible and thus purposefully uses them to enable ELLs to make sense of mathematical content.

P3: *Support for learning English while learning mathematics*

1. Is aware of and attends to students' struggles to make sense of, and to participate in, the classroom discourse by—

   a. planning ahead for use of gestures and visuals and anticipating students' gestures and use of visuals;

   b. allowing processing time and wait time for students to comprehend questions, think about answers, and formulate oral answers;

   c. preparing the students to give answers aloud (letting them know that they will be called on, rehearsing answers, etc.);

   d. inviting students to go beyond brief, single responses, both written and oral, when appropriate;

   e. translating or asking other students to translate when possible; and

    f.   giving time for the use of resources to enable access to the mathematical concepts and tasks.

2. Facilitates the acquisition of the English language by placing ELLs with monolingual English speakers. Gives tools and suggestions to facilitate student-to-student conversations (see chapter 13: Triangle Lesson video clip at www.nctm.org/more4u).

3. Uses sentence frames that require completion or fill-in-the-blank sentences with simple language structures that focus on both mathematical and linguistic development.

4. Purposefully alternates the grouping of students.

5. Uses approaches that facilitate ELLs' engagement in group work (e.g., making sure that the students understand the task, assigning roles for students, requiring different representations).

6. Provides experiences with mathematical concepts while introducing terminology. Does not use or teach mathematical terminology before students have had the opportunity to understand concepts. Reinforces previously experienced concepts and mathematics terminology. Front-loads (SIOP) with the mathematical terminology that students have already experienced.

7. Positions students as competent problem solvers (Empson 2003) and supports their nonlinguistic ways of communicating ideas and solutions to the class.

8. Is aware that the absence of student questions does not indicate understanding and therefore continually observes students' actions and gestures.

9. Assesses students' mathematical knowledge in their first language, if applicable. (Teachers should not assume that students who speak a language other than English can also read that language or that they know all mathematical terms in that language. Some ELLs know mathematical terms only in English.)

10. Recognizes that participation in reflection may be limited to gestures, nonverbal explanations, or a few words. May use individual activity or support to effectively engage the student in reflection.

P4: *Mathematical tools and modeling as resources*

1. Focuses on making sense of mathematical concepts by—

    a.   continually using mathematical terminology while using gestures or descriptions to make meaning of words;

    b.   implementing activities that require students to match, label, and repeat words that correspond to mathematical concepts;

    c.   creating a classroom mathematical environment that uses vocabulary and key visual models to enhance students' ability to engage in discourse (e.g. hundreds chart, part/part/whole mat, place-value chart, anchor charts for current learning);

    d.   providing graphic organizers to develop understanding of mathematical concepts and to learn terminology (see chapter 6: HS_2_Graphic Organizer video clip at www.nctm.org/more4u);

    e. using examples and non-examples to prevent and challenge misconceptions;

    f. writing what is said and asking the class to read; and

    g. identifying and making available appropriate resources (e.g., list of cognates, book in Chinese, electronic dictionaries); consulates may be able to provide useful language and mathematics resources.

2. Uses tools to make lessons comprehensible and to enhance discourse (e.g., software programs, websites, concrete materials, tables, graphs, graphing calculators) (NCTM 1991, 2007).

3. Facilitates students' use of models and drawings to—

    a. assess what students know; and

    b. communicate mathematically with the students.

P5: *Cultural and linguistic differences as intellectual resources*

1. Finds ways to use the students' first language for the purpose of—

    a. developing conversational and mathematical language;

    b. conceptually communicating mathematical ideas; and

    c. connecting English terms to the students' first language by using cognates from the first language when possible.

2. Recognizes a need for and uses various resources (e.g., school-family liaisons, cultural centers, consulates) to gain understanding and to validate what the students bring to the classroom in terms of the following: language, home culture, prior school culture, and mathematical experiences.

3. Recognizes the challenges that students face because their identities are constantly changing in alignment with different contexts (Nieto and Bode 2011)—in a classroom setting, at home, in recreational activities.

4. Helps develop a sense of belonging by—

    a. encouraging students to integrate their cultural selves into the classroom community;

    b. inviting students to share their culture, language, or artifacts;

    c. helping students embrace both worlds, thus acculturating but not assimilating to the new culture. (Assimilation requires a person to "give up cherished values and ways of behaving to become a part of the mainstream" [Igoa 1995, p. 44], whereas acculturation allows an individual to be part of the new culture "without discarding past meaningful traditions and values" [ibid.].)

Intermediate Stage

Characteristics of an ELL

- Experiences this stage for approximately 2–4 years.
- Uses simple sentences in the present tense.
- Speaks in phrases and sentences in first language and English (code-switching) while making sense of mathematical concepts (Moschkovich 2007).

- Speaks to convey simple messages and is understood by those who are acquainted with him or her.
- Frequently requests repetition or clarification of mathematical concepts or linguistic structures.

Common Student Actions

- Uses simple sentences to express mathematical ideas with support of tools for written and oral explanations (e.g., sentence frames, sentence stems, graphic organizers, mathematics vocabulary lists, electronic whiteboards, document cameras).
- Often participates in an internal dialogue, attempting to identify first-language terminology or clarify meanings for terminology in use in the classroom (see chapter 3).
- May or may not already know the mathematical concepts or related terminology in his or her first language.
- Keeps records of terminology and mathematical concepts by using various tools, such as graphic organizers and journals that include or require simple sentences, examples, and drawings. In writing, uses both languages, but may make a greater effort to use English.
- May use different procedures or notations to solve problems (see Mathematical Notations and Procedures and Mathematical Notation Comparison at www.nctm.org/more4u).
- Reads simple sentences that use high-frequency vocabulary and familiar mathematical terminology.
- Writes simple sentences. Requires support for writing about abstract ideas.
- Continues to need extended processing time to respond to questions and engage in different mathematics tasks.
- Raises questions with simple language structures and may ask clarifying questions (e.g., "Can you tell me that again?").
- Responds to and with multimodal communication (gestures, pictures, and models) to demonstrate understanding of mathematics concepts.
- Interacts in groups by using simple sentences to initiate and respond to mathematical ideas and questions. May need to use models and drawings to communicate with peers.
- Presents thinking by using simple sentences and nonverbal representations.
- Reflects briefly in written form.

Appropriate Teacher Actions

P1: *Challenging mathematical tasks*

The tasks for students at different levels of English proficiency do not differ. Teacher actions that support P1 at this stage of language development are the same as those described in the section "Essential teacher actions with all ELLs" (see pp. 22–24).

P2: *Linguistically sensitive social environment*

1. Uses processes such as cooperative learning structures to allow ELLs time to listen and talk with partners or within a small group.

2. Facilitates ELLs' use of gestures to enable the acquisition of both language and mathematical concepts.

3. Provides practice in the pronunciation and use, written and oral, of mathematics terminology. Often requires the use of specific mathematics terminology and encourages the use of information from journals, word walls, etc. (see Bridging the Language Barrier at www.nctm.org/more4u).

4. Models pronunciation of conversational and mathematical language, using compound sentence structure.

5. Provides sentence frames that give only the beginnings of sentences and require students to complete thoughts and give reasoning in oral or written format.

6. Provides opportunities to read, listen to, and respond to sentences using different verb tenses.

7. Provides opportunities for listening to and reading complex sentences and paragraphs. Follows up with tasks, holding students accountable for understanding the content.

8. Allows processing time and wait time for students to reason about their answers and formulate them for oral delivery.

9. Facilitates and encourages the rehearsing of presentations.

10. Recognizes that participation and reflection may be limited to the use of simple sentences and nonverbal explanations and may require support such as sentence stems and diagrams.

P3: *Support for learning English while learning mathematics*

1. Is aware of and attends to the linguistic cognitive demand on students to participate effectively in listening to, speaking and writing about, and comprehending mathematical ideas.

2. Purposefully alternates the grouping of students by—

   a. occasionally placing students who share the same language together to lower the linguistic cognitive demand to enable engagement in challenging tasks, in-depth mathematical discussions, and reflections;

   b. placing ELL with monolingual English speakers to facilitate the acquisition of the English language. Gives tools and suggestions to enable student-to-student conversations (see chapter 13: Triangle Lesson video clip at www .nctm.org/more4u);

   c. making grouping decisions on the basis of the cognitive demand of the task. Is aware that the higher the level of complexity, the more ELLs use their first language to think and reason (see case 4 by Morales in chapter 6);

   d. placing ELLs with peers who might be more inclusive and respectful of ELLs (Chval and Chávez 2011/2012);

e. using approaches to hold students accountable for participation in all aspects of the group's work.

3. Positions students as competent problem solvers (Empson 2003) and supports their linguistic and nonlinguistic ways of communicating a solution to the class (see case 5 by Chval in chapter 5 and chapter 5: ELL as a Competent Problem Solver video clip at www.nctm.org/more4u).

P4: *Mathematical tools and modeling as resources*

1. Uses tools such as concrete materials, tables, graphs, graphing calculators, and so forth to make lessons comprehensible and to enhance discourse (see Professional Teaching Standards—Discourse at www.nctm.org/more4u).

2. Provides graphic organizers, including note-taking templates, as tools to help students develop and record their understanding of mathematical concepts and to encourage them to use simple sentences in writing (see chapter 6: HS_2_ Graphic Organizer video clip at www.nctm.org/more4u).

3. Uses models and drawings to—

   a. assess what students know; and

   b. communicate mathematical concepts.

P5: *Cultural and linguistic differences as intellectual resources*

1. Finds ways to use the students' first language for the purpose of communicating mathematical ideas. Uses cognates and common prefixes and roots of words to emphasize meaning.

2. Continues to affirm the students' language and culture and uses the students' ways of being, thinking, and communicating to enhance the mathematical learning that occurs in the classroom (see chapter 5: Storytelling—Partitive Division video clip at www.nctm.org/more4u).

Advanced Stage

Characteristics of an ELL

- Experiences this stage for approximately 4–7 years. (The length of time varies, and students who enter high school as beginning ELLs require extra support.)
- Continues to require processing time for more advanced content-based terminology.
- Can read and write, using grade-appropriate written text containing all tenses.
- Speaks so that most listeners understand.
- Uses all tenses in speaking with few errors.
- Occasionally requests repetition or clarification of unfamiliar mathematical concepts or terminology.

Common Student Actions

- Generally uses familiar mathematical terminology in explanations and reflections.

- Requires extra time to process unfamiliar topics, concepts, or vocabulary.
- Occasionally participates in an internal dialogue, attempting to identify first-language terminology or clarify meanings for new mathematics terminology that is being used in the classroom (see chapter 3).
- Keeps records of mathematical concepts by using graphic organizers and journals for terminology, definitions, examples and non-examples, drawings, and so on. Continues to use his or her first language along with English (Morales 2004).
- Reads written text (with linguistic support) to make meaning of abstract mathematical concepts.
- Uses detailed sentences in both oral and written forms to explain mathematical thinking and defend reasoning.
- Interacts with other peers to construct mathematical knowledge and to plan and prepare for presentations.
- Actively participates in group work by listening, responding, verbally agreeing (or disagreeing), and offering alternatives.
- Records mathematical terminology and concepts, using more complex language, nonverbal representations, and examples.

Appropriate Teacher Actions

P1: *Challenging mathematical tasks*

The tasks for students at different levels of English proficiency do not differ. Teacher actions that support P1 at this stage of language development are the same as those described in the section "Essential teacher actions with all ELLs" (see pp. 19–21). However, the teacher actions vary to make the task accessible to students.

P2: *Linguistically sensitive social environment*

Models grade-level-appropriate sentence structures and provides opportunities for students to rehearse linguistically complex mathematical responses, both orally and in written form.

P3: *Support for learning English while learning mathematics*

1. Provides opportunities for students to read, listen, and respond, in written and oral forms, with different verb tenses.
2. Provides various types of linguistic support for students to make mathematical meaning of language with high levels of cognitive demand.
3. Supports students in providing detailed writings, presentations, and mathematical reflections, all including appropriate symbolic notations, precise mathematical language, and mathematical connections (e.g., working with other peers, using graphic organizers and visuals, modeling technical communication).

P4: *Mathematical tools and modeling as resources*

1. Provides opportunities for students to use tools, models, and other resource material in the students' first language and in English to aid ELLs in making sense

of mathematical text and in interpreting and analyzing content, thus increasing their linguistic proficiency and use of precise mathematical discourse.

2. Encourages students to use tools and models in explaining their mathematical thinking and describing connections between representations, thus increasing students' level of participation in MDCs.

P5: *Cultural and linguistic differences as intellectual resources*

Empowers students to enrich their cultural identities, develop positive academic identities, and continually grow as participants in the mathematics community.

The highly advanced English language learner

Although we do not focus on ELLs who are at the highly advanced level of English proficiency, we observe that ELLs at this level continually develop their proficiency in the English language and mathematics discourse as they enter new communities of learning. They continue to have internal dialogues in search of meaning for more complex mathematical ideas and sophisticated discourse. Chapter 3 presents Rea Goklish's story of her experience as an Apache doctoral student, and her account of her conceptual design develops a more in-depth understanding of the cognitive demands placed on ELLs, including those who are in the highly advanced stage.

Scenarios Showing ELLs in Mathematics Classrooms

We have presented teacher actions that foster mathematics discourse communities in which ELLs can successfully engage in learning mathematics by talking, doing, reading, writing, presenting, and representing. To help you apply what you have read in this chapter so far, we now present three scenarios and invite you to reflect on the teacher and student actions that they show.

Scenario 1

Isabel moved to the United States about six weeks ago. She is familiar with some common conversational English, and her replies involve one-word utterances. It is Isabel's third week in her school, and she is the only student in her fourth-grade class who speaks Spanish. She sits at her desk looking at what is happening in the classroom. She observes how students interact with the teacher and listens to the teacher and students as they pronounce different words emphasized during the mathematics lesson.

As the students work to find the area of a rectangle, Isabel is not clear about what to do, but when Mrs. Garza approaches her, she gestures to indicate that the students are trying to find the area of the rectangle, and Isabel immediately writes down the area, saying "*área.*" Mrs. Garza repeats, "Yes, the area is... square units," acknowledging the student's first language and modeling ways to participate in the mathematics classroom. The teacher finds out that Isabel actually knows the mathematics concepts but was not sure what the task itself entailed.

Mrs. Garza continues to work with Isabel on a one-on-one basis, taking time to translate into Spanish, using precise mathematical language in English, and continually assessing Isabel's understanding of concepts. The teacher looks for opportunities for

Isabel to present her mathematical thinking. As the weeks progress, Isabel begins to present her work in class by using diagrams, gestures, and mathematical notation.

Scenario 2

Mr. Edwards's high school class in first-year mathematics includes some ELLs who are at various stages of language development. Two students speak Vietnamese, one student speaks Russian, and three students speak Hmong. Before presenting the class activity, Mr. Edwards thought about different strategies that he should use to engage the ELLs in the task.

Mr. Edwards places a battery-operated car on the floor, turns it on, and lets it travel for a few minutes. He asks the students to think about what kind of data they could collect on the basis of what they observed. He rephrases his question by asking, "When you look at the car moving, what can you measure?" One student offers the idea that you could measure the time that it takes to reach certain distances. Mr. Edwards uses gestures and tools to indicate measuring time and distance. He summarizes the class discussion by *revoicing*—restating earlier comments to scaffold students' understanding and position them as contributors of knowledge—at the same time gesturing to indicate quantities that could be measured, and writing the students' ideas in clear, precise mathematical language in an effort to give the students access to that language. After the class decides to collect time vs. distance data, he organizes the students into groups that allow the ELLs to work with other students in the class. Mr. Edwards designs the activities so that all students have a role in setting up the experiments, timing, measuring, and recording the data. After the data are collected, Mr. Edwards asks students to "think-pair-share," partnering the ELLs who share the same language. Mr. Edwards facilitates the Russian student's participation in her group by encouraging the group to use gestures, diagrams, and an electronic dictionary.

Mr. Edwards asks students to share their observations. He provides stems (e.g., "As the length of time _____, the distance from the starting point _____.") to model the mathematical language and emphasize the mathematical concepts while facilitating the sharing of ideas by all students in the classroom. He then directs his students to return to their original groups and asks them to represent the data, using as many models as possible. Mr. Edwards encourages the students to refer to their 3-by-5 cards to review the different representations that they generated as a class. He observes the group work to determine if students represent the data with a table, a graph, or an equation.

All the groups prepare a presentation on a whiteboard to explain the relationship between the two variables and how those variables are represented in the different models. Mr. Edwards visits each group to assess their understanding and makes a point of rehearsing with the ELLs what they will present to the class. After all the presentations are completed, he asks all the students to reflect on the mathematical concepts that they learned during the day's lesson and to record diagrams and definitions in their journals. Some of the ELLs write mostly in their first language, and others use both languages.

Scenario 3

Mrs. Joy fosters a mathematics discourse community by focusing on discussions when problem solving. When she presents a problem, she typically asks the students the following questions: (*a*) "What do you understand about the situation of the problem?" and (*b*) "What do you know about the answer without solving the problem?" Mrs. Joy's middle school class consists entirely of Spanish speakers who are at various levels of English proficiency. The teacher poses the following problem: "Jeremy is three times older than his brother Juan. Jeremy's sister, Julia, is two years older than Juan. The sum of all their ages is 27. How old is Juan?"

Mrs. Joy typically leads a classroom discussion about a problem before the students begin working on it so that the students can understand what the task involves. She gives time for Roberto to discuss the problem situation with two new ELL students who speak very little English. She finds that when the students do this, they have a better understanding of what mathematical processes are involved. When she asks what students understand about the problem, some students say that there are three people who are brothers and sisters. Mrs. Joy says, "Yes, there are 3 siblings." When a student comments that Jeremy is the oldest, she asks, "How do you know that?" Another student then says that Juan is the youngest. The teacher asks the student to explain how he knows that this is true. Mrs. Joy asks the students to write or draw a diagram of what they understand about the relationships among the three siblings.

When Mrs. Joy asks students what they know about the answer, Monica shares her idea that the answer has to be less than 9. Mrs. Joy then asks the class, "Why do you think that Monica said that Juan has to be less than 9 years old? Talk to your partner, and decide if you agree with Monica. Decide if Monica is right." After the partners talk, the teacher asks Tony and Melissa to share. She asks Tony, who is at the beginning stage of language development, to share his illustrations, while Melissa, at the intermediate stage, explains how they thought about the problem. Tony's work shows the names of the siblings written in order with a 9 by each. Melissa explains that if they were all the same age they would each be 9. She says, "We know that they are not the same age. We already said that Jeremy is the oldest and Juan is the youngest. So we know that we have to take at least one year from Juan and give it to Jeremy. Tony then crossed off the 9 by Juan's name, wrote an 8, and crossed off the 9 by Jeremy's name and wrote 10. A few other students share their thinking and then begin to work independently.

The students discuss their work in small groups. As they talk, Mrs. Joy decides who will present their work, depending on the strategies that she observes students using. The student who presented first shared a table using a check-and-guess strategy; the second student used a bar model, and the last student presented an algebraic equation developed on the basis of a diagram.

Mrs. Joy challenges her students to think about how the equation is connected to the bar model. After the students make presentations, Mrs. Joy asks students to write about and compare their solutions with their initial understanding of the problem. She asks Melissa to translate the instructions and encourages Tony to write in Spanish.

Many classrooms contain students at multiple levels of English proficiency, and teachers have to make decisions about which strategies to use, when, and how often. Although creating MDCs is demanding, in the next chapters we present cases of practice, points to consider in designing lessons, and other tools, including analysis and observation protocols for mathematical tasks, teaching, and learning, as well as links to video clips and other vignettes that can increase understanding of the teaching of ELLs.

References

Application of Common Core State Standards for English Language Learners (2010). http://www.corestandards.org/assets/application-for-english-learners.pdf.

Common Core State Standards Initiative (CCSSI). *Common Core State Standards for Mathematics. Common Core State Standards (College- and Career-Readiness Standards and K–12 Standards in English Language Arts and Math)*. Washington, D.C.: National Governors Association Center for Best Practices and the Council of Chief State School Officers, 2010. http://www.corestandards.org.

Cummins, Jim. *Language, Power, and Pedagogy: Bilingual Children in the Crossfire*. Clevedon, UK: Multilingual Matters, 2000.

———. "Challenging the Construction of Difference as Deficit: Where Are Identity, Intellect, Imagination, and Power in the New Regime of Truth?" In *Pedagogies of Difference: Rethinking Education for Social Change*, edited by Peter P. Trifonas, pp. 41–60. London: Routledge, 2003.

———. "BICS and CALP: Empirical and Theoretical Status of the Distinction." In *Encyclopedia of Language and Education*, 2nd ed., vol. 2, *Literacy*, edited by Brian V. Street and Nancy H. Hornberger. New York: Springer, 2008.

Chval, Kathryn B., and Óscar Chávez. "Designing Math Lessons for English Language Learners." *Mathematics Teaching in the Middle School* 17 (December 2011/January 2012): 261–65.

Chval, Kathryn B., and Lena L. Khisty. "Latino Students, Writing, and Mathematics: A Case Study of Successful Teaching and Learning." In *Multilingualism in Mathematics Classrooms: Global Perspectives*, edited by Richard Barwell, pp. 128–44. Clevedon, UK: Multilingual Matters, 2009.

Echevarría, Jana, Mary Ellen Vogt, and Deborah J. Short. *Making Content Comprehensible for English Learners: The SIOP Model*. 3rd ed. New York: Pearson, 2007.

Edelsky, Carole. *With Literacy and Justice for All*. 3rd ed. Mahwah, N.J.: Lawrence Erlbaum, 2006.

Empson, Susan B. "Low-Performing Students and Teaching Fractions for Understanding: An Interactional Analysis." *Journal for Research in Mathematics Education* 34 (July 2003): 305–43.

Gee, James P. *Social Linguistics and Literacies: Ideology in Discourse*. 2nd ed. New York: Routledge Falmer, 1996.

Gottlieb, Margo, Lynore Carnuccio, Gisela Ernst-Slavit, and Anne Katz. *PreK–12 English Language Proficiency Standards*. Alexandria, Va.: Teachers of English to Speakers of Other Languages, 2006.

Igoa, Cristina. *The Inner World of the Immigrant Child*. Mahwah, N.J.: Lawrence Erlbaum, 1995.

Krashen, Stephen D., and Tracy D. Terrell. *The Natural Approach*. New York: Pergamon, 1983.

Lesser, Larry M., and Matthew S. Winsor. "English Language Learners in Introductory Statistics: Lessons Learned from an Exploratory Case Study of Two Pre-Service Teachers." *Statistics Education Research Journal* 8, no. 2 (2009): 5–32.

MacSwan, Jeff, and Kellie Rolstad. "Linguistic Diversity, Schooling, and Social Class: Rethinking Our Conception of Language Proficiency in Language Minority Education." In *Sociolinguistics: The Essential Readings*, edited by Christina B. Paulston and G. Richard Tucker, pp. 329–40. Oxford: Blackwell, 2003.

Morales, Hector, Jr. "A Naturalistic Study of Mathematical Meaning-Making by High School Latino Students." PhD diss., University of Illinois at Chicago, 2004.

Morales, Hector, Lena L. Khisty, and Kathryn B. Chval. "Beyond Discourse: A Multimodal Perspective of Learning Mathematics in a Multilingual Context." In *Proceedings of the 2003 Joint*

Meeting of PME and PMENA, edited by Neil Pateman, Barbara J. Dougherty, and Joseph T. Zilliox, vol. 3, pp. 133–40. Honolulu: Center for Research and Development Group, University of Hawaii, 2003.

Moschkovich, Judit N. "Using Two Languages While Learning Mathematics." *Educational Studies in Mathematics* 64, no. 2 (2007): 121–44.

National Council of Teachers of Mathematics (NCTM). *Professional Teaching Standards.*Reston, Va.: NCTM, 1991.

—————. *Principles and Standards for School Mathematics*. Reston, Va.: NCTM, 2000.

—————. *Mathematics Teaching Today: Improving Practice, Improving Student Learning.* 2nd ed. Updated, revised version, edited by Tami S. Martin, of *Professional Standards for Teaching Mathematics* (1991). Reston, Va.: NCTM, 2007.

—————. *Teaching Mathematics to English Language Learners.* NCTM Position Statement. Reston, Va.: NCTM, 2008. http://www.nctm.org/about/content.aspx?id=16135.

National Research Council (NRC). *Adding It Up: Helping Children Learn Mathematics.* Jeremy Kilpatrick, Jane Swafford, and Bradford Findell, eds. Mathematics Learning Study Committee, Center for Education, Division of Behavioral and Social Sciences and Education. Washington, D.C.: National Academy Press, 2001.

Nieto, Sonia, and Patty Bode. *Affirming Diversity: The Sociopolitical Context in Multicultural Education.* 6th ed. Boston: Pearson, 2011.

Thomas, Wayne P., and Virginia P. Collier. *A National Study of School Effectiveness for Language Minority Students' Long-Term Academic Achievement.* Santa Cruz, Calif.: Center for Research on Education, Diversity, and Excellence, University of California–Santa Cruz, 2002. http://www.crede.ucsc.edu.

Willey, Craig. "Teachers Developing Mathematics Discourse Communities with Latinas/os." In *Proceedings of the 32nd Annual Meeting of the North American Chapter of the International Group for the Psychology of Mathematics Education*, edited by Patricia Brosnan, Diana B. Erchick, and Lucia Flevares, pp. 530–38. Columbus: Ohio State University, May 2010.

Chapter 3

Language and Learning: A Conceptual Design from an Apache Perspective

by Rea Goklish

I stumbled on the conceptual design that I describe in this chapter as I came home one night distraught and irate from one of my doctoral courses. The instructor in my class had asked me a high-level question on the topic—discourse—that we were discussing this evening. I was unable to give an answer or response in a timely manner. As an ELL— a native Apache speaker—I had overcome the idea that this inability to respond quickly indicated a lack of ability to understand or learn. Instead, I realized, it simply indicated a need to follow a thinking process different from those who are not ELLs.

There were numerous times that I experienced a need for processing time as a student in my higher education career. During a lecture I was often not able to comprehend a word, statement, or expression. As a result, I did not understand the main concepts of the lecture or discussion. For example, if the lecture was on what research tells us about effective teaching methods, I would sit and listen intently as the professor discussed the research methods and the findings. Even though the statistics and charts were presented as visuals, my brain was so lost that it quit functioning, or "shut down." I would be oblivious to the ideas or statements, and, like a child, I became disengaged and frustrated.

At this point, I would often become frustrated with myself and angry at my professor and everybody else because of my needing to speak English and having to struggle to make sense of this new learning. It almost felt like I was a puzzle piece trying to force myself to fit into a place that wasn't natural for me. I experienced a feeling of wanting to scream in rage because I felt stuck while everyone was moving on without me.

My Conceptual Design

So, it was on this particular evening when I was angry at the world that I decided to "see" what my thinking process was like. I drew a diagram to illustrate how I perceived my brain or cognition to function as it dealt with language acquisition. I began by designing a flowchart (see fig. 3.1) to illustrate my processing of language and depicting conversations in Apache and English.

The three components of the conceptual design are spoken words, comprehension, and response. The "spoken word" is the language of the speakers, "comprehension" is the direct understanding between people as they talk, and "response" refers to the reply in either Apache or English, depending on who is talking to whom. This design describes the paths that my brain follows when it is conceptualizing a word or phrase.

Because my first language is Apache, naturally I think in Apache first. Therefore, in a conversation with another Apache speaker, I understand easily and respond accordingly, just as in the example I provide later. The conversation or dialogue is informal (small talk), and the response is quick and does not require any extra thinking time. Examples of this occur when I am with my mother and sisters. We talk, and the conversation flows naturally since the dialogue is in Apache. We do not have to think about what to say and how to respond as we carry on this conversation. In addition, because the tone is informal, we are comfortable and relaxed in this setting. We might be joking and laughing, or we might be discussing a family issue that requires some attention. Nonetheless, we don't worry or feel concerned about how we should present ourselves, what we should say, or how we should be feeling. Everything—the setting, the language, and the people—are all connected in a way that is completely natural. Therefore, since understanding is immediate, quick responses follow, and the conversation progresses.

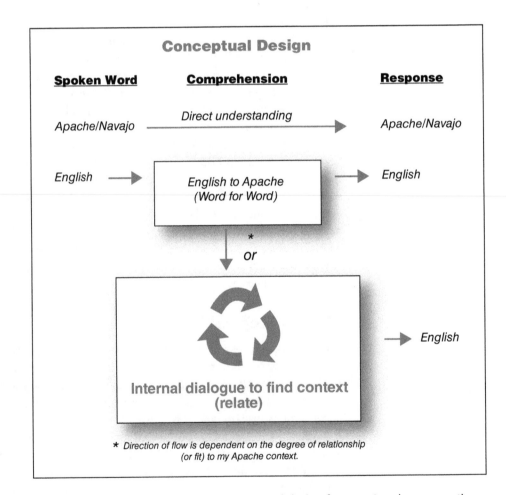

Fig. 3.1. Language and learning: a conceptual design from an Apache perspective

However, if the spoken word is English, it requires an English response. That is, in a conversation with an English speaker, the responses will be in English. As we talk, I understand what we're talking about, and I mentally "decode" the English words to Apache before I make a response. This thinking occurs in a split second since I do not stress over the topic or concept, nor do I find it difficult to understand what this person is saying to me. Comprehension occurs when I translate the English words to Apache. However, this is a relatively uncomplicated process because of my prior knowledge and familiarity with the ideas. For example, if the topic of discussion is different teaching strategies and cooperative learning, I am able to discuss these strategies easily because, as an educator, I am familiar with these terms and their meanings. The conversation is not complex for me and does not require much processing or shifting of language modes. The shift from my "Apache brain" to my "English brain" is smooth since the connections are easily made to the vocabulary, information, or knowledge that was previously stored in my brain. Thus, the path from spoken words in English to responses in English is not complex because of the prior experiences with and knowledge of the vocabulary and the associated concepts.

A third type of situation occurs when my brain requires more complex thinking and processing time. The box with the curved arrows in figure 3.1 indicates this level of the conceptual design, with the arrows tracing a circular path to show that internal dialogue is occurring and working to find relationships between the two languages. I think of the hourglass icon that is displayed when the computer is trying to locate something or is commanded to do something. The brain is trying to make sense of the words and is searching, searching, searching. For instance, when another English speaker talks to me, I naturally attempt to make sense of the words or syntax. This English speaker's vocabulary and articulation may be at a higher level of thinking or on a topic that I know little about. In this case, the path to arriving at an answer or providing a response is much different for me from the previous paths. The rate of the processing time slows down significantly, and the comprehension path is different from the previous ones. The path to a response enters this box where I try to figure out what was said, the meanings of the words, and their relation to what I know. My brain searches for a connection in order to make sense of the communication and understand the dialogue.

This struggling with the meanings of the words or terms requires extra time as I work to decipher the words and relate them to a familiar context. At this particular moment, my brain is trying to find out what this word or words mean, and the arrows in the box are moving in an attempt to make connections. Furthermore, new words that are abstract, like *disposition, character, criteria, concept, opportunity, objective,* and so on, are very difficult to interpret and understand.

This internal dialogue was more apparent than ever when I was participating in coursework in my master's and doctoral programs. Because I was familiar with my learning style, I was able to scrutinize or assess what style worked or didn't work for me. One of my classes in my first year in the master's program was a research course. The class material and vocabulary were all new to me; thus, I had to work harder than everyone else to take the time to study the vocabulary. In addition, most of the new words were abstract and theoretical, which made the work of understanding them that much more complicated.

In my doctoral course I recall I had trouble with *qualitative research* and *quantitative research* when these terms were first introduced to us. Furthermore, there were more complex words to follow as I progressed in my doctoral program—terms such as *phenomenology, heuristic, ethnography, grounded theory,* and *hermeneutic.* It seemed that most of the vocabulary was about methods and approaches, and they were confusing at first and so foreign to me. I eventually gained insights into these concepts and had an idea about the meanings of each of these methods or approaches.

Consequently, this struggle with language during my studies caused me to develop the conceptual design to understand my thinking processes. I can readily say that the design has helped me tremendously in my higher education career. I am also hoping and know that it will definitely help students, teachers, and other people in their studies and different fields of work. The design provides a visual picture of how some of us learn concepts when we are processing information in two languages, and it gives both the learners and their teachers a way to visualize the learning processes that are occurring.

I think teachers need to get their students to become cognizant of their thinking and learning. Students will then know what their strengths are as well as their weaknesses in regard to their learning and speaking of the English language. I wish I had been aware of some of the things I mentioned about my thinking process earlier in life rather than at the "end" of my education. If I had known, the awareness would have alleviated some of the situations I experienced in my classes as well as out of the classroom when I questioned my ability to think, reason, and learn.

My Learning Process

The protocol that I use when I experience this particular phenomenon of not knowing the meaning of words is to take the words apart and look in the dictionary to find some contextual meaning. I do this by repeating to myself in Apache what the professor said in English to see if that can help me understand. I also think about how these words are used in a sentence, along with its context. I am doing all these "extra" processes and steps in class while the lecture has continued and not slowed down to accommodate my learning style. I then have a lot of catching up to do. I write the words or phrases in my notes and start my "investigation" as soon as I get my hands on a dictionary or other reference books. Usually, this occurs at home during my studying time or at the Arizona State University Library. If and when this process is successful, I am able to provide a response in English. This processing time varies, with understanding occurring anywhere after ten minutes, three hours, or even a day or days.

I believe that this slow rate of comprehension is due to the new vocabulary that is not known or easily translated to the Apache language. In many cases, Apache vocabulary for the English words used in the dialogue or lecture does not exist. As a result, the brain of an Apache speaker is not able to relate or make connections; it can identify no prior knowledge, no related experiences or uses. Consequently, the Apache speaker has to slow down and work harder to comprehend the topic of discussion.

The Apache speaker has to shift his or her thinking so that he or she is thinking in Apache; the individual has to reiterate and translate what was said in English to Apache. This means literally translating what was said word for word, along with repeating the phrases that were said in English and trying to say them by using the Apache language.

I recall many times when I called my mother on the phone to see what she could tell me about a specific English word and its translation to Apache. We discussed the word, and she suggested a meaning, and sometimes she hit it right on target. Then I got all excited and took notes so that I could go back to my lecture topic and "plug in" the meaning I had just discovered.

Strategies that I used to cope with this type of learning—my learning style—are repeating everything in Apache to myself, as I just explained in the last paragraph, and being aware of wait time. This second strategy helped me to know that the comprehension would occur—just at a slower pace. I learned to be patient after I realized the mental processing that was occurring. It was not necessary to get upset or frustrated. Now that I understand my learning processes, I consider them special and of interest. Also, I realize that there are a lot of students and adults who experience this exact thing and do not know how to deal with it.

This phenomenon is neither a setback nor a dilemma. I am simply aware of how one processes words when developing a second language and the importance of understanding the rate of response or wait time. From my experience, more wait time may be required than what research currently tells us, which is about three to five seconds. If you notice, my understanding often took hours or days; therefore, the wait time is very critical. I encourage teachers to wait more than the five seconds, keeping in mind what is going on in the minds of our Apache students or other ELLs. I want to emphasize how many times I finally understood the details or the topics of discussion after several hours or a day (or even days). In the end, I learned to be nice to myself, and to be patient, knowing that understanding would come sometime soon.

I've also discovered that one of my learning styles is being very quiet at first when something is being taught or presented. I am like a digital camera, taking in every shot from every angle then viewing all the shots and editing them several times later before I am satisfied with a photo. My observation skills are a strong point in my learning, so at a meeting I'll be sitting and taking notes diligently, all the while listening and observing everything. Then later, using my conceptual design, I'll go over my notes and develop a series of questions, which I ask at the next meeting. This self-paced learning process allows me to become familiar with the topic, and I feel comfortable asking questions.

One of my major concerns when it comes to our Apache language and acquisition of a second language is the need for a strong "base" language, which *should* be our Apache language. However, most of our Apache students now speak English that is intermingled with Apache. This language is often not recognized as a valid form of communication but seen as a deficit. Teachers need to acknowledge and respect the language that students come with to school and use that to build a foundation for learning the English language in a more formal context.

When I was in high school, I had to take four years of formal English courses. These English courses were difficult for me since we had to learn about grammar, sentence structure, and all the ways of English usage. It may have been in my freshman or sophomore year that I got so frustrated about not knowing the terms, such as *interrogative, pronoun, participles, comparative, superlative,* and so on, that one day I just grabbed my English workbook and "dissected" it and studied each chapter as I never had before. This took me a while, but I made sure it stayed in my brain. I did this by saying the words, looking up the definitions, studying how they are used in sentences, and knowing parts of sentences. I did this out of frustration, but at the time I was not aware of what was going on, and I had no idea how it tied in with my Apache language.

English is a difficult language, with all its rules and exceptions. I know that our English teacher taught us the English content from a green workbook, and we worked on each page in class. Most of the words that detail sentence structure and parts of speech are abstract. Therefore, I got tired of trying to do the work and not knowing what the words meant and their usage. The frustration caused me to take the extra time to learn about the English language.

I grew up speaking only the Apache language. When I entered Head Start, most of my classmates were from the community, and we all spoke Apache fluently; it was a good thing that our teacher and instructional assistant spoke Apache. This made us feel at ease and comfortable because we could communicate with them. However, as I progressed through elementary school, I had no choice but to learn the English language in order for me to learn and be successful in school.

I had Apache as my strong base language, and English was and is my second language; therefore, I think I picked up the English language easily. Because of my fluency in the Apache language and my awareness of my culture, I was a healthy, well-rounded, whole person when it came to my identity or knowledge of who I was. In addition, as I stated earlier, I had no choice but to learn English as my second language, and if students learn their native Apache language first, they will also have to learn the English language. However, parents and students think that if their child learns English first, they'll be smarter, and life will be easier. In reality, it is the other way around. They need to learn Apache first, and then English. Doing so will be a long-term benefit. I made it through high school, college, and graduate school and eventually earned my doctoral degree, and I give partial credit to my strong Apache language foundation and cultural identity.

Over the course of my educational career, I've experienced a huge learning curve in the formal courses that I took at Arizona State University and in the jobs that I've had. As I reflect, I realize that I do not go to the box with the arrows in my conceptual design as much as I used to. I believe it is because now I know more about leadership, professional development, K–8 education, school systems, budgets, and so on. This list could go on and on. My point is that I've accumulated and stored so much information from my experiences that I can retrieve information when I need to. I hardly visit that place of the unknown these days, but when I do need to revisit the conceptual design, I make every effort to proceed with the process that is so well known to me.

One of my colleagues and I talked about this design, and I was explaining the details and the flow of information to her. After my introduction and explanation of the process, she said to me, "But Rea, you're fluent in English, you speak so well, and the way you switch the languages, one would never have known what was going on in your head or the difficult process you just explained to me about your design." She was suggesting that it was hard to believe that I actually struggled with the language and took the extra time to analyze the words. The extra time and extra skills I applied also helped to refine my English language acquisition.

Furthermore, I took a trip to China one summer with some of our Apache students from the reservation. This was a leadership and cultural exchange camp that was hosted by the Chinese in partnership with our school district. I, along with a colleague, had to

Reflection 3.1

What were some of Rea's feelings and attitudes that resulted from her experiences as an ELL?

If a highly educated individual must use so many strategies to be successful at learning in an English environment, what might ELLs need in order to learn effectively? Do these needs vary for mathematics students at different grade levels?

How might you help your ELLs recognize, manage, and take advantage of the internal dialogue that occurs as they learn mathematics?

present and talk about our Apache culture to the Chinese group. After our PowerPoint presentation, we had a question-and-answer session. Most of the students asked great questions and wanted to know more about our tribe. One of the Chinese counselors asked me about my English language; he questioned me about the fact that I speak English so well when English is not even my first language. My explanation was that I am an American, but I am also a Native American. I had to learn the English language from the time I entered school. In addition, in America everyone has to know the English language to survive and be successful. He was really intrigued about this, since students in China struggle with learning the English language.

I have had a few opportunities to present my conceptual design to audiences in different venues. I always receive positive feedback after my presentations, and there is always at least one individual who has experienced the same difficulties that I did. Furthermore, the design makes a lot of sense to some people. Teachers see how it could help them in their instruction, and, at the same time, they realize how the design would help and benefit their students. As I share the conceptual design, I describe it and provide examples so that my audience will be able to follow along. I find that every time I present this design, I say the exact same words verbatim as I have in another place and time. I am fond of this conceptual design because it opened my eyes and provided understanding to my thinking process; in addition, it reminds me of my struggles and how I overcame them. I also treasure it because it tells me that I can take control of my learning and that I do not have to feel helpless and vulnerable.

I hope that this design will help others to understand the processing that is occurring as an ELL is learning. I know that being cognizant of one's learning will be of benefit and that it will make life easier to know what is taking place in one's head. I challenge mathematics educators to use this conceptual design to help ELLs understand and accept the mental processes that are occurring in them. In doing so, ELLs will not question their ability to learn but will be empowered to think and reason in both languages.

Chapter 4

Elements of an Effective Mathematics Community for ELLs

by Sylvia Celedón-Pattichis and Nora G. Ramirez

---

more**4U**
- **Those Kids!** (journal article)

Consider the following views of an effective mathematics teacher who works with ELLs in an elementary school:

> "Consistency is important…. If I expect something from my students, I don't say I expect it one day and let it go for two, three days. It's every day." (Razfar, Khisty, and Chval 2011, p. 202)

> "I tell them [the students] the reason why we're in school is because we are learning, and if we make a mistake, that's great. Let's put it up on the board so that we could figure out how we could fix it." (Ibid.)

> "There is a lot of analysis they have to do. They have to think about their own thinking." (Ibid.)

> Sara was immersing students in an environment filled with sophisticated talk. When asked why she used sophisticated language with her ELLs, Sara replied: "When are they going to learn it? How are they going to learn it? They encounter those words in books. I'm angry with the notion that students are not competent to learn." (Chval and Chávez 2011/2012, p. 263)

It is clear that this teacher has high expectations for all of her students. These expectations are exhibited in the daily demands that she makes on students in using sophisticated language and writing to foster metacognition. This teacher also poses challenging mathematical tasks that are beyond grade level and that help students achieve at high levels on standardized tests (Razfar, Khisty, and Chval 2011; see also case 5 by Chval in chapter 5). In addition, she creates a mathematics discourse community that exemplifies the five guiding principles presented in chapter 2 for teaching mathematics to ELLs.

We recognize that the quality of the classroom environment has a big impact on the mathematics learning of ELLs. We described several aspects of the classroom community in chapter 2, and now we specifically address four areas of the learning environment:

1. Beyond setting high expectations
2. Taking time to listen, observe, and learn
3. Understanding individualistic vs. collectivistic value systems
4. Affirming ELLs' cultures in the mathematics classroom

Beyond Setting High Expectations

Even though we recognize that many educators are adamant in stating that they have high expectations for students, often their practices in classrooms with ELLs do not indicate that these are in place. Teachers of ELLs might examine their practices to determine whether their actions in the classroom parallel their stated expectations. If not, the teachers should have a means of determining what the issues are. We present a teacher's journey in uncovering her bias in a mathematics classroom and the actions that she took to address inequities that she observed in her interactions with students. We thank her for her honesty in allowing us as educators to learn from her experience and self-analysis.

Maryann Wickett, a teacher of third and fourth graders, shared the story of her self-examination as she scrutinized her behaviors during class discussions to determine whether they were hindering some students while giving access to others. As part of her routine, she recorded the students' mathematical contributions on chart paper. Doing so allowed Ms. Wickett to keep track of the teacher-student interactions in her classroom and provided ways for the students to have access through auditory and visual modalities. It also showed students that she respected their thinking.

What Ms. Wickett found from doing a self-analysis of the teacher-student interactions recorded in the charts was that she called on two boys before girls, she called on third graders before fourth graders, and she called on ELLs last. On the basis of her findings, she focused on giving "all children opportunities to respond first and equally in all class discussions" (Wickett 1997, p. 104). She continues to monitor her teaching by analyzing the chart-paper records and inviting visitors to make notes on her classroom discussions. Furthermore, she pauses to observe who has had an opportunity to talk and who has not. This strategy provides students with time to think and process. After a year of making an effort to engage more students in class discussions, this teacher learned the following:

> By understanding myself and looking at my biases openly and honestly—without self-condemnation—I am trying to figure out better ways to educate children. I am giving more students respect and opportunities. I also know that this is just the beginning of my journey. (Wickett 1997, p. 106)

We want to reiterate that all of us set high expectations. However, what needs to be addressed is the alignment of high expectations with teacher actions. Teachers should constantly monitor their actions and make a plan to explicitly change behaviors when necessary. Coaches and administrators can support the self-analysis, model lessons that exemplify high expectations, and assist teachers as they make changes.

Reflection 4.1

1. How might you determine if your teacher actions are aligned with the expectations that you have for all students in your classroom?

2. Complete the following sentence, thinking of as many possibilities as you can:

   If I have high expectations for my students, then in my classroom I would

   _____ .

3. Ms. Wickett's journey involved self-analysis of her interactions with her students. In your role as a teacher, coach, or administrator, how can you support—

   a. self-analysis in your educational community?

   b. teachers in developing classroom communities where high expectations are the foundation of the mathematical tasks and the discourse?

In addition to monitoring their actions, teachers should examine the mathematical task that they are posing and the manner in which they are engaging students in the task to determine whether these are in alignment with the high expectations that they have set for their students (see the Task Lens and the Power and Participation Lens in chapter 12 and the tools at www.nctm.org/more4u).

Chapters 5 and 6 present cases of practice and research from effective classrooms that demonstrate what high expectations look like and sound like. In addition, we invite you to read and listen to a few cases related to high expectations at www.nctm.org/more4u. Jana Ward's Triangle Lesson video clip, found in the online materials for chapter 13, shows fourth-grade students working on a task that engages them in exploring the triangle inequality theorem. This task exemplifies high expectations and involves content often covered in middle or high school.

Taking Time to Listen, Observe, and Learn

Teachers should listen with both a "mathematical ear" and a "personal ear." Using the personal ear, they should attend to getting to know the students in a way that addresses their language and culture. To listen effectively, often they must ask questions that show concern for and interest in students' day-to-day experiences. In middle school and secondary classrooms, some students may feel invisible and never talk directly to a teacher. Because of the structure and time limitations in secondary classrooms, it is imperative to have effective and efficient strategies to get to know students. Consider the following examples of classroom strategies for understanding students' personal and mathematical experiences:

- A secondary teacher uses a strategy called Check-In and Check-Out with her students. At the beginning of class, she takes five minutes to check in with students about how their day is going and what is happening in their lives. At the end of class, she has students check out by allowing them time to reflect on what they understood in the day's lesson. In doing so, she has learned that students appreciate the space that she creates for them to share their thoughts and feelings, and she is able to connect with them on a more personal level. This space also allows students to reflect on what they have learned about mathematics. In addition, what this teacher has learned from implementing this strategy is that students engage more easily in the mathematics task once they have had the time to share their personal experiences.

- A high school mathematics teacher built relationships with students when he replaced the desks with tables to have students work in cooperative groups. The teacher spent half the class time walking around and talking to students at their tables and leading them in significant mathematical discourse. He commented that this was the first time that he had talked to all students and was able to know students on both a personal and a mathematical level.

- An Arizona teacher became aware of her students' personal struggles with the passage of Arizona House Bill 1070 in the spring of 2010. After this tough immigration bill had passed, this teacher found it necessary to pull the class together and give them time to ask questions, discuss their concerns and feelings, and let them know that she cared about them. This teacher is an example of someone who listens to and cares about students' personal and emotional needs and knows that these often must be addressed before any learning can occur (Valenzuela 1999). This example also relates to the teacher actions that are essential for teaching ELLs in advocating for students' human and educational rights.

Chapters 5 and 6 present examples of teachers listening to and observing students. Teachers gain insights about what students understand in mathematics and the linguistic support needed to help ELLs develop English as a second language. In addition, chapter 7 provides an opportunity to listen to parents struggling with differences in culture, language, and schooling—particularly in mathematics. Examples of how we can learn from students as we conduct personal interviews appear in chapter 8.

Individualistic vs. Collectivistic Value Systems

To help teachers understand students' cultural tendencies, we draw on the work of Rothstein-Fisch and Trumbull (2008, p. 10):

> It can be very useful for teachers to understand the dominant tendencies of a cultural group as a starting place for exploration and further learning.

Rothstein-Fisch and Trumbull explain that there are two value systems—individualistic and collectivistic—that may distinguish different ways of being, knowing, and interacting. For example, in an individualistic value system, children are raised to be independent, whereas in a collectivist value system, children—many from immigrant families—are raised to be part of a group. In a collectivistic value system, choices are made on the basis of what is best for the family, and completing tasks as a group is important. Although considering the value system of a culture is important, listening to students will enable teachers to avoid making generalizations based on a student's ethnicity, language, and culture. "Every culture has both individualistic and collectivistic values," according to Rothstein-Fisch and Trumbull (2008, p. 9), who note that in a culture, one system is not valued more than the other. Rather, there are degrees of emphasis.

Traditionally, schools in the United States have tended to be more aligned with an individualistic value system, which represents mainstream U.S. culture. However, in the mathematics discourse community, as proposed in chapter 2, both systems are valued and necessary. Students learn from working collectively on a mathematical task while being held accountable individually for explaining their thinking and demonstrating understanding. For instance, one might consider placing a student as a competent problem solver in an individualistic process while having students use each other as resources in a collectivist setting. When ELLs are trying to make meaning of mathematics, they are more successful if they operate in a mathematics discourse community (Chval and Khisty 2009; Morales, Khisty, and Chval 2003; Moschkovich and Nelson-Barber 2009;

Reflection 4.3

1. Does your classroom have characteristics of both an individualistic and a collectivistic value system? Think of specific examples.

2. How do you become aware of the type of value system that is emphasized in the students' home life? How does that translate to your interactions with families and students?

Willey 2010), which has many characteristics of a collectivistic value system. This does not mean that ELLs should never work independently in a classroom. Teachers should observe students to gain insights on the ways in which they engage in this community and provide students with opportunities to participate both individually and in a group. More important, teachers should accept a student's value system and give opportunities for students to navigate within both systems. Teachers may make parents and students aware of the expectations in their classroom by showing the need for students to perform both individually and collectively.

Affirming ELLs' Cultures in the Mathematics Classroom

We draw on Nieto's (1999, p. xix) work to define culture:

> Students of all backgrounds deserve the very best our society can give them ... their cultures, languages, and experiences need to be acknowledged, valued, and used as important sources of their education. It is unfortunate that too many young people continue to be disenfranchised, disrespected, and devalued in our schools, and the result is that we all lose bright futures, the hope for something better, and even real lives in the process.

Culture encompasses the traditions of a group, its language, identities, sexual orientation, socioeconomic status, race, and so on. Culture is not static; it even varies for people from a specific group. According to Moschkovich (1999), it is critical for teachers to consider the culture of their classrooms to find out ways in which students have engaged in past mathematics classrooms and also to let them know what the norms are for engaging in the present classroom. Teachers should affirm students' cultures and ways of doing mathematics.

Affirming a student's language and culture can have such a major impact on ELLs' mathematics learning that we identified it as a guiding principle in chapter 2—P5: Cultural and linguistic differences as intellectual resources. Using the students' language and culture as intellectual resources requires that teachers build relationships with the students and guide students in building relationships with one another so that having respect for, listening to one another, and questioning and critiquing the work of others become norms in the mathematics classroom. We take the stance that teachers and students should take advantage of opportunities for integrating a student's culture in a natural and not an artificial way. Learning about a way in which students dress may not be as important as finding out about ways in which they handle conflicts. Students' cultural practices of interacting with one another and resolving conflicts, for example, might be at odds with the demands of a mathematics classroom when students are asked to agree or disagree with a solution. Thus, teachers need to support mathematics discourse practices, yet acknowledge that these practices may differ from students' cultural norms of respecting the ideas of others (Valdés 1996).

Validating, valuing, acknowledging, celebrating, nurturing, and *showing interest in* students' lives are words and phrases that come to mind when we think about affirming students in the mathematics classroom. We acknowledge that teachers may not get to know all the cultures represented in a mathematics classroom and that not all mathematical tasks may be culturally relevant. However, observing, listening, and asking authentic questions will enhance the teacher's ability to build relationships with ELLs, among ELLs, and with other students. We share some examples of how this might play out in the classroom:

- A second-grade mathematics teacher has her students provide a compliment or a question about a strategy used when sharing solutions to a mathematical task. Students listen and respect one another as they share their strategies. These norms may be different for ELLs who come from countries where asking questions may be seen as being disrespectful. However, this teacher expects all students to engage in a mathematics community that fosters the practice of offering compliments as a way of creating a nurturing environment.

- Recognizing that some of the ELLs in his seventh-grade classroom come from a collectivist value system and thus prefer to work in groups, Mr. Lee makes plans for these students to work on a project together while others might be working alone. At the same time, he fosters the ELLs' independence by requiring them to turn in individual papers and plans for them to present their work as a group, making sure that all students have a part in the presentation.

- Ms. Marik is working to develop as a classroom norm the practice of students asking questions of other students when they present in her high school geometry class. She recognizes that Su, her ELL student, never asks questions or causes any disequilibrium in the classroom. Before the students' presentations, she comments that even though they might not feel comfortable asking questions of their classmates, she wants them to think about a question to ask because from their questioning of one another the whole class will learn more. To facilitate Su's engagement in questioning, she pairs students to formulate one question to ask of the student presenter.

Reflection 4.4

1. What actions do you take to affirm students' identity? What do you do to build relationships with ELLs in the mathematics classroom?

2. To what extent do you build relationships with ELLs and their families *outside* of the mathematics classroom?

We recognize that a student might also come from a different educational culture. Valdés (1996) explains that Latino parents are frequently concerned about the need for children to have a broader perspective on what it means to be "educated." In their view, to be educated means to show respect toward others and to place others above self. What this means for teachers is that parents from collectivist societies are often concerned about how students are behaving in the mathematics classroom. This does not mean that they are not concerned about their children's learning, but their children's social interactions may be paramount. This raises important implications for teachers, who need to be prepared to address with parents not only the mathematics achievement of the student but also the student's ability to work with others. We invite you to read about parents' perspectives on their children's mathematical learning in chapter 7.

In addition, Gutiérrez's work in chapter 6 (case 6) focuses on getting to know students beyond the mathematics classroom. In chapter 1, we discussed the thoughts that Rebecca Merkel's ESL students share in their Prezi presentation on culture and language and specific actions that teachers can take to address their needs (see chapter 1 and the accompanying materials at www.nctm.org/more4u). As described in chapter 13,

Chval's TODOS LIVE presentation at www.nctm.org/more4u offers examples that illustrate mathematics teachers' need to be aware of the importance of affirming students' culture and language.

References

Chval, Kathryn B., and Óscar Chávez. "Designing Math Lessons for English Language Learners." *Mathematics Teaching in the Middle School* 17 (December 2011/January 2012): 261–65.

Chval, Kathryn B., and Lena L. Khisty. "Latino Students, Writing, and Mathematics: A Case Study of Successful Teaching and Learning." In *Multilingualism in Mathematics Classrooms: Global Perspectives*, edited by Richard Barwell, pp. 128–44. Clevedon, UK: Multilingual Matters, 2009.

Morales, Hector, Lena L. Khisty, and Kathryn B. Chval. "Beyond Discourse: A Multimodal Perspective of Learning Mathematics in a Multilingual Context." In *Proceedings of the 2003 Joint Meeting of PME and PMENA*, edited by Neil Pateman, Barbara J. Dougherty, and Joseph T. Zilliox, vol. 3, pp. 133–40. Honolulu: Center for Research and Development Group, University of Hawaii, 2003.

Moschkovich, Judit N. "Supporting the Participation of English Language Learners in Mathematical Discussions." *For the Learning of Mathematics* 19 (January 1999): 11–19.

Moschkovich, Judit, and Sharon Nelson-Barber. "What Mathematics Teachers Need to Know about Culture and Language." In *Culturally Responsive Mathematics Education*, edited by Brian Greer, Swapna Mukhopadhyay, Arthur B. Powell, and Sharon Nelson-Barber, pp. 111–36. New York: Routledge, 2009.

Nieto, Sonia. *Affirming Diversity: The Sociopolitical Context of Multicultural Education.* 2nd ed. New York: Longman, 1999.

Razfar, Aria, Lena Licón Khisty, and Kathryn B. Chval. "'Re-Mediating Second Language Acquisition: A Sociocultural Perspective for Language Development." *Mind, Culture, and Activity* 18, no. 3 (2011): 195–215.

Rothstein-Fisch, Carrie, and Elise Trumbull. *Managing Diverse Classrooms: How to Build on Students' Cultural Strengths.* Alexandria, Va.: Association for Supervision and Curriculum Development, 2008.

Valdés, Guadalupe. *Con Respeto: Bridging the Distances between Culturally Diverse Families and Schools: An Ethnographic Portrait.* New York: Teachers College Press, 1996.

Valenzuela, Angela. *Subtractive Schooling: U.S. Mexican Youth and the Politics of Caring.* Albany, N.Y.: State University of New York, 1999.

Wickett, Maryann. "Uncovering Bias in the Classroom—a Personal Journey." In *Multicultural and Gender Equity in the Mathematics Classroom: The Gift of Diversity,* 1997 Yearbook of the National Council of Teachers of Mathematics (NCTM), edited by Janet Trentacosta, pp. 102–6. Reston, Va.: NCTM, 1997.

Willey, Craig. "Teachers Developing Mathematics Discourse Communities with Latinas/os." In *Proceedings of the 32nd Annual Meeting of the North American Chapter of the International Group for the Psychology of Mathematics Education,* edited by Patricia Brosnan, Diana B. Erchick, and Lucia Flevares, pp. 530–38. Columbus: Ohio State University, 2010.

Chapter 5

Cases of Practice: Teaching Mathematics to ELLs in Elementary School

Chapter 5 is intended to make the points in chapter 2 come to life at the elementary level. The chapter presents five cases of elementary practice by different authors. Some of the authors point readers to video clips, available at www.nctm.org/more4u, to illustrate teaching strategies that they describe.

Celedón-Pattichis and Turner open the chapter with case 1, which presents video clips of two kindergarten teachers, one an English-speaking teacher and the other a bilingual teacher. These examples show how teachers support ELLs and bilingual students as they explain their mathematical thinking as well as how teachers position students as competent problem solvers.

In cases 2 and 3, two teachers at Monte Vista Elementary School in Las Cruces, New Mexico, and their university collaborator, Cathy Kinzer, point to the need to create language-rich environments by sharing the teachers' personal stories of their experiences first as English language learners and then as teachers of ELLs. Case 2 shares the strategies that Maricela Rincón uses to engage her third-grade students in making meaning of fractions. Four accompanying video clips illustrate how Maricela creates a mathematics discourse community that affords students opportunities to talk about fractions and demonstrate the use of graphic representations to make sense of fractions. Two of the clips show how students at the "bridging" or "advanced" stage of language development present their work in decomposing numbers to facilitate mathematical computations. Case 3 shares the concept map approach that Ricardo Rincón uses with his fourth- and fifth-grade students to build background knowledge of number lines. The accompanying video clip shows how the teacher draws on students' in- and out-of-school experiences as the base for the background knowledge that he builds on to launch an activity on adding and subtracting fractions by using a number line.

In case 4, Marco Ramirez and Chris Confer share how they work with teachers in ELL classrooms to prepare and support ELLs before making presentations to the whole class. This vignette exemplifies a method of ensuring that ELLs have the mathematical language and support needed to explain their thinking.

Last, in case 5, Kathryn Chval presents what she has learned from an extraordinarily effective fifth-grade teacher of ELLs. In particular, she illustrates how this teacher facilitated the participation of ELLs in mathematics by posing challenging mathematical tasks and fostering an MDC that supports ELLs as they participate in the classroom discourse, communicating with and listening to one another.

Case 1

Using Storytelling to Pose Word Problems in Kindergarten ESL and Bilingual Classrooms

by Sylvia Celedón-Pattichis and Erin Turner

more4u

- Kinder Study Prediction (worksheet)
- Kinder Study Results (table)
- ELL as a Competent Problem Solver (video clip)
- Storytelling—Partitive Division (video clip)

Consider the following word problems:

- Carla has 7 dollars. How many more dollars does she need to earn so that she will have 11 dollars to buy a puppy? (Problem type: Join Change Unknown)
- Robin has 3 packages of gum. There are 6 pieces of gum in each package. How many pieces of gum does Robin have altogether? (Problem type: Multiplication)
- Nineteen children are going to the circus. Five children can ride in each car. How many cars will be needed to get all 19 children to the circus? (Problem type: Measurement Division with Remainder)

In the online materials for chapter 5 at www.nctm.org/more4u, you will find the Kinder Study Prediction worksheet. Use it to predict what percentage of kindergartners you think would be able to solve each of the three problems. Once you have recorded your prediction for each problem type, check your percentages against those provided in Kinder Study Results, also at www.nctm.org/more4u. What trends do you observe in the results?

The study by Turner, Celedón-Pattichis, and Marshall (2008) shows that Latina and Latino kindergarten students can engage in solving problems of a variety of types when afforded the opportunity to do so. Most students can solve problems of the easier types, such as Join and Separate Result Unknown. About half of the students can solve problems of the types Join Change Unknown, Multiplication, Multi-Step, and Division. Compare and Division with Remainder problems tend to be more difficult for students, but about one-fourth of the students can solve these problems. The different problem types are included in Kinder Study Prediction at www.nctm.org/more4u. Although the wording of the problems is different in the Common Core State Standards (2010), their structures are similar. The percentages in the study by Carpenter and colleagues (1993)

The research for case 1 was supported by the National Science Foundation, under grant ESI-0424983, awarded to the Center for Mathematics Education of Latinos/as (CEMELA). The views expressed here are those of the authors and do not necessarily reflect the views of the funding agency.

indicate even higher percentages for students from white, middle-class backgrounds. The point of this comparison is that young children from different cultural and linguistic backgrounds can solve challenging mathematical tasks.

The case of practice presented below illustrates how two kindergarten teachers—one an ESL teacher and the other a bilingual teacher—used storytelling to engage all students in problem solving in order to support their development of language in explaining their mathematical thinking while developing their basic mathematics skills, and to position them as competent problem solvers.

Context of the Classrooms

We focus on two vignettes drawn from the larger kindergarten study by Turner, Celedón-Pattichis, and Marshall (2008), Turner et al. (2009), and Turner and Celedón-Pattichis (2011). Both vignettes include video clips (see ELL as a Competent Problem Solver and Storytelling—Partitive Division at www.nctm.org/more4u). The two schools studied consisted predominantly of Latina and Latino student populations (75 percent and 87 percent), and almost all students (over 90 percent) qualified for free or reduced-price lunch. The teachers whose classrooms were studied are identified as Ms. Field and Ms. Arenas; all names are pseudonyms. Ms. Field, who was trained in English as a second language (ESL) strategies, taught mathematics in English. Almost half of Ms. Field's students were ELLs, and the rest were native English speakers. Ms. Arenas, a native Spanish speaker, followed a bilingual model of instruction, and all of her mathematics lessons were in Spanish. All of her students were native Spanish speakers with varying degrees of English language proficiency. Both teachers taught in an all-day kindergarten program and had approximately 18 to 20 students in their classes.

We selected these classrooms because the teachers had participated in professional development focused on young children's mathematical thinking (i.e., cognitively guided instruction, see Carpenter et al. [1999]), and they were interested in conducting problem-solving lessons with their students. This was the first year that both teachers used what they had learned about children's thinking to plan and implement problem-solving tasks.

Findings

Although we did not focus on storytelling in our professional development with teachers, one practice that we found to be common to both teachers in our kindergarten study was the use of authentic, "story-like" conversations to generate mathematical problems. For example, in the spring of the school year, Ms. Field used books to talk about honeybees in an informal, conversational manner that provided rich contextual information. This informal approach afforded students the opportunity to share their own personal experiences and prior knowledge about honeybees. At some point in the lesson, Ms. Field showed her students a honeycomb. One student, Bernardo, noticed that the honeycomb was the same shape as a hexagon pattern block, and Ms. Field took advantage of his observation by posing the following multiplication problem: "Then how many sides would 3 hexagons have?" What is important to notice is how Ms. Field used the story of honeybees and informal conversations to build a new, shared experience, examining the geometry of a honeycomb, which then allowed her to generate other mathematics word problems.

Similarly, Ms. Arenas drew on events that were occurring in the community as a way of posing word problems. The video clip Storytelling—Partitive Division illustrates this point, showing how the teacher elicited and built on her students' experiences of celebrating Easter with their families.

Video Clip

ELL as a Competent Problem Solver (ESL Classroom)

Ms. Field drew from contexts and events that were familiar to students' lives, such as playing with marbles at school and finding pennies, to pose Multiplication and Separate Result Unknown problems. The following transcript shows how Ms. Field draws from the context of marbles to pose Join Result Unknown problems, how she positions an ELL as a competent problem solver, and how she supports this student in explaining her mathematical thinking (see ELL as a Competent Problem Solver at www.nctm.org/more4u).

Ms. Field: You need one more? Put a thumb up when you are ready to go. OK. Ready? OK. Everybody, erase your board. Here we go. Let's see. Alma had 3 marbles, OK? And Nickie had 4 marbles. How many did they have altogether? So how many did Alma have? 3. And Nickie had? 4. So how many did we have altogether? OK. Samantha, what did you do? May I hold this? Could you tell us what you did? [*The teacher shows the whiteboard to the group.*] You knew it was 3, and you counted on? And how did you count on?

Student 1: 4, 5, 6, 7.

Ms. Field: Ah, very good. So 3 and 4; count again and see. Who got it a different way? Samantha counted on; who did it a different way? Lázaro?

Student 2: [*Inaudible.*]

Ms. Field: Go ahead; show me how you counted.

Student 2: …I go backwards and counted…

Ms. Field: So you knew that was 4 [*points to his board*], so what's the next number? 5.

Student 2: 7.

Ms. Field: OK, everybody, erase. Oh, wait. Would you tell us what you did, Alma?

Student 3: I put a 3 and 4.

Ms. Field: [*Takes her whiteboard to show*] Everyone, look at Alma's. Cap your marker. Alma, tell us what you did.

Student 3: [*Inaudible.*]

Ms. Field: And show us how you got your answer.

Student 3: I put 2, this first and this first …[*inaudible*].

Ms. Field: And how did you get your answer? What did you do? What's your answer? This is good. Did you count, or how did you do it? [*She has 3 and 4 written on her board and corresponding lines above.*] Show us.

Student 3:	I count 1, 2, 3, then 1, 2, 3, 4.
Ms. Field:	And then what's your answer? How did you do it? Did you count them? Show me. How did you do it? Oh, you used this [*referring to hundreds chart*]? Come up and show us how you did it. Everyone, hold your hands, and see what Alma is doing. [*Alma goes to the hundreds chart.*]. Show us.
Student 3:	1, 2, 3, [*points to numbers as she counts*] 4.
Ms. Field:	So you had 3, and then you knew you had 4 more, so you counted 4 more, so count 4 more. [*Together with Alma:*] 1, 2, 3, 4. So what was your answer? [*Alma points to 7.*] Very good, very good, thank you.

This example shows how Ms. Field valued the contributions of an ELL at the beginning stage of English language development. This teacher action is critical; research has shown that the more students are positioned as competent problem solvers, the more rapid is the trajectory to their participation in explaining their mathematical thinking (Empson 2003). In fact, by the end of the school year, we noticed the generative power of this practice, when one ELL posed a Separate Result Unknown problem for her teacher and her peers to solve: "Ms. Field, wait; let's try another one! Let's try this one. One girl have [sic] 10 rings, and then one [other] girl take[s] 3. So how many is left?"

Video Clip

Storytelling—Partitive Division (Bilingual Classroom)

Ms. Arenas typically began her lesson by asking students to listen carefully (*"Fíjense amorcitos"* [Listen, my little loved ones]) because she was going to share a story (*"Pues les voy a contar una historia"* [I am going to share a story]—see Turner et al. [2009]). The following transcript illustrates how Ms. Arenas built a story around a classroom activity that involved decorating and filling Easter baskets (See the video clip Storytelling—Partitive Division at www.nctm.org/more4u). The structure of the problem that she generated ($9 \div 3 = ?$) reflected an actual classroom event in which the student teachers needed to distribute nine eggs equally among three people.

Ms. Arenas:	*Vamos a ver otra. Fíjense, que estamos ya comprando los huevitos de pascua para sus canastas. Los huevitos de pascua. Y tenemos—* (Let's do another one. Listen, you know we're already buying the little Easter eggs for your baskets. The Easter eggs. And we have—)
Julieta:	*Maestra, mi mamá y una prima ya compraron las canastas.* (Teacher, my mom and a cousin already bought the baskets.)
Ms. Arenas:	*¿Ya compraron las canastas?* (They already bought the baskets?)
Julieta:	*¡Sí!* (Yes!)
Ms. Arenas:	*Ah, Ms. Marta y Ms. Antonia* [*two classroom assistants*] *ya las van a empezar a decorar. ¿Verdad? Las canastas de pascua. Entonces, adentro les vamos a poner unos huevitos.* (Oh, Ms. Marta and Ms. Antonia [classroom assistants] are going to start decorating them now. Right? The Easter baskets. Then, inside, we are going to put some little eggs.)
Alonso:	*¿Maestra? ¿Maestra?* (Teacher? Teacher?)

Ms. Arenas:	*¿Sí?* (Yes?)
Alonso:	*Mi mamá me va a comprar una canasta de basquetbol.* (My mom is going to buy me a basketball basket.)
Ms. Arenas:	*¿Para la pascua?* (For Easter?)
Alonso:	[*Nods.*]
Ms. Arenas:	*¡Ay, qué bonito!* (Oh, how nice!)
Student:	*Y maestra, mi mamá ya le echó dulces.* (And teacher, my mom already put the candies in.)
Ms. Arenas:	*¿Ya le echó huevitos? Pues ahora, Ms. Anabel y Ms. Crisanta* [*student teachers*] *trajeron 9 huevitos.* (She already put in little candy eggs? Well, today, Ms. Anabel and Ms. Crisanta [student teachers] brought 9 little [candy] eggs.) …
Ms. Arenas:	*Escuchen. Pero los quieren repartir, escuchen. Primero escuchen. 9 huevitos trajeron. Pero los quieren repartir entre Ms. Marta, Ms. Antonia y Ms. María. ¿Cuántos le van a quedar a cada una?* (Listen. But they want to share them, listen. First, listen. They brought 9 eggs. But they want to divide them among Ms. Marta, Ms. Antonia, and Ms. María. How many is each one going to get?)

This example shows how using storytelling with a context that was very familiar to students provided multiple entry points for students to contribute to the story by offering comments or posing questions as Ms. Arenas told the story. In other word problems, students co-constructed the story with the teacher by offering the number of people sharing twelve cookies or the price of a toy airplane. Although the process is not illustrated in this video clip, students were able to solve this problem by drawing nine eggs and three people, distributing one egg at a time to each person, and obtaining an answer of three eggs for each person.

Lessons Learned

What we learned from conducting the kindergarten study is that teachers use storytelling to connect students' home and community experiences with formal mathematics knowledge, to create spaces for students to co-construct stories with the teacher, and to help students explain their mathematical thinking as they also developed problem-solving and basic number skills. We emphasize the need to pose challenging mathematical tasks in kindergarten *before* students master basic mathematics skills. By the end of the year, students were competent and more confident not only as problem solvers but also as problem posers.

On the basis of the lessons that we learned, we offer suggestions of what teachers can do in the kindergarten classroom and what mathematics educators can do to prepare preservice elementary teachers working with young children. The need is urgent to challenge preconceived notions and deficit views of what young children can do mathematically—especially children who have historically been marginalized, including ELLs.

What teachers can do with young children in mathematics

Implementing the following suggestions can support ELLs in developing mathematical confidence and competence:

1. Provide ELLs with mathematical tasks that range from addition to subtraction, comparison, and division with remainder. (See problem types in Kinder Study Prediction at www.nctm.org/more4u.)
2. Use storytelling as a natural approach to make the mathematical tasks culturally relevant for young children. This allows multiple points of entry for students to engage with the stories and the mathematical task.
3. Observe the strategies that young children use to solve problems, and use their understanding to advance their mathematical thinking.
4. Position ELLs as competent problem solvers, and support them as they explain their mathematical thinking to others.

How an elementary mathematics methods course can use this work

We pose the following questions to preservice elementary teachers when we are covering a unit on children's early thinking about number in a mathematics methods course:

- What percentage of kindergarteners do you think can solve the following word problems by April of the school year? (Write down your prediction.)
- Which problems would be the most difficult? The easiest? Why?
- Think about how a young child (kindergarten, early first grade) might solve each of the problems?

The problems that we ask students to consider are found in Kinder Study Prediction in www.nctm.org/more4u. We provide the contexts of the kindergarten studies by Carpenter and colleagues' (1993) and Turner and colleagues (Turner, Celedón-Pattichis, and Marshall [2008], Turner et al. [2009], and Turner and Celedón-Pattichis [2011]). Carpenter and colleagues studied seventy white, middle-class children, whereas Turner and colleagues studied forty-five Latino and Latina low-income children. Kindergarten students in both studies were provided with several tools to solve the problems, and the interviewers conducting the pre- and post-assessments could read the problem to a child as many times as needed. We also let preservice teachers know that in the case of the work by Turner and colleagues, kindergartners could request that the problem be read in English or in Spanish.

After giving preservice teachers an opportunity to reflect on the questions for about ten minutes, we ask them to compare their predictions with the results of both studies (See Kinder Study Results in www.ncmt.org/more4u). Most preservice teachers are surprised to find that kindergartners can solve problems of types such as Comparison, Multiplication, and Partitive Division, including Division with Remainder. Our goal in presenting this activity in an elementary mathematics methods course is for preservice teachers to realize the underestimated capacity of young children to engage in challenging mathematics tasks and to take note of the teacher actions involved in facilitating classroom discussions with students who are learning English in different contexts.

In addition, we also ask preservice teachers to discuss which problems they think may be easier or more difficult for kindergarteners and why they think so. We ask them to notice differences between the wording of Join Result Unknown and the Comparison types of problems. Preservice teachers observe that problems of the Join Result Unknown and Separate Result Unknown types are often easier than problems of the Comparison and Start Unknown types, for example, because problems of the former types involve actions that can be modeled directly with different tools. Comparison problems, by contrast, involve a relationship between two numbers, and it is more difficult to know what to model directly, since no action is involved. Similarly, young children may not know how to begin to make a direct model if that is the only strategy they rely on to solve a Start Unknown type of problem.

Most preservice teachers notice that young children can engage in thinking about problems of the easier types by using direct modeling strategies, such as working with cubes to solve the following problem:

> Juan has 4 toy cars. His mother gives him 7 more. How many toy cars does Juan have altogether?

Young children can model the problem directly by forming a group of 4 cubes and another group of 7 cubes and then can solve by counting one by one or using other counting strategies to make 11. Or they can draw the toys. However, preservice teachers' predictions indicate that they do not believe that young children can solve more challenging problems.

After preservice teachers discuss the three points posed at the beginning, they have many more questions about how to engage ELLs—especially those in the early stages of language development—in solving challenging mathematics tasks. The video clip ELL as a Competent Problem Solver illustrates how a teacher who does not share the native language of the student positions a beginning ELL as a competent problem solver. The video clip Storytelling—Partitive Division shows how a bilingual teacher presents stories in an informal, conversational manner, including rich contextual information, and invites students to respond with questions or comments.

We include these video clips to offer counter evidence to the deficit views often voiced about what young children from culturally and linguistically diverse backgrounds can do. The video clips provide examples of teachers successfully creating mathematics discourse communities for young children. These videos also offer opportunities to identify practices described in chapter 2 with the language demand in mathematics lessons (LDML) tool discussed in chapter 10.

Case 2

Fostering an Equitable Classroom for English Language Learners

by Cathy Kinzer and Maricela Rincón
as told by Maricela Rincón

· ·

more**4**u
- Fractions Lesson (Beginning) (video clip)
- Fractions Lesson (Group Work) (video clip)
- Decomposing 1 Valerie (video clip)
- Decomposing 2 Georgieann (video clip)

· ·

According to NCTM (2000), "In this changing world, those who understand and can do mathematics will have significantly enhanced opportunities and options for shaping their futures" (p. 50). In contrast, NCTM continues, "A lack of mathematical competence keeps those doors closed."

My Story as an English Language Learner

Growing up in a large city—Chicago, Illinois—and attending an overcrowded inner-city school were not easy. Being an English language learner (ELL) made it more difficult because at that time ELLs were generally considered "less smart" than their Caucasian counterparts. In fact, we were treated as though we were *invisible*. I remember feeling even more invisible in mathematics. The teacher would rarely call on me, and it was obvious that my answers did not have the same value as those of my peers. My peers would find validation in the teacher's praise, bestowed in comments like, "Very good," or "Very smart," while my correct answers would go unacknowledged. I remember hating mathematics, not because it was hard, but because it was not engaging. The teacher was always at the board doing, and we, the students, were always watching. It was boring and frustrating because the teacher would look for *the* correct answer, and when I did not give the exact answer she wanted, I would be punished by not being called on again for a long time. To make matters worse, I was in a class where we had the same mathematics teacher for four years, beginning in second grade and continuing through fifth grade. This teacher taught me many things, but even as an ELL who spoke little English, I was aware of one thing that is still vivid in my mind: I never wanted to teach like my mathematics teacher.

Today, I am a teacher too, and I teach mathematics to students, including ELLs. My students are not invisible, and the ideas of equitable opportunities, engagement, and motivation are important to me as a teacher. I want *all* my students to become confident and competent in expressing their mathematical thinking and showing their reasoning skills. I make sure that ELLs feel successful and important as they acquire skills to think critically. As an educator in pursuit of a master's degree in mathematics, I have learned the value of sitting in a classroom as a learner of mathematics. As I gain confidence and flexibility in teaching the content, I find myself fostering a socio-constructivist approach with a student-centered classroom.

Using a socio-constructivist approach based on Vygotsky (1978), I consider the students' culture, language, and context, and I create lessons relevant to the students. For example, knowing that some of my students assist their parents in cultivating *chile* (chili plants) in the summer, I design mathematics problems that include the division or distribution of *chile*. Because of their familiarity with *chile*, students bring in their personal connections and proudly share how they distribute the *chile* to different markets. The lessons become richer and deeper as students make the content relevant to their own lives. Having these connections allows the students to develop problem-solving strategies that work for them.

Today, all my students, including ELLs, are empowered in the classroom. They have the freedom to take over the lesson and show their peers newly discovered strategies with confidence. Students are encouraged to analyze problems and to conjecture about how they arrived at their responses. They justify their solutions by making sense of the mathematics.

Current School Context and Demographics

Monte Vista Elementary is a new school, located approximately fifty miles north of the Mexican border in Las Cruces, New Mexico. The school serves a semi-rural community with an increasing home development project under way. Monte Vista is a Title I dual language (50/50 model in English and Spanish) K–5 elementary school, with over 75 percent of the students receiving free or reduced-price lunch. My classroom is a multicultural monolingual English setting with students who are Caucasian, African American, Puerto Rican, and Mexican, and they come from different parts of the United States. The majority of the students were born and raised either in New Mexico or in El Paso, Texas. Most English language learners participating in the dual language program are Spanish speakers who have immigrated to the United States from Mexico. My classroom has a total of twenty-four third-grade students. Of the twenty-four students, three students have IEPs (individualized education programs), and four ELLs are at Level 3–Developing and Level 5–Bridging, according to the levels of English language proficiency identified in the WIDA standards (World-Class Instructional Design and Assessment 2011). This assessment is used to measure students' academic language development on the basis of specific standards set by the consortium.

Learning challenges in the classroom include students who have been diagnosed with behavioral issues and two students who have been identified as learning disabled. To meet the learning needs of the students, it is necessary for me to make accommodations on the basis of individual student needs. It is also necessary for me to differentiate instruction and make modifications for students on IEPs. To maintain student engagement and motivation, it is necessary for me to continually build background based on student cultural experiences and prior learning and to provide links to content knowledge in mathematics. Technology available in the classroom includes an interactive whiteboard, five computers, and a document camera. Students are able to interact with content in different ways, allowing them to learn in different modalities. Having these opportunities is also a key element in maintaining student engagement and motivation. Parental support is moderate to high, with parents actively sponsoring community involvement activities for fund-raising. Parents also participate regularly in school-based activities, including numeracy and literacy nights, and they attend monthly PTA meetings.

Successes and Challenges in Teaching Mathematics to ELLs

Having taught ELLs in dual language settings and in a sheltered instruction setting, I can say that the challenges have been many. Sadly, most of the challenges have not been with the students themselves but rather with the myths that are often unchallenged about ELLs and the stigma that is often attached to being an ELL. I encountered one example of this when I team-taught with a colleague in a dual language program. Her philosophy was that the curriculum had to be differentiated because the ELLs were not able to meet the mathematics content standards. She worked very hard to differentiate the mathematics curriculum because she was convinced that the *pobrecitos* (poor, pitiful) students were not capable of achieving or thinking critically at the same cognitive level as their monolingual English-speaking counterparts.

Changing her perspective was among the most difficult challenges that I faced because I was the new teacher, and she had been teaching at the same grade level for many years before I arrived. Addressing this challenge took work, time, and patience. Because we shared students by switching every other week, I taught the Spanish component, and she taught the English component. I had to build on what she taught students each previous week. The change came about when the disparity in test scores began to decrease to the point where the ELLs surpassed their monolingual English-speaking counterparts.

This was the beginning of my success as an educator of ELLs. I refused to buy into the idea of ELLs being *pobrecitos,* and I began to produce evidence that ELLs were able to achieve, given the opportunity. ELLs began to notice the positive attention that they were receiving and were excited and stood proud when their work was posted next to that of their monolingual English counterparts. This was something new because, before this time, individual mathematics work of ELLs was deemed unworthy of being posted but was instead kept tucked away in their portfolios; only their group projects, such as fraction quilts, were posted.

Today, as a sheltered instruction teacher and a bilingual lead teacher, I find that although teachers continue to underestimate ELLs, we are making progress. There is no question that leveling the playing field will continue to be a challenge for educators. However, as a teacher of ELLs, I hope that I have empowered my students to be confident in standing up for what they know and are able to do in the face of educators and peers who may question and demean their wealth of knowledge, experience, and strategies, or what González, Moll, and Amanti (2005) call their "funds of knowledge."

Policies and Practices Supporting or Hindering My Teaching of ELLs

During my time as a teacher, my school district has instituted policies and practices that have supported my teaching of mathematics to ELLs. At one time, my school district employed a full-time mathematics professional development coach, who would come to schools and observe in the classroom for the purpose of providing guidance and expertise specifically for teaching mathematics. My district also formed a team of teachers to design standards-based mathematics assessments. As a result, schools were mandated to administer "benchmark mathematics testing" to report how students were performing in specific strands in mathematics. These practices were short-lived, but they were a great start, helping schools to focus on mathematics, the importance of mathematics data collection, and student performance specifically in mathematics. These practices supported my teaching of mathematics to ELLs because the testing was available in both English and Spanish, and all students were being tested on the same skills across the district. Student scores were broken out into subgroups and shared with schools, allowing teachers to do comparative analyses and to make changes based on what worked for other teachers who were successful.

In my school, I am proud to say that I don't think that my teaching of mathematics has been hindered by district policies and practices. However, teachers within the district have expressed the view that the popular practice of requiring grade-level teams to be on the same page on the same day in the mathematics curriculum is a hindrance to their teaching. They believe that this policy has inhibited the implementing of innovative ideas that can potentially increase student motivation, engagement, and achievement.

In the world of mathematics, we have excellent thinkers and philosophers who have made monumental contributions in mathematics. However, our students have never heard of them. Such individuals exist even in our community. We have mathematicians at our local state university who are willing to share their passion about mathematics but are not invited to interact with students because of the limited time that teachers have to teach the curriculum. The exclusion of these experts is a hindrance—these educators will not have a chance to inspire students by sharing challenges that mathematicians such as Albert Einstein or Charles Babbage faced in their efforts to prove their theories and take our world to a new level of mathematical thinking and reasoning. There is no question that Eric Carle, Dr. Seuss, and other renowned authors have made a contribution to the way that children view literature, but they are known *because*, as educators, we have presented them to our students, giving them great value and respect. It would be exciting to have the opportunity to do the same with our scientists and mathematicians, and I wonder whether this would make a difference in the way that our students approach and view mathematics. If the same amount of effort that is given to teaching literature were invested in teaching mathematics, might students no longer be intimidated or low-performing in mathematics?

Advocating for ELLs in the School and Classroom Setting

Advocating for our ELLs is critical to leveling the playing field. In my classroom, I advocate for ELLs by always keeping their best interests at the forefront. When my grade-level team plans common assessments, I make sure that the mathematics assessment is based on mathematical skills and not on language proficiency. Furthermore, I have found that it is also important to examine assessments for cultural bias.

Understanding the cultural experiences of an ELL is key to administering fair and equitable assessments. For example, asking questions about the difference between the number of players in a basketball game and the number of players in a baseball game requires that students have contextual experiences. Such questions add cultural bias to a test, placing ELLs at a disadvantage in relation to native English speakers. Also, using word problems that require students to leave out of consideration difficult language that is beyond their level of language proficiency can make an assessment inaccessible to ELLs.

When ELLs have not reached an academic level of proficiency in the second language, it is fair to provide the assessment in the students' native language. This would ensure that language barriers do not compromise the skills that are being tested. Carefully reviewing test questions in advance to ensure that students are given an equitable opportunity to score as well as their counterparts is one way that I advocate for my students. I make sure that students have ample opportunities to use the mathematics content vocabulary in context. If ELLs are administered the mathematics assessment in English, they are allowed to ask language-based questions requesting translations of words that may impede their understanding of the problem.

Teaching Strategies—Video Clips

Providing explicit instruction for ELLs is a strategy that is widely misunderstood. Making content accessible to all students requires explicit instruction so that students make connections. For example, opening a lesson by asking students questions such as, "What comes to your mind when you think about fractions?" or, "Where in the real world do you use fractions?" allows teachers to tap into their students' personal experiences and background knowledge. Thus, this explicit instruction requires students to think, make connections, and relate to the content in ways that are vivid and connected to their current lives (see the video clip Fractions Lesson [Beginning] at www.nctm.org/more4u).

Purposeful student interaction is critical in teaching ELLs. Planning and preparing questions that elicit critical thinking are key to getting students hooked on mathematics. Posing inquiry-based problems to students requires them to use different problem-solving approaches, resulting in multiple solutions and enhancement of student engagement. As students work in interactive groups, I facilitate instruction by posing questions such as, "Can you explain your thinking on that strategy?" or, "Can you think of another strategy to work the same problem?" Using "what if" questions as students experiment with different strategies helps students think about other possibilities, leading them to think more deeply, take risks, and make discoveries as they share their thinking within their groups (see the video clip Fractions Lesson [Group Work] at www.nctm.org/more4u).

Using graphic representations to explore problem-solving methods can help students visualize and make connections to the content. A graphic representation that is paired with content vocabulary can become a mnemonic device that helps students relate to the content. Mnemonic devices can take the form of illustrations that students draw to help them remember a concept or idea. Mnemonic devices may also be word initials, which can help students recall a sequence or order. For example, the sentence "Never Eat Soggy Waffles" is often used as a mnemonic device to help students remember cardinal directions. In my classroom, I always present relevant content vocabulary at the beginning of the lesson. Vocabulary cards with graphic representations are available for students to manipulate and use in formulating ideas to explain their thinking. (See the video clip Fractions Lesson [Group Work] at www.nctm.org/more4u.)

Purposeful planning and purposeful posting of graphics around the classroom can also complement the teaching and learning of mathematics for ELLs. The use of scavenger hunts, which send students around the classroom to find objects that relate to the content, can serve to anchor student understanding of mathematical concepts. For example, my classroom has a bulletin board with congruent objects posted. In a scavenger hunt, students had to find congruent objects within the classroom. Today, they continue to look for congruent objects in the environment. They have done similar activities with angles, polygons, area, volume, and perimeter. When students use vivid images and have hands-on experiences, teachers can access their learning throughout the year and use it to link to and build understanding of new mathematical language and concepts. This learning is evident as students explain and share their mathematical understanding through classroom presentations.

I use total physical response (TPR) and chants as other mnemonic techniques that benefit all students, including ELLs. Students engage in TPR when they create body movements or sing chants that prompt them to think about specific mathematics formulas or procedures. In using TPR, students access their knowledge and apply it in problem solving. In teams, students can practice and formulate specific movements to help them remember the definition of important mathematical terms. One example of TPR is students' use of movement to remember the features of a polygon. When they need to identify polygons, they can eliminate answers by going through the motions or singing their chant.

When students have a vocabulary bank stored in the form of TPR, it is fascinating to see how they use it during testing or when they are solving problems on their own. Supporting ELLs by providing them with opportunities to create movements to help them link the vocabulary to mathematical concepts has proven to be effective in giving students understanding that transfers when they move to the upper grades. I have students who continue to approach me—three years later—to tell me how much TPR has helped them in learning new vocabulary in middle school.

In mathematics instruction, high expectations for students should never be compromised. The label "culturally disadvantaged," used in identifying culturally and linguistically diverse (CLD) students who qualify for gifted programs, has been used to justify *watering down the content* for ELLs. The content is "dumbed down" because of the belief that the standards are set too high for ELLs to meet. This reflects a deficit view, which effective teachers dismiss.

In fact, teachers who understand the value of cultural background will capitalize on their ELL students' funds of knowledge (González, Moll, and Amanti 2005), consistently drawing on student cultural experiences and validating the ways in which students think about and relate to the content. González, Moll, and Amanti's research on funds of knowledge is based on the idea that ELLs come into the classroom having rich background experiences that teachers should draw on to help students relate and make sense of the content.

Effective teachers of ELLs also provide students with diverse ways to share their learning in the classroom. As is evident in the accompanying video clips, ELLs who have opportunities to interact in meaningful ways—through dialogue, hands-on learning to make sense of mathematics, and peer teaching—are empowered and excited to demonstrate their understanding of mathematical content, thus enriching the learning for *all* students (see the video clips Decomposing 1 Valerie and Decomposing 2 Georgieann at www.nctm.org/more4u).

Case 3

Building Background Knowledge to Teach Mathematics in an ESL Classroom

by Cathy Kinzer and Ricardo Rincón
as told by Ricardo Rincón

 • **Number Line Prior Knowledge (video clip)**

The NCTM Position Statement on Teaching Mathematics to English Language Learners states, "Schools and teachers that serve ELL students must not only identify and use instructional strategies that make content more accessible in a second language, but also consider how to implement culturally relevant pedagogy in mathematics classrooms" (NCTM 2008). I first discovered the truth of this statement in my own experience as an English language learner.

My Story about Teaching Mathematics to ELLs

I arrived in our great nation as a young adult whose English proficiency placed me several levels below core classes at a community college. After three semesters of ESL courses, I was approved to take other classes that did not involve language development. At that time I learned that our educational system was not perfect and more was needed to address the learning needs of English language learners (ELLs). A student's level of English language proficiency influenced the teacher's evaluation of his or her content proficiency. The system did not differentiate, recognizing that, at least in my case, I would have been able to take mathematics courses while I developed English language skills. After all, I would have been able to use cognates and numbers to understand the science and mathematical ideas presented in the instruction. However, the approach focused mostly on my deficits in the English language and not on my ability to understand mathematical ideas. This issue in our educational system helped me to develop a sense of urgency to advocate for our ELLs and study the work of linguists such as Cummins, Krashen, and Collier.

A few years afterward, and now an educator myself, I learned to access and apply students' "funds of knowledge," as described by González, Moll, and Amanti (2005), during everyday instruction. This approach opened my eyes. I learned that students come into our classrooms with plenty of lived experiences and background knowledge that I can access and use to make my lessons applicable to their lives. By this, I mean that I have learned the importance of valuing students' strengths and building from their language, ways of knowing, and culture while using them as resources for learning. Understanding my students' funds of knowledge helped me modify my idea of my role and view myself as both a learner and a teacher of ELLs.

During the past nine years, I have had the opportunity to serve as an elementary teacher of English language learners. During this time, I have learned that many of the preconceptions that teachers have about ELLs are actually misguided and ill-conceived. ELLs come into our classrooms with plenty of background knowledge, which, if accessed, can be used to facilitate their understanding of new academic concepts. Their culture, everyday experiences, and language play an important role in daily instruction. As an educator, I have evolved from having a *deficit* philosophy and expecting limited work from my ELLs, to consistently challenging them to excel because I have seen that they too can achieve and exceed my expectations.

Demographics of Monte Vista Elementary School

My classroom at Monte Vista Elementary School, like the Monte Vista classroom described in case 2, is a dual language classroom in which instruction is in English one week and in Spanish the subsequent week. I serve twenty-five fourth- and fifth-grade students, 100 percent of whom are of Hispanic descent, with English language skills that range from Level 1–Entering to Level 6–Reaching, according to the levels of English proficiency identified in the WIDA standards (World-Class Instructional Design and Assessment 2011). Three students in my class have IEPs.

Monte Vista is a Sheltered Instruction Observation Protocol (SIOP) school (Echevarría, Vogt, and Short 2004) and addresses four language domains: speaking, reading, writing, and listening during instruction. These domains have been essential to the students' academic success as well as to the development of their second language. An example of this approach is the teachers' practice at Monte Vista Elementary of posting and reviewing content and language objectives several times to establish a clear understanding of the purpose and focus of the lesson. The purposeful use of technology during instruction is also very evident at any given point in a mathematics lesson.

Successes and Challenges in Teaching Mathematics to ELLs

Many of the successes that I have experienced in teaching mathematics to ELLs are connected with the fact that they enjoy the challenge associated with finding multiple strategies for solving a problem. In particular, ELLs want the opportunity to engage in cognitively demanding mathematics tasks that require thinking and reasoning. They also want opportunities to be active contributors to their own learning and to show what they know. Although they may need some assistance in understanding the terminology introduced in word problems, once they figure out the mathematical ideas, they enjoy trying different approaches to solve the problem.

I am currently teaching a fourth- and fifth-grade bilingual combination, and the students' eagerness to try the most complex approaches to solve a problem is evident. They are sure to approach a simple multiplication problem, such as 345×68, with several strategies, including the use of an area model, an algorithm, multiple towers, or arrays to make a graphical representation of their work. Although the expectation is to try a minimum of two approaches, students usually exceed this expectation, in the process showing their creativity and independent thinking. The students use graphical representations, mathematical models, language, and one another as resources for making sense of the mathematics.

One particular aspect of our approach that I think is important to student success is our use of higher levels of the revised version of Bloom's taxonomy, which places analyzing, evaluating, and creating as the three highest domains (Anderson 2001; Bloom 1984). Like other students in our educational system, ELLs are aware that a knowledge-based response places them at the lowest level in Bloom's taxonomy. That is why they regularly aim to generate a response that reflects understanding, application, and analysis of new concepts presented. This is also a reason why creating a graphical representation, providing a solid rationale for their approach, applying new concepts in everyday situations, and analyzing the effectiveness of their approach in the form of an explanation are all very important. Their competitive spirit drives them to work beyond a simple response to a complete response that shows in-depth understanding, which is important if they are to succeed on our standardized test.

Our state assessment requires that students explain and make sense of the mathematics in responding to open-ended questions. These tasks require a greater depth of knowledge and move students beyond giving just a basic knowledge-based answer. This approach is parallel to the approach to mathematics education that lies behind NCTM's (2000) Process Standards for problem solving, representation, reasoning and proof, communication, and connections in mathematics. Performance on questions that assess students' proficiency with these processes accounts for about 50 percent of their total scores on the test. Simply put, students must be ready to provide answers that include reasoning and proof, a graphical representation, and a written rationale for their approach to problem solving. To help students develop these skills, it is important for us to provide instruction that supports the Process Standards so that students can be successful on the state test. The test requires skill in the mathematical processes as well as understanding of the mathematics content for a proficient response.

Challenges that I have experienced in teaching mathematics to my ELLs, like those described in case 2, are mostly associated with word problems. To address these challenges and ensure that all students have equal access to the content, I have designed seating configurations that provide peer support as well as opportunities to for all students to interact, use language, and contribute their thinking. These components play an important role in team discussions. As an ELL teacher, I understand the benefits associated with opportunities to use new terminology. I have found that team discussions are excellent venues for ELLs to use or apply new terms and listen to other students whose level of proficiency in English is more advanced than their own. I have observed that team discussions have helped my ELLs to develop high levels of confidence and become more active contributors to the discussion. In my classroom, I purposefully group students to use their language skills and content knowledge and develop their confidence as a way of building a learning environment where all students have access to rigorous mathematics.

Policies and Practices Supporting or Hindering Teaching Mathematics to ELLs

One of the district and school policies that has played an important role in my ability to build working relationships with parents is the idea of "one positive phone call per day." As an educator and as a parent, I strongly believe that the role of the parents in their child's education is essential. I am fully aware that without the parents' support, I would not be able to instill in my students a love for learning mathematics. Making a phone call each day has made a substantial difference in the way my students show up to class each morning ready to learn. In addition to making the phone calls, each year, after a few months of teaching in an elementary classroom, I normally try to get to know my students and their families. I enjoy having casual conversations, visiting with them at home, and occasionally participating in their family traditions and celebrations (see also case 6 by Gutiérrez in chapter 6). This approach has given me a better understanding of my students' cultures, values, and traditions. Incidentally, what I learn in their homes tends to appear in word problems. Visiting or talking with parents on a regular basis has been key to my ability to understand their situational reality and make strong working relationships that connect home and school, students, parents, and educators.

Advocacy for ELLs in the School and Classroom Setting

As a bilingual lead teacher, I attend monthly meetings and workshops for the purpose of updating my practice on the basis of current events and academic research. One of the most influential learning experiences that I have had is learning about what González, Moll, and Amanti (2005) call "funds of knowledge." As stated in the research, all students come to school with a plethora of knowledge to offer, based on their academic and cultural experiences, as well as drawn from their situational reality. To help our colleagues learn to access and apply these experiences during their instruction, the school administration asked several of us to provide professional development for all staff, using an online platform. The approach was very effective; concepts such as building background knowledge and everyday applications became a common practice during all instruction. Needless to say, what our ELLs had to offer provided the foundation for lesson planning that emphasizes consistent student engagement during the lesson.

The video that I would like to share is called Number Line Prior Knowledge (see www.nctm.org/more4u), and it provides an example of the building background knowledge strategy of SIOP. In the video, we see how students share what they know about a topic, drawing on what they have learned in the school setting as well as on what they have experienced in relation to the same topic at home or in some other non-school environment. The video also shows how we can use the same approach for vocabulary development. As regularly occurs when I access students' personal experiences, the connections that students make to everyday situations are much more in tune with their lives than what I can personally offer.

In this case, the objective of the lesson was to use a number line to add or subtract fractions. During the launch, I decided to use a concept map approach to build background knowledge. I started by asking students what they knew or remembered about a number line from what they had learned at school. The answers varied from "A number line is a line" to "A number line is a graphical representation of whole numbers and fractions." After asking students what they knew about a number line from what they had learned at school, I asked students to share experiences with number lines outside of the school setting. The responses were much more varied and rich than what I could have offered. Students started by associating a number line with a tape measure and ended by noting the implicit number line located on a clock. I acknowledged the children's insight in connecting the attributes of a number line with the attributes of a clock, observing that both use equal measurements to represent distances.

From my personal experience, I can say that building background knowledge is an essential component of any instructional approach in a language-rich classroom environment. Asking students to share what they know helps to level the playing field because it gives other students who may not know or remember as much the chance to start making associations between the new concept and something as real as—in the case of my students—a tape measure or a clock.

Message from This Example

The message that this video clip sends to other teachers is that ELLs have funds of knowledge that can enhance their own and their peers' understanding of new concepts. Without the ideas and experiences of my students, I am confident that I would not have been able to think of examples such as the speedometer or a clock to talk about a number line. Accessing their everyday life experiences with number lines of all sorts helped my students connect an academic concept to something real and tangible.

Case 4

From "Plussed" to "Added": Supporting English Language Learners

by Marco A. Ramirez and Chris Confer

David was a third-year teacher. "With three years of teaching under my belt, I can tell you one thing," he commented. "There's way more to teaching than I ever realized."

David's third-grade class had twenty Native American students and ten Hispanic students. The school was located on an urban-area reservation in Tucson, Arizona. David often taught mathematics from a textbook, but he was stepping out by teaching a few new strategies for addition. He realized that many of his students didn't understand the traditional procedure, and their accuracy was low.

Overall, his classroom functioned a lot like the classrooms of his childhood, with the teacher doing most of the talking and the students doing the listening. David was starting to try to change this through class discussions—and he wasn't very pleased with the results. David's brow furrowed as he described his dilemma.

"A small group of boys always has the answers," he explained to Jennie, the mathematics coach, who had walked into his room just in time to see him shaking his head over his lesson plans. "They call out the answers. Even when I make sure they raise their hands, the other students just sit silently, waiting for one of those five boys to answer. " "Hmm," Jennie said, pausing to think about David's difficulty. "I wonder why the others don't answer. Is it that they can't solve the problem, and so have nothing to say? Or is it that they don't have the words to form an answer and explain their thinking? Or maybe we need to just slow down the discussion to give them more time to think."

Jennie was well aware that David's students were mostly English language learners. About 60 percent of the students had a primary language other than English. Some spoke mostly Yoeme, the Yaqui native language, others spoke a combination of Yoeme and Spanish, and still others included English in their mix. Some students, like Darrin, were in the "silent period." They would listen and do the work and occasionally talk to another student—but never to the whole group.

"Well," David answered Jennie, "probably some students have trouble with the math, but I'm guessing a lot of them need support with language." "Let's plan tomorrow's lesson," Jennie suggested. "Then we can make sure that all the students have visual models to solve the problem. Next, we can try out ways to support our ELLs so that they have the language to explain their thinking."

Not all schools are so fortunate as to have mathematics coaches. Had David been without Jennie's help, he might well have gone back to his old way of teaching, with the rationale that "these new ideas just don't work." However, a school site with a skilled mathematics coach has an effective way to provide real-time, job-embedded professional development for teachers of English language learners. As it was, David and Jennie put their heads together to plan the next day's lesson.

Planning to Support English Language Learners with Mathematics Concepts

In preparation for the lesson on strategies for addition, Jennie and David themselves worked to solve 37 + 49 mentally in as many ways as they could. "Turn the 49 into 50 and the 37 into 36," contributed David. "That makes it easy: 36 + 50 = 86. "That might make sense to some of your students," Jennie said, nodding, "but you'll have to clearly record where those number changes came from so the ELLs can follow what the others are saying. And you'll have to be explicit about connecting what the students say to the diagram. This diagram might work." Jennie quickly made a sketch on a sheet of paper (see fig. 5.1).

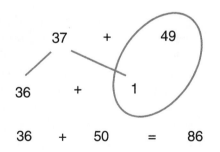

Fig. 5.1. Mapping out possibilities of student thinking

"What other strategies might your students use? And what models might they need?" continued Jennie. David brought out his hundred chart and showed Jennie a strategy that he thought was more accessible to his students—starting with the larger number, 49, then jumping to 59, 69, and then 79. Then David counted forward 7 more spaces to get to 86; figure 5.2 illustrates his process. "That works," Jennie commented. "Again you'll have to be explicit about why jumping down on the hundred chart increases a number by ten."

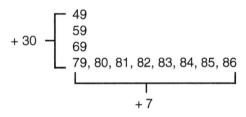

Fig. 5.2. Additional possibilities of student thinking resulting from collaborating

Jennie encouraged David to consider yet another strategy. "How about adding the tens and ones separately?" she asked. "I'm guessing that if we get out the place value blocks, they'll add thirty and forty to make seventy, and then add the ones. But on the other hand," Jennie considered, "the students might also begin with 37, then add the tens blocks—47, 57, 67, 77, and then add the ones to get to 86."

"What is really important," David agreed, "is that the kids have the opportunity to see the mathematics through the visual models. But what about the kids who get the mathematics but don't have the language to participate in a whole-group discussion? And how do we slow down the kids who just jump in and tell the answer?" David had brought up a critical point for teachers of English language learners: Mathematics is a language of its own, with its own unique vocabulary, sentence structures, paragraph and story structures, and symbols. Furthermore, homophones abound—for example, *sum* and *some*—as do words that have completely different meanings in mathematics from their meanings in everyday language—for example, *set*. English language learners must explicitly be taught each of these language tools if they are to participate fully in the classroom mathematics community.

Supporting English Language Learners in Developing Mathematical Language

Jennie and David discussed how students usually talked about mathematics. Although the students could say, "I added it," they more often said, "I plussed it." Without a doubt, the word *added* was in the students' memory banks. Although that word was in their receptive vocabulary, the students did not readily produce it when speaking. The students needed some guidance and practice so that they could efficiently retrieve the appropriate words and construct sentences.

Jennie began to coach David in how to provide language tools to English language learners. "It's important to begin by using everyday language," she told him. "You might begin by telling a student, 'You broke 37 into 30 plus 7.' Then model the mathematical terminology," Jennie explained, "so the kids can practice with you before they speak to the whole group."

Jennie began modeling as though the student were present: "I want you to say it like me: 'I decomposed 37 into 30 plus 7.' Your turn." Jennie gave the student's response: "I decomposed 37 into 30 plus 7," and then resumed modeling: "Great! Now listen again: '*Next*, I decomposed 49 into 40 plus 9.' Your turn." Again responding as the student, Jennie said, "I decomposed 49 into 40 plus 9."

Jennie explained to David how she would discuss adverbs that signal sequence. "Did you hear me say the word *next?* Why did I say *next?*" Jennie then told David, "It's important to explicitly teach English language learners adverbs that help them describe sequence. You can connect the word *next* to the word that a student might more easily use—*then*. Model for the student the language that she might use to share in front of the class, and help the student practice it so that she is successful."

Jennie and David planned to support a few students who didn't typically speak during discussions. Then they planned to invite those students privately to share during the discussion. Jennie and David agreed to honor the students' decisions about whether or not to accept the invitation to share. However, they were certain that the students would feel confident enough, given the additional support. In fact, Anisa did agree to share, and David smiled as he watched her from across the room as she practiced what she would say.

Teaching the Lesson: A New Kind of Discussion

The next day during mathematics time, David and Jennie consciously practiced modeling language as the students solved their addition problems. David and Jennie could hear each other say, "Now repeat after me," or, "Let's practice saying it this way." Every now and then they would glance proudly at each other as if to say, "This is really working!"

"You all worked hard on the problem," David said to open up the discussion when he got the whole group's attention. As he started talking, the five boys inevitably waved their hands. "All of you thought in different ways," David continued, focusing his attention on the whole class. "Who thinks they would be confident enough to share their thinking about how they solved the problem?" About half the students in the class raised their hands, including a number of girls. Yes, the same five boys raised their hands, but as those boys looked around, they were surprised to see that many other students were willing to share. Those boys were no longer the "mathematics keepers" of the classroom!

The first child who shared did so with social language typical of David's third-grade class. "I plussed the tens," she explained, showing how she used the base-ten blocks to model adding the tens first. "Mine's different," called Anisa. The other students looked at her in surprise: Anisa never shared. Anisa came to the front and placed her paper under the document camera. She began to speak. "My strategy for solving the problem is this. I de-, *decomposed*, the 37 into 30 + 7. Next...." She paused just slightly to glance at David with a little smile. "Next, I decomposed the 49 into 40 + 9. Then I added 40 to 30 to get 70 and 7 + 9 to get 16. I added 70 and 16 together to get 86. Eighty-six is the answer."

Jennie, Anisa, and David all looked at one another as if something truly remarkable had happened, because something amazing did in fact happen. All three realized that this was the beginning of a new kind of classroom discussion, a powerful kind of classroom discussion that would transform the way in which David's English language learners would learn mathematics. For teachers, the litmus test is the evidence: how much of the language that students practiced does the student use while sharing in front of the class? Does the student do it exactly as practiced? Does the student use even 80 percent of the language? David now had a way to gauge the extent to which his English language learners had internalized mathematical language.

Later that day David checked in with the girls who previously had rarely participated in classroom discussions. "What did you think about the class mathematics discussion?" David asked. "I liked it," answered Dianira. "It's not always the same kids." "Yeah, we got a turn," nodded Valeria. "What did you like about sharing?" David asked, turning to Anisa. "I like how I sounded," Anisa said. "I felt smart."

Summing It Up

Each classroom has a unique culture, a culture that includes all the students or excludes some of the students. Any teacher can imagine sitting alone at a desk, hearing Russian or any other unknown language, while trying to learn a difficult subject. Unfortunately, far too many English language learners live that reality during mathematics instruction. Providing for the needs of ELLs requires teachers to plan for language supports on a daily basis and then consistently use those supports.

Lesson plans must require teachers to pre-think the vocabulary and sentence structures that the students will need to use. They must require teachers to plan for the visual models that will help English language learners have access to the mathematics. ELLs depend on teachers to unpack the structures of questions and word problems. These students depend on teachers to elicit the prior knowledge that will help students make sense of mathematical concepts.

David had the support of a qualified mathematics coach who understood the role of language and who could effectively help him shift to an inclusive classroom culture. As a result, Anisa not only *felt* smart but her contributions gave her the evidence she needed to convince herself that she was indeed smart.

Case 5

Facilitating the Participation of Latino English Language Learners— Learning from an Effective Teacher

by Kathryn Chval

Throughout my career, I have collaborated with dedicated and hard-working teachers who have opened their classrooms so that others could learn from them. Yet, one teacher, Sara, stood out from all the others. From the first time I visited Sara's classroom in 1992, I knew she was extraordinary—a teacher who could inspire a Hollywood production. Sara taught Latino English language learners (ELLs) in a low-income urban neighborhood in ways that I had not observed or read about in the literature. She did not reduce the curriculum's level of complexity, especially its language, even though the students were ELLs. Instead, Sara engineered a mathematics learning environment where students actively engaged in collaborative problem solving, oral and written communication and justification, and independent thinking. To give other practitioners insight into how Sara facilitated the participation of ELLs during mathematics, I share my experiences of researching Sara's fifth-grade classroom and provide images of her teaching.

Sara's Classroom

Sara is Latina, and at the time of the study she had been teaching for twenty-one years. To investigate Sara's teaching, I made audio recordings of 119 mathematics lessons over the course of one school year. I also observed 66 of those lessons and carefully documented what transpired with field notes and examples of student work.

Year after year, Sara's students consistently outperformed their peers on standardized assessments. For example, table 5.1 shows how the students in Sara's class compared with other fifth-grade classrooms at her school and throughout the district, as measured by the Iowa Test of Basic Skills for Mathematics during the year of the study. Although her students began the school year below the other two groups, they left Sara's classroom outperforming the other two groups as well as the national norm.

Table 5.1

Growth in one year, measured by median grade equivalent on Iowa Test of Basic Skills

Comparison groups	End of fourth grade mathematics total	End of fifth grade mathematics total	Gain
Sara's class (N = 22)	4.3	6.1	1.8
Other fifth graders in Sara's school (N = 56)	4.6	5.8	1.2
District (N = 23,479)	4.6	5.6	1.0
National norm	4.8	5.8	1.0

Sara's students also made significant improvement in their oral and written communication related to mathematics, as evidenced in the transcripts and examples of student work. For example, late in the school year, the students were given two problems, one of which was the following: "A three-quarter circle has an area of 100 square centimeters. Calculate the perimeter of the three-quarter circle." Students had already solved similar problems involving full circles; however, the three-quarter element was completely new. Violetta volunteered to present the solutions for both problems at the board to the class. She drew a sketch of a three-quarter circle on the board and then wrote the calculator keystrokes for her solution to the first problem (see fig. 5.3). As she wrote each keystroke, she explained the meaning behind it, as demonstrated in the transcript of Violetta's presentation. To find the perimeter of the three-quarter circle, Violetta calculated three-fourths of the circumference (she referred to this as "the curvy part") and then added the lengths of two radii (she referred to this length as "the diameter").

100	÷	3	=	×	4	=	÷	π	=
$\sqrt{x}$	×	2	=	STO	×	π	÷	4	×
3	=	SUM	EXC

Fig. 5.3. Violetta's calculator keystrokes for first problem

Violetta: We are going to find the perimeter of the three-quarter circle. The area of the… The area of the three-quarter circle are 100 square centimeters. Now, we are going to go backward from the area to the perimeter. One hundred divided by three equals the area of one quarter circle. Multiply by four to get the area of the whole circle. Divide by π to get the area of the square built on the radius. You take the square root to get the radius. And then you multiply by two to get the diameter. Then we store it [*a reference to the calculator*]. Then we multiply by π to get the circumference of the circle. Then we divide it by four to get the quarter circle. Then we multiply by three to get the curvy part of the three-quarter circle. Then we sum it—sum it to memory [*another reference to the calculator*]. So we can get the circumference, the perimeter, of the three-quarter circle.

Throughout Violetta's presentation, she used drawings of the problem, calculator keystrokes, gestures, and oral communication to explain how she solved the problem—all critical components of Sara's teaching that Violetta appropriated. Moreover, we see the mathematical challenge of the problem that was posed—atypical for fifth grade and for ELLs—demonstrating Sara's high expectations.

Establishing Expectations for ELLs' Participation

The transcripts of Sara's classroom at the beginning of the school year were quite different from Violetta's example. Students answered questions by using numbers or short phrases. They did not know how to work productively in groups. They did not exhibit the mathematical practices identified in the Common Core State Standards for Mathematics (CCSSI 2010, p. 10):

1. Make sense of problems and persevere in solving them.
2. Reason abstractly and quantitatively.
3. Construct viable arguments and critique the reasoning of others.
4. Model with mathematics.
5. Use appropriate tools strategically.
6. Attend to precision.
7. Look for and make use of structure.
8. Look for and express regularity in repeated reasoning.

Yet, by second semester, the CCSS mathematical practices were the norm in Sara's classroom. As I began to work with other teachers in professional development settings to help them learn about Sara's teaching, they commented on prevalent, unproductive interactions that hinder ELLs' participation, including encounters in which their native-English speaking peers disrespect them, ignore their questions or requests, do their work for them, or do not understand their mathematical misconceptions. Unfortunately, too often ELLs are left to work in isolation or to participate as spectators (Brenner 1998). Therefore, teachers need to be purposeful and act strategically to build a classroom community that values ELLs' contributions and enhances ELLs' participation in mathematical activities. This invites the question, What did Sara do to facilitate the participation of Latino ELLs in her mathematics classroom?

From the first day of school, Sara immersed ELLs in an environment filled with words, both written and spoken. She created an environment in which students experienced and used language in the context of collaborative activity and problem solving. She ensured that every student paid attention to spoken and written words and supported them as they began to use those words. Specifically, Sara—

1. spoke and wrote sophisticated words;
2. used these words frequently and in the context of solving problems; and
3. helped students build understanding of the meanings of these words.

During the whole-group discussions in the first twelve days of school, Sara prominently used words such as *tell, dictate, explain,* and *write.* Sara used these words 779 times, an average of 65 times per lesson. Such repetition is significant because it demonstrates that Sara expected her students to communicate while learning mathematics.

Sara developed an environment that was not only filled with communication, but also valued its often forgotten inverse—listening. Cazden (1988) argued that in a typical U.S. lesson, students look at the teacher, even when classmates speak. Sara, on the other hand, built an environment in which students were expected to look at their peers when they spoke. She explicitly discussed the value of listening and how it should take place. For example, on the first day of school, Sara taught a lesson comparing hearing and listening. Furthermore, to establish the importance of listening, Sara related her classroom to a family—a family that shares, cares, helps, and respects. Four examples from August 27 demonstrate this approach.

Example 1

Sara:	You care about your family. Is there anyone here who does not care about their family? [*no response*] Ah, everybody cares about their family. Do you care about school?
Chorus:	Yeah.
Sara:	Do you? How do you show that you care about school? Violetta is annoyed. I can see it in her face. Hold on a second. Her face is all crunched up, and I know she wants to listen, and she's reacting to something that Matthew is doing. Is Matthew showing us that he cares?

Chorus:	No.
Sara:	Is Violetta hearing what all is going on?
Chorus:	No.
Sara:	No, she's busy taking care of a problem here. And Matthew is not listening very well. Matthew, we care about you, so what can we do to help you out? Because this is a family right here. We spend lots and lots of hours together, don't we?
Matthew:	Yes.
Sara:	So we are a family. When you do something, it affects all of us, doesn't it? All of us, right now, are paying attention to you, because you cannot pay attention. We have to pay attention because we care about you. Do you care about us?
Matthew:	Yeah.
Sara:	How are you going to show us that you care about us?

In example 1, Sara compared the class to a family. She also compared Matthew's behavior—his not listening—to not caring. During the first week of school, Sara began to establish the need for listening as she built the foundation for creating an environment where students cared about what was said.

Example 2

Sara:	If I show you respect, I expect respect right in return. If I work very, very hard, I expect the same from you… that you work very, very hard. If I listen to you, then I want you to listen to me. I show you that I care by the work that I do. You show me that you care by the work that you do. That's how I want you to show me respect. How do you want me to show you that I care? Alejandro? Is there anything special that I should do, or am I already doing what you think I should do?

In example 2, Sara established important expectations, including respect, hard work, listening, and caring. In the following example, the students were working in pairs while Sara circulated and provided guidance. In this example, she emphasized that the students should ask for help when needed and that they should teach one another.

Example 3

Sara:	There is a rule up there on the good rules. Which is the rule you should be looking at right now?
Students:	Move quietly.
Sara:	No, you're being very good about noise. Noise is wonderful.
Students:	Be a good listener.

Sara:	Be a good listener. Oh, something else I think.
Students:	Move quietly.
Sara:	Can we go down to the purple rule?
Students:	Encourage participation.
Sara:	Encourage participation. Are you allowed to move around the room quietly?
Students:	Yes.
Sara:	Yes. So Dalia was asking Alejandro, and Alejandro didn't know what to do. Alejandro wasn't participating because he never asked for help. So somebody over here. Anybody. You move around. I'm only one person. Move around quietly and ask each other. You can teach each other. Walk around. Help each other. I can't help all of you at the same time.

Example 4

Sara:	We have to share things. That's how we learn. That's how we show people that we care for them.

The four examples above illustrate how Sara established a sense of family in her classroom—a family that shares, cares, helps, respects, and listens. Sara modeled effective listening, but also explicitly talked about how to do it. She made students responsible for articulating reasoning and for working hard to understand the reasoning of others—critical elements of the CCSS Standards for Mathematical Practice and the NCTM (2000) Process Standards. She emphasized looking at the speaker to demonstrate respect and good listening. She explained that good listening can lead to additional ideas, which in turn can increase the quality of the discussion. She also discussed the fact that good listening involves tone of voice, facial expressions, and gestures. From the first day of school, Sara discussed effective features of listening and the importance of listening. The following two excerpts provide examples:

Example 1: September 1

Sara:	Which rule are we practicing right now?
Students:	Good listeners.
Sara:	We're going to be good listeners. What is a good listener? Someone who?
Students:	Listens.
Sara:	How do I know you're listening carefully? How does anyone know that you're listening carefully? What must you do when you are listening carefully?
Students:	By looking at the person.

Sara: You look at the speaker and you focus your attention on the speaker completely. You're not playing with anything inside your desk. You're not looking through a folder. You're not chatting with a neighbor; you're listening.

Example 2: September 9

Sara: You're going to be a good listener. So you are going to look at whoever answers, or whoever completes an answer. Because sometimes people have part of the answer, and another person helps out and completes an answer.

At this early point in the year, Sara reminded the class to look at the speaker as he or she approached the chalkboard to present. (Early in the year, pairs of students would present solutions to the class, providing an opportunity for ELLs to communicate with a peer if they struggled during the presentation and to build their confidence with public speaking.) In the September 9 example, Sara emphasized looking not only at the first person who answers, but also at the next student, who may add to that answer. Later in the year, such reminders were nonexistent. Students followed the dialogue of the respective speakers with their ears and their eyes. Sara had developed an environment of talk and listening and had created a family that showed respect and caring by talking and listening. Sara had high expectations for her students—all of her students. Every student was expected to participate and contribute to the learning of everyone in the classroom—including the teacher. Sara established a collaborative environment—a family—rather than a competitive environment.

A teacher can establish disagreement or argumentation as a negative, confrontational classroom practice; however, Sara carefully created an environment whereby disagreement was cooperative, positive, and valued. In an interesting way, she used disagreement as a mechanism for developing cognitive processes such as reflection, analysis, reasoning, and justification. Thus, a family that shares, cares, helps, respects, and listens is in a position to "construct viable arguments and critique the reasoning of others" (CCSS Mathematical Practice 3).

At the beginning of the school year, the participation of Sara's students in these types of processes was restricted by their lack of experience. The following examples show Sara establishing the foundation for these processes—a critical element in the students' mathematical development. Sara used a simple teaching strategy to establish this practice in her classroom early on in the school year. For example, consider the progression of Sara's statements over the course of a few days, as shown in the following list:

September 1:	Are the [calculator] keystrokes correct?
September 2:	They don't agree with you.
September 3:	I disagree.
September 4:	Do you agree with that? Yes or no?

Sara began with a word familiar to her students—*correct*. In the second example, several students have stated that an answer is "not correct." Sara revoiced this response by saying, "They don't agree with you." In the third example, Sara modeled a desirable response for her students by saying, "I disagree," instead of saying, "You are wrong." Then Sara moved on to give the students a choice. At this point, the question is still phrased in a yes-or-no format. Not until September 16 does Sara go beyond that format (seven new students entered the classroom on September 10) as the following transcript demonstrates:

September 16

Marisa:	We got our triangle, our right triangle in there, we got to multiply one leg times the other leg to find the area of one triangle.
Sara:	Marisa, can you stop and say what you've done so far?
Marisa:	Yes, we multiplied one leg times another leg on the triangle, and *N* equals twelve. And the area is the whole rectangle, and we don't want the whole rectangle. We want the triangle. So you have to divide by two—equals six. Six is the area. Centimeters. Is the area.
Sara:	I disagree. Anybody else disagree?
Chorus:	Yes.
Sara:	You have to say that. When you see something you don't agree with, you say, "I disagree." If we don't disagree, then we don't have to discuss it.
Marisa:	Square centimeters.
Sara:	Yes. You corrected yourself. Good.

Here Sara established the importance of stating disagreement when it is observed. She also explicitly explained that disagreements warrant discussion. At this moment, Sara granted permission to her students not just to raise their hands when they saw a mistake, but to state it verbally. From this moment forward, students eagerly and consistently said, "I disagree." A few moments later, a student took the plunge and became the first to say the magic words. Sara did not praise the student for saying them, but challenged him to justify his response.

Sara:	Really? How are you going to find the…
Student:	I disagree.
Sara:	You disagree with *what*?

A few moments later, the following dialogue ensued in the classroom:

1. *Sara:*	Stop, stop, stop. Well, let's pretend that he said three times five. If he says three times five, Yomara, would you say you agree or disagree?
2. *Yomara:*	Disagree.
3. *Sara:*	*Why?*
4. *Yomara:*	Why?
⋮	
13. *Sara:*	Well, Mark, he said three times five. And he meant this length times this length. *Why* do we disagree with that? One person. *Why* do we disagree with that, Yomara?
14. *Yomara:*	Teacher?
15. *Sara:*	Lucia, *why* do we disagree with that? Tell her the problem.
16. *Lucia:*	Because she multiplied the hypotenuse.
17. *Chorus:*	Yes.
18. *Sara:*	Do we need the hypotenuse?
19. *Chorus:*	No!

Not only did Sara's students have to say "I disagree," but they also had to describe what they disagreed with and present an argument for their position. In the preceding dialogue, Sara extended their talk, but more important, she involved students in discussions in which they justified solutions. This aspect of Sara's teaching was significant because students who justify solutions, especially while facing disagreement, will gain better mathematical understanding as they work to convince their peers about differing points of view (Hatano and Inagaki 1991; NCTM 2000). Sara recognized the importance of justifying and worked carefully to establish it as a classroom norm—a norm that appeared to be foreign to these students in the first few weeks of school.

During the first three weeks of the year, Sara stood near the chalkboard as students presented their ideas, and she circulated among the tables as her students worked together. During the second semester, she continued to circulate as her students worked, but as students presented, she withdrew to the side of the classroom, away from the chalkboard. She continued to guide the discussions; however, when disagreement or uncertainty arose, students stepped in and approached the board to help their peers instead. Sara's students took risks, made mistakes, and looked to one another for help.

Using Calculators to Facilitate ELLs' Participation

Sara introduced the term *keystrokes* in the context of a specific machine: the scientific calculator. In working with the calculator, Sara used this term in two distinct ways: (1) to denote the striking of calculator keys; and (2) to denote—in speaking or writing—the symbols representing the calculator keys. Sara required students to present keystrokes both orally and in writing to accustom them to communicating and discussing mathematical thinking.

In Sara's classroom, using keystrokes to discuss and negotiate meaning was more important than using the calculator to compute answers. The following excerpts from transcripts illustrate how Sara established these practices:

Sara: On your paper write the keystrokes that you would need to put into your calculator to find the area of that rectangle. Don't take the calculators out, I didn't say that. I asked you to write the keystrokes.

Sara: Your keystrokes are very important to me because they tell me what you are thinking. I cannot be inside your head. Oh, unless I open his head. [*class laughter*] I can't do it. But if I see your work, I know what you are thinking.

Figures 5.4 and 5.5 help establish the context for Sara's comments and demonstrate the typical use of calculator keystrokes during the second half of the year in her fifth-grade classroom. Figure 5.4 shows a sample problem. Sara drew the figure on the board, asked her students to work in groups to calculate its area, and then circulated to assess students' progress.

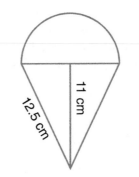

Fig. 5.4. Problem posed to Sara's students: What is the area?

After a short time, Sara asked for a volunteer to write the keystrokes on the chalkboard and explain his or her meaning for the first part of the problem. Marisa volunteered and came to the board to write the keystrokes to calculate the length of the radius of the semicircle (by treating the radius as one leg in a right triangle, with 11 cm as the length of the other leg and 12.5 cm as the length of the hypotenuse, and using the Pythagorean theorem), as shown in figure 5.5. Sara then asked for a second volunteer to continue where Marisa left off. Violetta volunteered to write and explain the second part of the solution, which involved calculating both the area of the semicircle and that of the isosceles triangle.

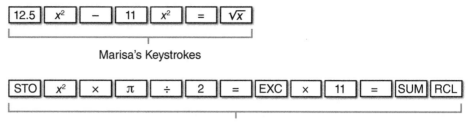

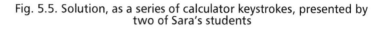

Fig. 5.5. Solution, as a series of calculator keystrokes, presented by two of Sara's students

Sara used calculator keystrokes as a common "language" that was central to the classroom discourse to mediate interactions in small-group and whole-class discussions. This common language was especially important to Sara's students who were learning English as a second language. Students presented keystrokes both verbally and in writing to communicate mathematical thinking, initiate conversations, pose questions to their peers and teacher, analyze their peers' solutions, and articulate corrections and modifications. The students used the keystrokes to plan and create strategies to solve mathematics problems and to create and articulate a process of reasoning to justify their solutions.

In fact, Sara's students became so proficient at thinking and problem solving with the keystrokes that they no longer needed the calculator itself. Sara's technique for using keystrokes in a typical mathematics problem is outlined in the chart in figure 5.6. Although Sara never explicitly articulated this technique herself, it was the process (with the exception of step 6) that she used in every observed lesson. (For further discussion of Sara's use of writing in the mathematics classroom, see Chval and Khisty [2009].)

Step 1	Students write a plan for solving the problem, using only keystrokes.
Step 2	Students use keystrokes to communicate plan.
Step 3	Students break down sequence of keystrokes into components and discuss the meaning of each component.
Step 4	Students listen to presentation of keystrokes, analyze keystrokes, and make a decision concerning agreement with that solution.
Step 5	Students suggest alternative keystroke sequences, including more efficient ones.
Step 6	Students write a narrative of how to solve the problem.

Fig. 5.6. Sara's process for her students for using calculator keystrokes

Through this process, Sara used keystrokes to facilitate her students' development of the functions of planning, problem solving, reflection, analysis, and writing. For example, Sara used calculator keystrokes to develop the students' planning function, or the ability to plan for the solution of a problem (step 1). Students were not only expected to write their keystrokes, but they were also expected to write them *before* they touched the calculators. In an important variation from common teaching practice, Sara did not have her students use keystrokes only to make a record of what they had already pressed. The keystrokes, as Sara used them in her classroom, served the students as a means of communicating and displaying their thinking and, more important, as a way to create a specific plan for solving a problem before they touched the calculators.

Once the students developed a plan for solving a problem, Sara used the keystrokes as referents for discussing mathematical ideas. As students presented sequences of keystrokes to the class, she challenged them to communicate their thinking by writing the keystrokes on the chalkboard and explaining their solutions verbally. Often, students presented part of the solution, like Marisa in the case above, and others, like Violetta in the same case, continued the solution. Sara used this public process to help students clarify their thinking and build meaning.

Once the keystrokes were on the chalkboard for all to see, every student had the responsibility to read them and analyze them. Even if students had written a different sequence on their own papers, they were responsible for understanding other solutions presented by peers. This responsibility included recognizing invalid methods, suggesting alternative methods, or determining more efficient methods. In this process, the students used the keystrokes as objects of reflection and analysis. Although some educators might think that Sara's emphasis on keystrokes would reinforce an algorithmic way of solving problems, analysis of student work indicated that students often generated anywhere from five to eight different solution strategies for many of the problems. This finding strongly suggests that students were not applying memorized procedures for solving problems.

Conclusion

Teachers need to consider how to support their students' development of proficiency with mathematics and language, enhance mathematical tasks, and at the same time establish, facilitate, and maintain productive classroom interactions specifically for ELLs if they want to achieve excellence and equity for these students in their classrooms. Sara provides a critical example of how to *support* ELLs as they simultaneously do advanced mathematical work and acquire a second language. She maximizes contextual supports, such as drawings, calculators, and other representations, which complement other supports, such as teaching for meaning and using students' thinking as learning resources.

Sara's teaching provides an example of how to use the potential of the calculator as a tool to enhance mathematical learning and understanding. She demonstrates how keystrokes can be used to promote and facilitate social activity among ELLs. She introduces the idea of using keystrokes as a common language to mediate interactions so that ELLs can negotiate mathematical meanings. Most important, Sara demonstrates the value of purposefully establishing a learning community where ELLs have the opportunity to participate in productive mathematical practices.

References for Chapter 5

Anderson, Lorin W., and David R. Krathwohl, eds. *A Taxonomy for Learning, Teaching, and Assessing: A Revision of Bloom's Taxonomy of Educational Objectives.* Complete ed. New York: Longman, 2001.

Bloom, Benjamin S., and David R. Krathwohl. *Taxonomy of Educational Objectives: The Classification of Educational Goals.* Handbook 1: *Cognitive Domain.* New York: Longman, 1984.

Brenner, Mary. "Development of Mathematical Communication in Problem Solving Groups by Language Minority Students." *Bilingual Research Journal* 22, nos. 2–4 (1998): 103–28.

Carpenter, Thomas P., Ellen Ansell, Megan L. Franke, Elizabeth Fennema, and Linda Weisbeck. "Models of Problem Solving: A Study of Kindergarten Children's Problem Solving Processes." *Journal for Research in Mathematics Education* 24 (November 1993): 428-41.

Carpenter, Thomas P., Elizabeth Fennema, Megan L. Franke, Linda Levi, and Susan B. Empson. *Children's Mathematics: Cognitively Guided Instruction.* Portsmouth, N.H.: Heinemann, 1999.

Cazden, Courtney. *Classroom Discourse: The Language of Teaching and Learning.* Portsmouth, N.H.: Heinemann, 1988.

Chval, Kathryn B., and Lena L. Khisty. "Latino Students, Writing, and Mathematics: A Case Study of Successful Teaching and Learning." In *Multilingualism in Mathematics Classrooms: Global Perspectives,* edited by Richard Barwell, pp. 128–44. Clevedon, UK: Multilingual Matters, 2009.

Common Core State Standards Initiative (CCSSI). *Common Core State Standards for Mathematics. Common Core State Standards (College- and Career-Readiness Standards and K-12 Standards in English Language Arts and Math).* Washington, D.C.: National Governors Association Center for Best Practices and the Council of Chief State School Officers, 2010. http://www.corestandards.org.

Echevarría, Jana, Mary Ellen Vogt, and Deborah J. Short. *Making Content Comprehensible for English Language Learners: The SIOP Model.* Upper Saddle River, N.J.: Pearson Education, 2004.

Empson, Susan B. "Low-Performing Students and Teaching Fractions for Understanding: An Interactional Analysis." *Journal for Research in Mathematics Education* 34 (July 2003): 305–43.

González, Norma E., Luis Moll, and Cathy L. Amanti. *Funds of Knowledge: Theorizing Practices in Households, Communities, and Classrooms.* Mahwah, N.J.: Lawrence Erlbaum, 2005.

Hatano, Giyoo, and Kayoko Inagaki. "Sharing Cognition through Collective Comprehension Activity." In *Perspectives on Socially Shared Cognition,* edited by Lauren B. Resnick, John M. Levine, and Stephanie D. Teasley, pp. 331–48. Washington D.C.: American Psychological Association, 1991.

National Council of Teachers of Mathematics (NCTM). *Principles and Standards for School Mathematics.* Reston, Va.: NCTM, 2000.

———. *Teaching Mathematics to English Language Learners.* NCTM Position Statement. Reston, Va.: NCTM, 2008. http://www.nctm.org/about/content.aspx?id=16135.

Turner, Erin, and Sylvia Celedón-Pattichis. "Problem Solving and Mathematical Discourse among Latino/a Kindergarten Students: An Analysis of Opportunities to Learn." *Journal of Latinos and Education* 10, no. 2 (2011): 146–69.

Turner, Erin, Sylvia Celedón-Pattichis, and Mary E. Marshall. "Cultural and Linguistic Resources to Promote Problem Solving and Mathematical Discourse among Hispanic Kindergarten Students." In *Promoting High Participation and Success in Mathematics by Hispanic Students: Examining Opportunities and Probing Promising Practices,* TODOS Research Monograph, edited by Richard Kitchen and Edward Silver, pp. 19–42. Washington D.C.: National Education Association Press, 2008.

Turner, Erin, Sylvia Celedón-Pattichis, Mary E. Marshall, and Alan Tennison. "'Fíjense Amorcitos, les voy a Contar una Historia': The Power of Story to Support Solving and Discussing Mathematical Problems with Latino and Latina Kindergarten Students." In *Mathematics for Every Student: Responding to Diversity, Grades Pre-K–5,* edited by Dorothy Y. White and Julie Sliva Spitzer, pp. 23–41. Reston, Va.: National Council of Teachers of Mathematics, 2009.

Vygotsky, Lev. *Mind and Society: The Development of Higher Mental Processes*. Cambridge, Mass.: Harvard University Press, 1978.

World-Class Instructional Design and Assessment (WIDA). English Language Proficiency Standards. http://www.wida.us/.

Chapter 6

Cases of Practice: Teaching Mathematics to ELLs in Secondary School

Like chapter 5, chapter 6 presents cases of practice that are intended to exemplify the points in chapter 2. Six cases highlight essential strategies for teaching mathematics to ELLs at the secondary level. A common misconception is that secondary teachers need to focus only on teaching the content of mathematics (Gutiérrez 2002). However, as Cathy Kinzer, a university collaborator, and David Lee Ubinger, a high school teacher, emphasize in case 1, secondary teachers need to attend to both language and content objectives to address the needs of ELLs. In addition, they illustrate through a series of video clips how David uses sheltered instruction strategies in teaching a freshman algebra 1 class composed predominantly of ELLs.

In case 2, Cynthia O. Anhalt and Jennifer A. Eli demonstrate how an eighth-grade teacher helps ELLs make connections between whole number and polynomial long division.

Next, in case 3, Bill Zahner shows how a high school algebra teacher uses the unit "The Overland Trail" from the first year of the Interactive Mathematics Program (IMP) curriculum (Fendel, Resek, and Alper 1996) to teach a unique student population of recent immigrant ELLs and bilingual students taking algebra a second time. This case gives us insight into how ELLs engage in conceptually demanding mathematics in whole-class and group discussions.

Similarly, in case 4, Hector Morales Jr. shows how bilingual students use their native language while working in groups to make sense of highly advanced mathematics from another IMP unit, "The World of Functions" (year 4; Alper et al. 2000).

Cases 5 and 6, the last two cases of secondary practice in chapter 6, illustrate the need to advocate for ELLs' educational rights (Celedón-Pattichis 2004) and to build relationships (Kitchen et al. 2007). In case 5, Matthew Winsor shares the role he took as an advocate for an ELL who was initially misplaced in his pre-algebra class. In case 6, Rochelle Gutiérrez provides lessons learned from her research on effective high school mathematics teachers and poses questions that engage teachers in reflection on power and identity issues in teaching mathematics to Latina and Latino students.

Case 1

My Story about Teaching Mathematics to ELLs

by Cathy Kinzer and David Lee Ubinger
as told by David Lee Ubinger

- HS_1_Learning Goals (video clip)
- HS_2_Graphic Organizer (video clip)
- HS_3_Mathematical Language (video clip)
- HS_4_Word Wall (video clip)
- HS_5, HS_6, HS_7: Language and Content Objectives 1, 2, 3 (3 video clips)
- HS_8, HS_9, HS_10: Exit Task 1, 2, 3 (3 video clips)
- HS_11, HS_12: Students as a Resource 1, 2 & Gesture (2 video clips)
- HS_13_Students as Competent Problem Solvers and Listening Skills (video clip)
- Task involving DVDs (PowerPoint presentation)
- Task involving Temperature (PowerPoint presentation)
- Task on Teacher's and Brother's Race (PowerPoint presentation)

I was born and raised in El Paso, Texas, a border city adjacent to Juarez, Mexico. Throughout my own K–12 school experience, I was accustomed to being immersed in a learning environment with language learners whose primary language was not English. I share the culture of my students as I teach at a high school in Chaparral, New Mexico, minutes from where I graduated from high school in El Paso. Being around language learners has always been a part of my life. I have found strategies for teaching ELLs that have been both effective and ineffective. Most of the effective strategies are practices for teaching mathematics that one would want to use with all students, although some are essential for working with ELLs and go beyond the needs of the general education classroom.

Within the learning culture, several explicit strategies have been useful for work with ELLs:

- *Providing students with a snapshot of the big picture of a lesson* by beginning with the end in mind and stating the content and language objectives for each lesson (not just what we are going to learn but the mediums in which we will communicate our learning) and reflecting at the end of the lesson on how the objectives were or were not met. (See HS_1_Learning Goals; HS_5, HS_6, HS_7:

Language and Content Objectives; HS_8, HS_9, HS_10: Exit Task—all at www.nctm.org/more4u.)

- *Using comprehensible input* (presenting material in an understandable way) by modifying contextual questions, shortening sentences, and removing confusing words while not lowering mathematical or linguistic expectations for the lesson, and by modifying problem-solving scenarios to make them culturally relevant. (See Task PowerPoint presentations at www.nctm.org/more4u.)

- *Increasing wait time between questions* to allow students the opportunity to formulate a response that accurately represents their understanding and to allow students opportunities to discuss ideas in small groups and possibly in their native languages before sharing in English with the whole group. (See HS_11 and HS_12: Students as a Resource, at www.nctm.org/more4u.)

- *Explicitly teaching vocabulary* through a dual language word wall that enables the transition from student-friendly language to correct mathematical terminology; providing a language-rich environment with many formal and informal opportunities for using vocabulary and the language of mathematics; and using words, numbers, pictures, and graphs to communicate the meaning of new mathematics terminology. Providing visual representations offers ELLs ways to communicate mathematics concepts and ideas. (See HS_3_Mathematical Language and HS_4_Word Wall, at www.nctm.org/more4u.)

- *Creating cooperative and interdependent groups to support first- and second-language development* by grouping ELLs at times with English-speaking students and at times with other ELLs; encouraging group members to ask clarifying questions of each other in native languages and using discourse to make sense of mathematics and communicate their mathematical thinking. (See HS_11 and HS_12: Students as a Resource 1, at www.nctm.org/more4u.)

- *Encouraging nonlinguistic representations for communicating proficiency in mathematics* (including but not limited to words, numbers, pictures, gestures). For example, students finding the solution to a system of equations might draw a graph to identify an intersection point, might use their arms to indicate two lines intersecting, might use numbers to find the solution algebraically, or might use words (in English or their native language, depending on their language proficiency) to communicate the meaning of their solution mathematically or within the context of the problem scenario. (See HS_2_Graphic Organizer and HS_12_Students as a Resource 2 & Gesture, at www.nctm.org/more4u.)

- *Using listening skills and positioning students as competent problem solvers.* (See HS_13_Students as Competent Problem Solvers and Listening Skills, at www.nctm.org/more4u.)

School Demographics

Chaparral High School (CHS) is a Title I school located in Chaparral, New Mexico, approximately ten miles north of El Paso, Texas. Of the eleventh-grade students who took the state math assessment in 2009, 90 percent were Hispanic, and 51 percent were designated as English language learners (ELLs). Ninety-eight percent of these students were designated as "economically disadvantaged," and 100 percent received free meals. Many of the students at CHS will be first-generation college students, and some will be first-generation high school graduates. A large number of students at CHS speak English only at school; their native language is spoken both at home and with peers, offering little to no practice of English outside the educational setting.

Successes and Challenges in Teaching Mathematics to ELLs

Throughout my teaching of mathematics to ELLs, I have experienced successes and struggles. Because I am an English-only educator, I have had moments when I have felt that I could not communicate wholly with students who are emerging in their English language proficiency. I think this problem has given me a better understanding of different ways in which students can communicate their learning of mathematics. One of the beauties of developing problem solvers through teaching mathematics is the number of tools that students have for communicating their learning. Using English is not the only way for students to communicate their ideas and experiences. Just because a student might not know how to express himself or herself in English does not mean that there is not another appropriate medium that he or she can use. I have learned to encourage not only ELLs but all students to communicate multiple problem-solving strategies. Students are able to express their learning through words, numbers, pictures, or gestures. I am constantly looking for alternate ways to communicate my own teaching and facilitate assessments. I am also looking for opportunities to model English usage and mathematics terminology for my students. Students themselves must be supported to serve as resources for one another in our classroom discourse and communication.

Policies and Practices Supporting or Hindering My Teaching of ELLs

As I search for ways for ELLs to practice and refine their English usage through their learning of mathematics, I have experienced moments when students best express themselves by using their native language. It has been in these situations that I have found that connections can be made between a student's native language and English through a student translator. Sometimes there might not be a word that directly translates specific mathematics terminology between languages. In some of these instances I have observed students using gestures or pictures to communicate with one another their learning and understanding of mathematical concepts taught in class. Our school has not always supported students' using their native language to communicate their learning within the classroom. At times, students not in a dual language class have been required to speak only in English, with the intent of forcing them to use and practice their English in everything they did. My experience has been that some students are not ready to express themselves fully in English, even when they are in an English-only classroom. Forcing them to speak and write only in English deprives them of the opportunity to make connections between their native languages and cultures and the new environment and culture that they might find themselves in someday.

Advocating for ELLs in the School Setting and Classroom Setting

By allowing students to communicate their learning in both English and their native language, teachers can create a safe, risk-free environment for ELLs. Efforts to create such an environment start from the first day of class. Norms are established to foster constructive student and teacher feedback for proper language usage. ELLs will make mistakes in their English usage when first taking the risk to use English in the mathematics classroom. These mistakes should be seen as learning opportunities, and both the teacher and the student should regard them as teachable moments in language usage in a constructive way, just as the mathematics teacher would view a student's misconception in mathematics reasoning as a learning opportunity. It is important to create a culture that supports ELLs by honoring what they bring to the classroom. ELLs can find success in communicating their learning and practicing English within the classroom learning environment.

Video Clips

I invite you to view a series of video clips that reflect my journey in developing strategies that engage ELLs in learning mathematics. (See HS_1–HS_13 at www.nctm.org /more4u.)

Context: Chaparral High School, ninth-grade freshman algebra 1

Purpose: The lesson was intended to allow students to demonstrate their understanding of solving a system of linear equations by using substitution to arrive at a precise answer. Prior experience with the task involved solving a system graphically or by using a table. The lesson provided an opportunity for students to make connections among the tools of algebra (creating a table, drawing a graph, finding intercepts, writing an equation). These visual representations are important ways to make sense of the mathematics and communicate mathematically.

Message: Students often come up with multiple problem-solving strategies in the mathematics classroom. Some of these strategies might potentially be more efficient, but the ultimate goal is for all students to make sense of the mathematics. Their strategies represent a continuum of understanding. By honoring students' ways of thinking and listening to their ideas, I am more able to support them and scaffold their next steps. It is important to give students time to think about the mathematics and develop ways to communicate their thinking. Language development takes time. Students need opportunities to make sense of the mathematics through conversations that develop language, representations, and other ways of communicating in a learner-focused environment.

Case 2

Building Connections from Whole Number to Polynomial Long Division—Teaching English Language Learners

by Cynthia O. Anhalt and Jennifer A. Eli

- **Figures 6.2, 6.3, 6.4 (as color images)**

There is little argument regarding the centrality of number and its operations in the mathematics curriculum throughout the history of schooling. As *Principles and Standards for School Mathematics* (National Council of Teachers of Mathematics [NCTM] 2000) asserts, "Historically, number has been a cornerstone of the mathematics curriculum" (p. 32). *Principles and Standards* emphasizes that understanding number and operations, developing number sense, and gaining fluency in arithmetic computation form the foundation of mathematics education for the elementary grades. Computational fluency is therefore foundational for all students, including those who are learning English and mathematics simultaneously.

The Common Core State Standards for Mathematics (CCSSM) place emphasis on number and operations—in particular, on division—on finding "whole-number quotients and remainders with up to four-digit dividends and one-digit divisors, using strategies based on place value, the properties of operations, and/or the relationship between multiplication and division" (Common Core State Standards Initiative [CCSSI] 2010, p. 30). For the purpose of this project, we use "long division" to refer to the standard division algorithm traditionally taught in the United States, involving a number with three or more digits in the dividend and a number with one or more digits in the divisor.

In learning algebra, students build on their knowledge of arithmetic to work with generalized forms of the processes. Students' understanding of algebra should build on the proficiency that they have developed in arithmetic. This is especially important to the success of English language learners (ELLs), who are learning algebra while continuing to develop English proficiency. "Nevertheless, for many students [including ELLs] learning algebra is an entirely different experience from learning arithmetic, and they find the transition difficult" (National Research Council [NRC] 2001, pp. 255–56).

In general, students' knowledge of whole number long division procedures is fragile at the elementary and middle school levels (NRC 2001). In our project, we found that eighth graders had difficulty in their initial attempts to make the transition from whole number long division to polynomial long division. In particular, these eighth graders remembered learning procedures for whole number long division in the fourth grade but had difficulties remembering how to carry out the algorithm, and more important, they lacked the conceptual understanding of underlying mathematical structure to make connections to algebra.

The standard whole number long division algorithm is traditionally taught as a procedure, with steps such as divide, multiply, subtract, and bring down. Yet, reform-oriented teaching emphasizes making meaning in tandem with learning the algorithms.

Thus, we set out to investigate and document effective ways to teach division of polynomials to a diverse student population that included ELLs.

Reflections from the Teacher

The teacher featured in this case study, Mr. Joseph Cuprak, has been teaching mathematics for more than twenty years, at multiple grade levels. His exemplary teaching inspires all students to learn mathematics, and we are grateful to him for graciously sharing his classroom with us so that we, in turn, might share his work with other educators.

Mr. Cuprak currently teaches all the eighth-grade mathematics courses at his middle school, as well as one period of mathematics each day at a nearby high school. He has taught mathematics courses at the university and community college level for a number of years in addition to teaching summer school to incoming middle school students. Over the years, Mr. Cuprak has had the opportunity to build a deep and flexible knowledge of the mathematics curriculum from the elementary through the postsecondary level while also developing teaching strategies that promote learning for all students and are especially crucial for ELLs.

We asked Mr. Cuprak to reflect on his experience in teaching these lessons and to carefully dissect and analyze his teaching. One of his initial reactions was that throughout his years of teaching he had seen many students struggle to remember the standard algorithm for whole number long division, even though, as he knew, they had seen it multiple times before reaching his classroom. He had often wondered, "Why don't students remember the long division algorithm? What specific things could I do to help them remember it better so that they can make a smoother transition to algebra?"

Mr. Cuprak has thought deeply about how to help students build connections to polynomial long division. He has also often witnessed the fact that some students are able to do the mathematics but have difficulty expressing the mathematics verbally—especially those students who are learning English while simultaneously learning mathematics. He has learned to be patient and continue to give ELL students opportunities to explain their thoughts.

In general, he has found that once students gain a better conceptual understanding of whole number long division, they are more able to build and understand explicit connections between whole number and polynomial long division. Mr. Cuprak believes that learning is cumulative and that, as a teacher, he needs to consistently make explicit connections within "old knowledge" and with "new knowledge" by embedding conceptual perspectives in familiar mathematics. By making those mathematical connections deliberately and explicitly in his teaching, Mr. Cuprak believes that all his students, including the ELLs, will deepen their understanding and retain the mathematics.

The Classroom Setting

The case study that we present comes from a middle school that emphasizes teacher-centered traditional approaches to teaching mathematics. Although Mr. Cuprak works within the parameters of a traditional school setting, his views on teaching and learning also incorporate reform-oriented strategies. The eighth-grade algebra classroom that we studied consisted of 34 students, with 22 female and 12 male students, of whom

53 percent were Hispanic/Latino, 44 percent were Anglo, and 3 percent were Native American. A total of 10 students came from families in which Spanish was the primary language spoken at home.

The students responded positively to the reform-oriented strategies that Mr. Cuprak used during a unit on polynomials. One main aspect of his teaching was his deliberate attempt to make the mathematics comprehensible to his students at every point in the discussion. Thus, he was mindful of appropriate pacing and the need to verbalize the mathematics in different ways, with clear articulation. His lesson demonstrated teaching strategies that promote learning for all his students, including students who are not fully proficient in the English language. Figure 6.1 presents some of the literature-based effective teaching strategies for ELLs (e.g., Barnett-Clark and Ramirez 2004; Carr et al. 2009; Coggins et al. 2007; Echevarría et al. 2004) and their connection to the teaching strategies that Mr. Cuprak used. Mr. Cuprak taught the lessons on long division that follow by using both traditional and reform-oriented approaches in which modern technology—specifically, the use of an interactive whiteboard—allowed the teacher to show connections—explicitly, efficiently, and smoothly—between the processes of whole number long division and polynomial long division. The strategies described in the figure are embedded in the description of the case study that we present.

Literature-Based Effective Teaching Strategies for ELLs	Specific Teaching Strategies Used by Mr. Cuprak
Making the mathematics more comprehensible and accessible to all students	• Related the mathematical concepts underlying the polynomial long division algorithm to help all students succeed in more advanced topics in algebra
Modeling a process explicitly and deliberately	• Used the interactive whiteboard to model the whole number division algorithm and the polynomial long division algorithm in tandem with drawing the parallels between the two • Color-coded the place values during the division process
Scaffolding—building students' abilities to complete tasks on their own, step by step	• In whole number division, pointed out the stacked partial quotients and combined them by adding the place values and the remainder as a fraction (see figs. 6.2 and 6.3)
Using visuals and graphic organizers	• Had students fold their papers vertically and work through the two division processes side by side • Color-coded the place values during the division process
Contextualizing the mathematical language; expecting students to listen for it and use it when possible with partners, in small groups, or in whole-class discussion	• Had students participate in naming the polynomials mathematically by degree and number of terms; • Made the mathematical language easy to understand and accessible to all • Talked aloud while working through the mathematics to model the thinking process • Specifically communicated mathematical terms, degrees of exponents, and place values
Clarifying the language to make the mathematics understandable; actively engaging students in discussions to help them develop mathematical discourse	• Asked students to explain their reasoning with relation to place value when describing the next step in dividing whole numbers and polynomials

Fig. 6.1. Summary of ELL teaching strategies used by Mr. Cuprak

Literature-Based Effective Teaching Strategies for ELLs	Specific Teaching Strategies Used by Mr. Cuprak
Establishing classroom norms that include a risk-free environment for students to ask questions	• Made students feel comfortable and confident in using mathematical language during discussions, especially in identifying and classifying polynomials in the context of long division
Drawing on students' prior knowledge and experiences to help them make connections, modeling connections explicitly, and teaching procedures with understanding	• Asked the students what they knew about whole number long division • Embedded conceptual perspectives in familiar mathematics that students bring to the classroom—specifically, gave attention to the role of place value in whole number long division and its connections to polynomial long division • Made the role of place value and its meaning in division algorithm clear
Helping students build relationships between mathematical concepts	• Emphasized the importance of the relationship between whole number and polynomial division
Setting high expectations and offering support for all students	• Supported and encouraged students to communicate the mathematical ideas aligned with expected outcomes for first-year algebra

Fig. 6.1—*Continued*

The Lessons on Polynomial Long Division

We videotaped several lessons that Mr. Cuprak taught in a unit on polynomial long division. In addition to helping students develop computational fluency with a focus on understanding the processes associated with polynomial long division, one main goal for each of the lessons was to scaffold and make explicit the mathematical connections between arithmetic and algebraic long division processes. The teacher structured the lessons in this unit on polynomial long division with an eye to providing mathematical motivation for the topic, drawing on students' prior experiences with arithmetic long division and co-creating the processes associated with carrying out whole number division and those needed for polynomial long division. We focus our discussion on the teacher's explicit efforts within these lessons to further students' computational fluency, to build connections from previously learned knowledge to new knowledge, and to develop students' mathematical language.

Prior knowledge, scaffolding, and connections

Mr. Cuprak began the lesson on polynomial long division by drawing on his students' prior experience and knowledge of arithmetic long division. He asked the students if they remembered when they learned about whole number long division in their elementary classes. The students indicated that they remembered doing long division in the fourth grade, a little more in the fifth grade, and not much more since sixth grade. At this point, the teacher realized that he needed to informally assess his students' knowledge of the standard U.S. whole number long division algorithm, thereby informing his instruction in order to help students build computational fluency in polynomial long division. One volunteer student, standing at the front of the classroom, created a problem on the board for the class to do. His problem involved a single-digit divisor: 15,111 divided by 3. After Mr. Cuprak asked him to solve his own problem, the student immediately turned to his classmates for help since he was having difficulty remembering how to begin the arithmetic processes associated with whole number division.

Students who do not retain the procedure illustrate NCTM's (2000) concern that "students who memorize facts or procedures without understanding are not sure when or how to use what they know, and such learning is often quite fragile" (p. 20). In particular, middle grades students' "computational fluency should develop in tandem with understanding the role and meaning of arithmetic operations in number systems" (p. 32). Having been reminded of the students' difficulties in remembering an algorithm for whole number long division, Mr. Cuprak focused on re-teaching and making the algorithmic process of long division explicit, with emphasis on place value and the relationship between multiplication and division, to promote understanding of the U.S. standard whole number division algorithm (see fig. 6.2). The goal was for the students to see the division process in light of conceptual understanding gained through attention to place value and relationships. Then they could more easily transfer that understanding to their thinking about dividing polynomials.

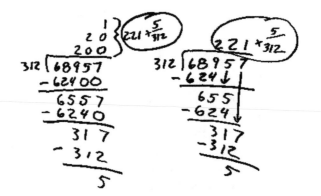

Fig. 6.2. Whole number long division

Once the students could bring current understanding to the division algorithm, the teacher could then draw parallels between the whole number long division algorithm and the algebraic polynomial long division algorithm to help students see the relationship and build connections. The teacher began by asking the students to fold a sheet of paper in half along a vertical axis and copy down the problem 68,957 divided by 312 on one half of the sheet. The teacher then actively engaged students in a conversation about how to divide 68,957 by 312, using the approach to division that is sometimes called the "stacking method" (illustrated in fig. 6.2). Through teacher questioning and guided practice, students began to make connections from their previous experiences with the whole number long division algorithm and were able to remember the procedure better as the teacher placed emphasis on a conceptual understanding of place value and its role in the process of long division.

An underlying belief of Mr. Cuprak's teaching is that understanding the whole number long division process is a powerful prerequisite for learning the polynomial long division process. After the discussion about how to work through the algorithm for 68,957 divided by 312, Mr. Cuprak presented the problem $(6x^3 + 7x^2 + 14x + 14)$ divided by $(3x + 2)$ and asked the students to copy it on the other half of the sheet of paper. He then presented these two problems on two different pages of the interactive whiteboard and worked through the standard algorithms of long division simultaneously. He switched back and forth between the two problems (see fig. 6.3 for the polynomial division) while asking students what to do next—and, more important, asking them to explain their reasoning. In one instance, a student explained that the first term of the polynomial in the dividend should be looked at first to "see" what the divisor should be divided into, a step similar to that of considering the first digit and subsequent digits in the dividend of a whole number first to "see" what the divisor should be divided into. For example, the 6 (and then the 69) in the dividend is the first consideration for dividing 52 into 6981 in the whole number long division algorithm.

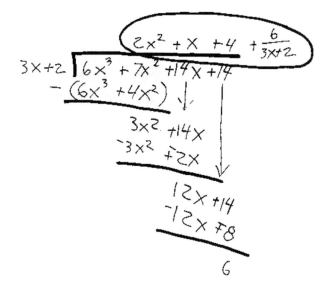

Fig 6.3. Polynomial long division

Mr. Cuprak also used the color tools of his interactive whiteboard to show explicitly the importance of place value, and he focused on the role of place value in carrying out the polynomial long division algorithm (see fig. 6.4; figs. 6.3 and 6.4 are also available at www.nctm.org/more4u). Although the notion of showing students the parallel algorithms may be widely used, the explicit use of language and color-coded place value cannot be underestimated in its power to make the process more deliberate for ELLs. The students were then given two different problems to solve to demonstrate their understanding of the parallel processes in whole number and polynomial long division: 587,392 divided by 31 and $(8x^3 + 10x^2 - 13x - 20)$ divided by $(2x + 3)$. A sample of student work is shown in figure 6.5.

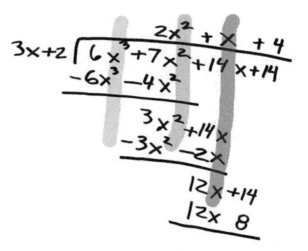

Fig. 6.4. Color coding polynomial long division

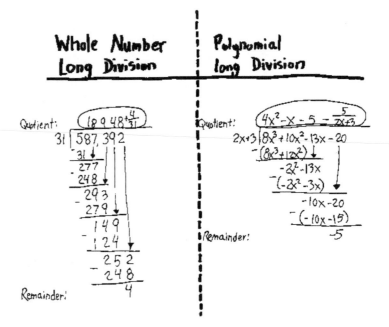

Fig. 6.5. Sample student work on a polynomial division problem

Mr. Cuprak's skill with the interactive whiteboard allowed him to present the mathematics efficiently and effectively. By working through the two problems with a focus on deliberate scaffolding, he was able to help students build mathematical connections between the processes. By having the students create a folded sheet with both problems, Mr. Cuprak enabled them to simulate his color-coded use of the interactive whiteboard, thereby helping them to make the mathematical connections between whole number long division and polynomial long division visually explicit.

A closely observed lesson segment

To show Mr. Cuprak's approach in more detail, we conclude by presenting a segment of the lesson, during which the teacher solved the problem $(6x^3 + 7x^2 + 14x + 14)$ divided by $(3x + 2)$ and the problem 68,957 divided by 312 in parallel to show the similarities in the thinking involved in both procedures.

Mr. Cuprak began by asking, "What are we going to do here to divide a polynomial by a binomial?" The students responded that the $3x$ needs to go into the $6x^3$, and the teacher continued modeling the procedure, saying things such as, "We're going to make a big deal about bringing down that next term, which happens to be plus $14x$. And then what do we do to do this?" Mr. Cuprak switched to the screen on the interactive whiteboard with the whole number long division problem and continued modeling both problems, making the processes explicit while asking questions.

At the end of the whole number division problem, Mr. Cuprak came to the solution and pointed to the stacked partial quotients (see fig. 6.2) and said, "Notice the 200, the 20, and the 1, and where they came from; combine that together, 221, and I still have my remainder of plus division, which is one important aspect of learning to think algebraically."

Because the concept of division is about number relationships and helping students develop a sense of quantity, it is important to teach whole number long division conceptually, since this conceptual understanding in turn helps students understand the algebraic ideas and the procedure for polynomial long division. At a minimum, teachers need to consider the crucial factors that will give all students, including ELLs, opportunities to continue to learn and to take higher-level mathematics.

Case 3

Discussing Conceptually Demanding Mathematics in a Bilingual Algebra Class

by William Zahner

Consider the following problem (Fendel, Resek, and Alper 1996, p. 272), set in the context of U.S. westward expansion:

> The Stevens family had a 50-gallon water container. In an effort to conserve water, they reduced their daily consumption to three gallons per day. If they began with a full container, how many gallons would they have left after three days? Eight days? Twelve days? x days?

The vignette that follows depicts how a bilingual algebra teacher supported the mathematical, linguistic, and social needs of English language learners as they engaged in solving this problem. In the following section, I introduce Ms. V and her students, describe a few key moments from one lesson, and then consider how Ms. V made conceptually focused mathematics accessible to all students in her linguistically diverse class. (All names in the vignette are pseudonyms.)

The Teacher and the Class

Ms. V's bilingual algebra class at Campo High School brings together two distinct student populations: recent immigrant English language learners (ELLs) and bilingual students not classified as ELLs who are repeating algebra. Ms. V's success as a teacher, recognized by peers and administrators, demonstrates that bilingual students, English language learners, and students who have been placed in a "remedial" class can all learn algebra by participating in cognitively demanding discussions of important mathematical concepts. Ms. V skillfully uses multiple resources to support her students' learning of algebra through group investigations and whole-class discussions. In the following, I introduce Ms. V and her students, examine one lesson from Ms. V's class, illustrate students' reasoning with examples from small-group and whole-class interactions, and then consider the resources (linguistic, curricular, and material) that Ms. V used to craft and teach this lesson.

Campo High School is located in a medium-sized school district in a semi-rural area of California. The total enrollment at Campo is approximately 1,550 students, and during the year of this vignette, the California Department of Education's statistics indicated that Campo High School's student population was overwhelmingly Latino (94 percent) and from low socioeconomic backgrounds (77 percent qualified for free or reduced-price lunch). Thirty-five percent of the students at Campo were classified as English learners, while 48 percent were classified as FEP, or "fully English proficient." (In California, a student is identified as an English learner until he or she achieves district-specified scores on state achievement tests and meets other academic criteria, at which point the student is identified as RFEP, or "reclassified fluent English proficient." FEP students are both RFEP students and students whose primary language is not English but who scored high enough on a state test of English proficiency to be considered "initially fluent English proficient," or IFEP.)

Ms. V's algebra class was one of the few bilingual mathematics classes at the school, and about one-third of Ms. V's thirty students were Spanish-dominant speakers. Ms. V teaches her class by using a mixture of teacher-led instruction, small-group discussions among students, and whole-class discussions. Most classes start with a whole-class introduction, followed by a group activity, in which the students work with peers, and a closing whole-class discussion. Ms. V's students work on non-routine group-worthy tasks (Cohen 1994) nearly every day. In an interview after my observations of her class, Ms. V explained that she started using group work because it actively engages her students in making sense of mathematical ideas. Her use of group work and non-routine tasks in a class with a high proportion of English language learners is notable because exploratory learning is often reserved for "advanced" students.

The Lesson in Curricular Context

In the episode that follows, Ms. V was teaching a lesson called "Water Conservation" from the unit "The Overland Trail" in the first year of the Interactive Mathematics Program (IMP) curriculum for high school (Fendel, Resek, and Alper 1996). The curricular focus of the unit included reasoning with data, creating and interpreting graphs of linear relationships, and interpreting and comparing the rates of change in linear graphs (Interactive Mathematics Program 2009).

The Water Conservation problem described how much water two families had and the rate at which the two families used their water supplies while crossing an arid region of the Overland Trail. One family in the story started with 50 gallons and used 3 gallons per day, whereas the other family started with 100 gallons and used 8 gallons per day. Given a description of the situation in words, the students were asked to generate a table of values showing how much water each family would have after a certain number of days, write a formula in terms of x for the amount of water each family would have after x days, graph the two equations, predict when the families would have the same amount of water, and predict when each family would run out of water.

Examples Showing the Discussion Unfolding

In the following section, I detail how Ms. V set up and taught "Water Conservation." I first focus on Ms. V's introduction of the problem, then look at two excerpts from the students' small-group interactions (one in English and one in Spanish), and then describe how Ms. V brought closure to the lesson.

Introducing the problem

Ms. V introduced the problem by asking her students to read it in Spanish and English. The introduction to the problem explained that two families traveling the Overland Trail used water at different rates as they crossed the Nevada desert. Question 1 was posed in the following manner (Fendel, Resek, and Alper 1996, p. 272; quoted at the beginning of case 3 and reproduced here for the reader's convenience):

> The Stevens family had a 50-gallon water container. In an effort to conserve water, they reduced their daily consumption to three gallons per day. If they began with a full container, how many gallons would they have left after three days? Eight days? Twelve days? x days?

After reading the problem aloud, Ms. V asked the students whether they could make an equation with the given information. She offered most of what she said in both Spanish and English. The following classroom excerpt starts after the class had read the problem aloud. Spanish utterances that the teacher did not translate are provided in English in parentheses, and observational comments appear in square brackets, in italics. Ms. V focused her questions to direct the students' attention to key quantities and relationships in the given information.

Ms. V:	OK, gracias. (Thank you) ¿Con cuánto empezaron? How much did they start with?
Students:	Cincuenta. (Fifty)
Ms. V:	Cincuenta galones, fifty gallons of water. How much are they using per day? ¿Cuánto están usando por día?
Students:	Tres galones. (Three gallons.)
Ms. V:	Tres galones al día. ¿Pueden hacer una ecuación con eso? (Three gallons per day. Can you make an equation with this?) ¿No? ¿No pueden hacer ecuación? Angélica sí puede. (No? You can't make an equation? Angélica can.) Sabemos con cuánto empezamos y cuánto estamos usando al día. (We know how much we start with and how much we are using per day.) So talk in your group and see if you can come up with an equation. Hablen en su grupo [*inaudible*] pueden escribir una ecuación con esa información. (Talk in your group and see if you can write an equation with this information.)

In this introduction, Ms. V used several resources to help all her students gain access to grade-level mathematics. First, Ms. V made this problem accessible to both her English-dominant and Spanish-dominant students by using both Spanish and English while introducing the problem. Second, Ms. V focused the discussion on the mathematical issues in the problem and used familiar terminology to encourage her students to make connections between what they had done previously in her class and the new activity. For example, Ms. V tapped into the students' prior knowledge by referring to the y-intercept as the "starting amount." This was terminology that she and the students used when writing linear equations in earlier classes. Finally, Ms. V allowed the students time to solve this problem in their groups. She could have taken the students through the steps of setting up the equation while lecturing and writing on the board. Instead, Ms. V made this problem more challenging and engaging for her students by asking them to set up the equations for each situation by discussing the problem in their groups. Ms. V did not simply tell her students that the equation was $y = 50 - 3x$ but instead named one student who she knew had already generated an equation. By naming a student who could do the task, Ms. V assigned competence to the students and indicated that they could use one another as resources rather than rely on her for the answers.

Group discussion

After the whole-class introduction, Ms. V's students worked on all five questions from the Water Conservation problem in their groups. As the students talked, Ms. V circulated among the eight groups, asking questions and offering help. In the following interaction, Ms. V talked with Susana, an English-dominant student who set up her second equation ($y = 100 - 8x$). Immediately before this interaction, Susana apparently misspoke and said that the second family started with 800 gallons (instead of the 100 gallons given in the problem). Rather than simply correcting Susana's error, Ms. V emphasized relating the quantities in the equation back to the situation. In her discussion with Susana, Ms. V also emphasized that the word *per* implies a rate of change that needs to be multiplied by the independent variable. Making this connection helped Susana see where each parameter (i.e., the slope and the y-intercept) should be written in the linear equation.

Ms. V:	How many gallons of water do they have to start?
Mateo:	A hundred.
Susana:	They have a hundred.
Mateo:	[*Whispered*] One hundred.
Ms. V:	One hundred, so write *y* equals one hundred.
Susana:	OK.
Ms. V:	And how much are they using per day?
Susana:	They're using… um… eight gallons. That's what I meant to say, but I said eight hundred.
Ms. V:	Per day [*emphasized*] per day. Say "per day."
Susana:	Per day.
Ms. V:	That's why we have to multiply. Per *x,* times *x.* So it's what? What's the equation?
Susana:	Minus?
Ms. V:	Yes, write minus.
Susana:	Eight *x?*
Ms. V:	Yes. Now you substitute three days, eight days, and twelve days.
Susana:	OK.

After this discussion with Ms. V, Susana and her group mates continued answering the remaining questions from the lesson "Water Conservation."

The next classroom excerpt comes from a group discussion that occurred later in the same class period. This discussion illustrates how a group of Spanish-speaking students supported each other as they solved a problem without Ms. V's help. At the start of this excerpt, Ms. V instructed Andrés to complete his table of values for the equation $y = 100 - 8x$ by substituting 3, 8, and 12 for *x.* She walked away telling Andrés that he had forgotten 12. After Ms. V left the group, Graciela began asking Angélica questions. Angélica explained the steps to Graciela, and then Angélica told Graciela to help Andrés because Graciela was closer to him.

Ms. V:	Sí, muy bien. Um… veinticuatro … setenta y seis. Ocho, OK. Falta una con doce. Doce días. Doce días. Ocho por doce. [*Walks away.*] (Yes, very good. Um… twenty-four … seventy-six. Eight. OK. You are missing one with twelve. Twelve days. Twelve days. Eight times twelve.)
Graciela:	[*To Angélica*] ¿Cuál era la- el ecuación? (What was the equation?)
Angélica:	Cien… [*pauses and corrects herself*] *y* es igual a cien menos ocho *x.* (100… *y* is equal to 100 minus eight *x.*)
Graciela:	[*To herself*] …Ocho *x* y este [*referring to the previous equation*] *y* es igual (… Eight *x* and this *y* is equal to…)

107

[*Inaudible exchanges continue among Graciela, Angélica, and Andrés.*]

Angélica: Explica la del doce. Graciela, estás más cerquita explícasela. [*Asks Graciela to explain.*] (Explain the one with twelve. Graciela, you are closer, explain it to him.)

Graciela: ¿Cuál? (Which?)

Angélica: La de doce. (The one with twelve.)

Graciela: [*Inaudible*] Aquí empieza, pon [*inaudible*] ocho por doce y ya de aquí son [*inaudible*] cien menos lo que encuentra en ocho por doce. (Here you start, put [*inaudible*] eight times twelve and then here it's one hundred minus what you get from eight times twelve.)

With Graciela's help, Andrés was able to complete his table and answer the questions from the task. After the conclusion of the group discussions, Ms. V wrapped up the lesson by displaying students' graphs and discussing the answers to conceptually demanding questions concerning when the two families in the problem would have had the same quantity of water, and when each family would have run out of water.

Conclusion: Mathematical, Linguistic, and Social Supports Used by Ms. V

In this brief example of a day in the life of Ms. V's class, we can see Ms. V skillfully combining multiple levels of support for her students. Her supports were mathematical, linguistic, and social. In particular, Ms. V—

- maintained a focus on important mathematical ideas;
- used the real-life context of the problem to support conceptual reasoning (e.g., "How much did they start with?" "How much per day?");
- allowed the students time to talk to one another in the language of their choice;
- provided opportunities for students to do conceptually demanding mathematics while learning English;
- created a group-work environment where students actively sought help from each other and provided help to one another.

Some teachers who see videos of Ms. V in action assume that because they are not bilingual, they cannot support students in the same way that Ms. V did. However, it is important to note that many of the supports that Ms. V provided were not dependent on her speaking Spanish. Monolingual teachers can also maintain a focus on important mathematical concepts, establish positive working environments in small groups, and provide time for students to talk through ideas with group mates in their preferred language.

Case 4

Twelfth-Grade English Language Learners and the Making of Mathematical Meanings

by Hector Morales Jr.

The observations that I share were part of a larger study of Latinos in mathematics (Morales 2004) and were made in a twelfth-grade mainstream class in a school that has a student population that is nearly 80 percent Latino. The students in this class are particularly interesting because they are all in an advanced mathematics class and are studying mathematics through a standards-based reform curriculum, Interactive Mathematics Program (IMP; for the particular IMP textbook that the class was using, see Fendel and colleagues [2000]). The students also represent varying degrees of proficiency in two languages.

Four of these students were selected for closer study. Some of the students in this particular group were in a bilingual education program in the early grades, and some were not; one is a fairly recent immigrant. This group of students—Carina, Jessica, Elena, and Inés—has worked collaboratively all year; they represent fairly typical students in the school and in most of the high school mathematics classes. Carina, Elena, and Jessica were all born in the United States, but their parents are from Mexico. They all grew up speaking both Spanish and English at home, but they are not comfortable reading or writing in Spanish. All three students have been observed speaking Spanish when explaining to others while doing mathematics and also speaking mathematically in both languages. Inés is the only student in the group who was born in Mexico, and she immigrated to the United States when she was 12 years old. She returned to Mexico to complete her ninth-grade education and later returned to the United States to complete her high school education.

The IMP curriculum expects students regularly to listen to and attempt to understand others' explanations, to communicate, explain, and justify their reasoning, and to use mathematical representations (e.g., numerical tables, algebraic expressions, images from a graphing calculator) to demonstrate their understandings. Students were observed as they worked on the unit "World of Functions" in the fourth year of IMP (Fendel et al. 2000). The purpose of this unit is to explore basic families of functions and various ways in which they can be represented, such as tables, graphs, algebraic expressions, and models for real-world situations. This unit also requires students to draw on their extensive previous work with functions from other units throughout the four years of their IMP experience. In the first two weeks of the unit—

- the students reviewed different ways to think about functions (as, for example, a graph, a table, an equation, a problem situation), sketched graphs of functions based on problem situations, and worked with data represented in a table;
- the teacher formally defined functions and families of linear, exponential, and sine functions.

The students were assigned the task of recalling some ways in which functions were helpful to them. To do this task, they had to select an IMP unit and a particular function that they had studied previously. Specifically, they needed to do three things:

1. Describe the problem context in which the function was used and explain what the input and the output for the function represented in the problem context.
2. Describe how the function was helpful in solving the unit's central problem or some other problem in the unit.
3. If possible, identify the function family for the selected function.

The students in the study group chose "All about Alice," a unit in the second year of IMP (Fendel et al. 2004). The unit starts with a model based on Lewis Carroll's *Alice's Adventures in Wonderland*, in which Alice's height is doubled or halved by her eating or drinking certain magic potions. The basic principles for working with exponents and an introduction to problems involving exponential growth and decay arise from this situation. The vignettes that follow show how students can use a variety of resources to make meaning of a complex mathematical situation involving exponential growth. Specifically, the problem is as follows (Fendel et al. 2004, p. 385):

> Alice's height changes when she eats the cake. Assume as before that her height doubles for each ounce she eats. A) Find out what Alice's height is multiplied by when she eats 1, 2, 3, 4, 5, or 6 ounces of cake. B) Make a graph of this information.

To solve this problem, students could represent the relationship in a table of values or a graph and consequently discover that if Alice's height is doubling for every ounce that she eats, then her height is multiplied by a power of two that depends on how many ounces of cake she eats. For example, if Alice's height is originally 3 feet and she eats 4 ounces of cake, her height is now 48 feet ($3 \times 2^4 = 3 \times 16$, or 48). This mathematical problem can also be represented by an equation of the form $y = ab^x$. In this case, Alice's height is doubling, so the base, b, is 2, and Alice's original height is represented by the variable a, giving the equation $y = a \cdot 2^x$.

Classroom Vignettes and Observations

This section presents three vignettes illustrating Latino students' processes of making meaning while doing advanced mathematics. English translations of Spanish utterances are provided in parentheses, and descriptions of students' actions appear in brackets, in italics. L1 indicates a student's first language (Spanish), L2 indicates his or her second language (English), and an arrow → indicates a shift between languages.

Vignette 1

The first vignette shows the students interpreting the Alice problem at the outset of the activity. It shows them discussing what is happening in the context and what the words and mathematical ideas mean.

Transcript	Observations of Student Actions
Jessica: ¿Qué era la primera, se hace así? OK, dice: Alice "changes when she eats the cake, assume as before that her height doubles for each ounce she eats," so that means if she eats one ounce, that means that she grows twice, dos ¿qué? Double, no double, two. (What was the first one, do you do it like this? OK, it says, "Alice changes when she eats the cake, assume as before that her height doubles for each ounce she eats," so that means if she eats one ounce, that means that she grows twice, two what? Double, no double two.)	Jessica uses— L1 to clarify the task; L2 to read text from the book; L2 to make meaning. She tries to make sense of the text "her height doubles" by saying, "She grows twice, dos ¿qué? Double, no double, two."
Carina: Yeah.	
Jessica: See, so when two is four, and then three is six, and four is eight, y así, y así vamos hacer la graph. Going like that para arriba [*gesturing*]. You get it? (See, so when two is four, and then three is six, and four is eight, like this, and this is how we are going to make the graph. Going like that, up [*gesturing*]. You get it?)	L2→L1→L2 Jessica explains that doubling means taking a number and making it twice as great, and she uses a gesture, as illustrated below, to show how the graph grows in an upward direction.
Elena: Um hmm. Pero, how do we times it? (But how do we times it?)	Elena wonders about the symbolic notation, or how this would be written mathematically.
Jessica: Porque mira, two, times two. Well, no. (Because look, two, times two. Well, no.)	2×2: two times two L1→L2
Elena: But that's what you were telling me yesterday y yo pensé que no. OK, so we... (But that's what you were telling me yesterday, and I didn't think so. OK, so we...)	Elena remembers discussion from yesterday; debates about the solution. L2→L1→L2
Jessica: Double it by, nómas double the number of ounces, so that means if she takes... [*Elena interrupts*]. (Double it by, just double the number of ounces, so that means if she takes...)	L2→L1→L2 "Double" → "nómas double the number of ounces"
Elena: Two times two, y luego four times two, y luego six times two; is that what you are saying? (Two times two, and then four times two, and then six times two; is that what you are saying?)	L2→L1→L2 Elena explains what doubling means to her in words, by using multiples of two.
Carina: Yeah.	
Jessica: Más o menos como... sumando el mismo número. (More or less like... adding the same number.)	L1 Jessica offers another way to think about multiplying by two as more or less adding the same number to itself.

Transcript	Observations of Student Actions
Carina: Pero es lo mismo de sumando si lo multiplicas por dos. (But it is the same as adding if you multiply by two.)	L1 Carina recognizes the equivalency of the ideas expressed by Jessica and Elena.
Jessica: Uh huh, yeah. OK, entonces la primera está fácil... [*inaudible*]. (Uh huh, yeah. OK, then the first one is easy.)	L2→L1
Inés: Lo que parece es como hicimos un IN/OUT table y ya lo sacamos. (It looks like we just did an IN/OUT table, and that's it.)	Inés uses the precise mathematical terminology, IN/OUT table, in English perhaps because the content was learned in English. The students' first representation appears below:
Carina: Yeah!!!	
Jessica: So viene siendo *x* times two equals *y*. ¿No? (So it comes out to *x* times two equals *y*. No?)	L1→L2 Jessica also expresses the equation symbolically "$x * 2 = y$."
Carina: IN times two equals OUT.	L2 Carina expresses the equation alternatively as "$IN \times 2 = OUT$."

The students' fluid movement between cultural languages is not trivial. It is a language practice that is a strategic meaning-making process and essential to creating and maintaining a culture of collaboration (Gutiérrez, Baquedano-Lopez, Alvarez, and Chiu 1999). Moreover, the movement between mathematical and everyday ways of speaking in L1 and L2 provide this group with the resources necessary to clarify their mathematical thinking regarding their interpretation of the problem in the textbook. For example, Elena, Jessica, and Carina all express what doubling means to them in different ways. Elena multiplies by two to double the ounces, Jessica says in Spanish that the doubling pattern more or less involved adding the same number, and Carina says in Spanish that multiplying by two is the same as adding (a number to itself). It is interesting to note that each student has her own interpretation, but then the students quickly agree on an equation that reflects their idea of multiplying by two.

Jessica expresses her equation in terms of x's and y's (x times two equals y), and Carina expresses her equation in terms of IN and OUT (IN times two equals OUT), as shown in both the transcript and figure 6.6 (taken from Jessica's notebook). When Carina uses the terms IN and OUT, she is drawing on her earlier experiences as a resource, reaching back to the first year of IMP. IN represents the variable x, and OUT represents the variable y, the independent and the dependent variables, respectively. It is interesting to note that both Carina and Jessica draw from their past experience in ways that allow them to express the equations interchangeably, using different genres. Unfortunately, what they do not realize is that they are multiplying the number of ounces of cake by two, instead of Alice's height.

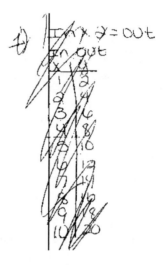

Fig. 6.6. The students' IN/OUT table (from Jessica's notebook)

The equation correctly spans the table of values, yet the students' representations do not properly model an exponential function. Shortly thereafter, the students realized that they were doubling the number of ounces of cake instead of Alice's height. This revelation helped move their discussion in a different direction that took into account Alice's initial height as demonstrated in the next excerpt.

Vignette 2

In the next vignette, Inés recalls her previous experience with the Alice problem from her sophomore year and brings up the issue of starting with an initial height for Alice. This helps others to rethink the problem in a way that then forces them to cross out their IN/OUT chart (in fig. 6.6) and start a new one, shown in the transcript of vignette 2 as well as in figure 6.7.

Transcript	Observations of Student Actions
Inés: [*Inaudible*] …Empezamos de cuatro pies. Si toma si come un pedacito son ocho, si come un pedacito son dieciseis, el tercer pedazo dieciseis y dieciseis. Treintaidos ¿no? (…We start at four feet. If she drinks, if she eats one piece, it becomes eight, if she eats one piece, it becomes sixteen, the third piece, sixteen and sixteen, thirty two, no?)	Inés uses L1 to hypothesize about a situation or to imagine an if… then… scenario. STARTING 4 feet $In^2 \cdot 2 = OUT = \quad y = x^2 \cdot 2$ In | OUT 1 | 8 ft 2 | 16 ft 3 | 32 ft 4 | 64 ft 5 | 128 ft 6 | 256 ft
Jessica: Pero, ¿cómo sacastes eso? (But how did you get that?)	Jessica uses L1 to ask how Inés obtained this table.
Inés: Porque si empezamos con cuatro pies, como yo les digo, si come un pedacito y sale, aumenta de altura de doble. [*Gestures with her hand to show Alice's height growing.*] (Because, if we start at four feet, like I'm telling you, if she eats one piece, and it comes out to, her height grows double.)	Inés uses L1, "doble," to justify her explanation from before about how Alice's height doubles.
Jessica: Ohh, her height doubles.	Jessica realizes what is meant by the problem.
Carina: That's what we are telling you.	
Elena: You know it's the same thing, mira. Dos, you multiply one times two is two, two times four is eight, y si pones two times two is four, four times four is sixteen. (You know it's the same thing, look. Two, you multiply one times two is two, two times four is eight, and if you put two times two is four, four times four is sixteen.)	L2→L1→L2 Elena moves fluidly between L1 and L2, using everyday language to describe how "dos," or two, is the same as squaring a number.
Carina: In squared, times two is equal to your OUT.	Carina expresses the equation symbolically as $IN^2 \times 2 = OUT$.

In this vignette, we see Inés trying to refocus the group to understand that Alice's initial height is necessary to compute subsequent heights as Alice eats each additional ounce of cake. Inés keeps reminding the other group members that if you start with Alice's height of four feet and you double that number, you get her new height of eight feet, and then if you double that number, you get sixteen feet, and so on. Finally, Inés says in Spanish, "The height grows by double," and at the same time, Inés gestures with her hand, demonstrating how Alice's height doubles for each ounce of cake that she eats. Immediately after Inés speaks, Jessica has her aha moment, realizing that she needs to double Alice's height—not the number of ounces of cake. What makes Inés's talk significant is the fact that she uses Spanish to help her group understand the problem. Inés makes specific connections to the textbook by incorporating elements of the Alice problem into her talk (e.g., if Alice eats one piece of cake, her height increases by a factor of two, or, in other words, it doubles). Inés also incorporates the idea of doubling (e.g., sixteen and sixteen are thirty-two) in a form similar to Jessica's previous way of thinking of it as "adding the same number twice," with an added gesture. It is the combination of all interactions that affords Jessica her aha moment and leads the students to express their mathematical thinking in a different way. Following this discussion, the students create a new table of values (see fig. 6.7) that correctly modeled Alice's exponential growth. Unfortunately, the equation is not correct and does not span all of their entries.

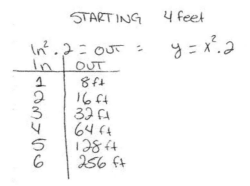

Fig. 6.7. The students' IN/OUT table and equation (from Inés's notebook)

Vignette 3

On the next day, Carina entered the group's equation, $y = 2 \cdot x^2$, into the graphing calculator and discovered that their table's values (see fig. 6.7) were not the same as the values that the graphing calculator generated (fig. 6.8). After this realization, the students immediately began another quest to find out what exactly had gone wrong, as demonstrated in the next vignette.

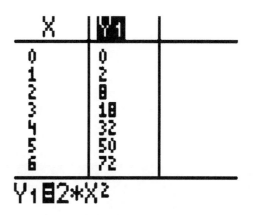

Fig. 6.8. Screen capture of the students' graphing calculator's display

Transcript	Observations of Student Actions
Carina: Mira, la pongo en la calculadora y luego pido la **TABLE** y me da otra answer de lo que nosotros tenemos aquí. (Look, I put it in the calculator and then I push **TABLE**, and it gives me a different answer from the one we have here.)	 L1→L2→L1 Students use technology to verify their solution.
Jessica: A ver. Ponla donde la pusiste el... (Let's see. Put it where you had it...)	
Carina: y equals x, quedamos al x squared times two, verdad? (y equals x, we have x squared times two, right?)	Carina verifies that the equation, $y = x^2 * 2$, is correct.
Jessica: Mhmm...	
Carina: Y luego fuimos a la **TABLE**. (And then we went to **TABLE**.)	Carina is referring to the **TABLE** key on the calculator.
Inés: No, no, no. Porque tú la pusiste.... [*inaudible*]. (No, no, no. Because you put it...)	
Elena: Three es nine... times two... is eighteen. (Three is nine... times two... is eighteen.)	Elena checks the calculations in the table generated by the calculator.
Inés: Pero ¿por qué?... [*inaudible*]. (But, why...)	Inés tries to figure out why there is a discrepancy between their IN/OUT table and the table that the graphing calculator generated.
Carina: Y es lo que sale aquí. Thirty-two. And out of three sale eighteen. (That's what comes out here. Thirty-two. And out of three gives eighteen.)	 Carina compares the tables to each other. When the input is 3, the output on the graphing calculator is 18 (ft), and the output on their handwritten tables is 32 ft.
Jessica: Mhmm. Entonces lo hicimos mal... Pero esto, el OUT [*referring to the output values*], tiene que ser así. (Mhmm. Well then, we did it wrong... but this, the OUT [*referring to the output values*], has to be like this.)	Jessica realizes that something is wrong, but she sees that the written table's output values are correct.

Transcript	Observations of Student Actions
Carina: Yeah … [*inaudible*].	Carina agrees.
Jessica: Oh, OK.	Jessica agrees.
Inés: Lo que está [*referring to the equation*] mal es esto. (This [*referring to the equation*] is what is wrong.)	Inés points to the equation as the mistake.
Jessica: Porque también el zero tiene que ser el cuatro, IN tiene que ser cero y luego el out tiene que ser cuatro. Así tiene que ser. Y primero el zero cuatro uno ocho dos dieciseis. (Well, the zero has to be four, IN has to be zero and then the OUT has to be four. That's how it has to be. And, first, the zero four, one eight, two sixteen.)	Jessica refers to the table to confirm that Inés is correct. Jessica connects her understanding of the problem situation, commenting that the zero term must be four (Alice is 4 ft tall before she takes the first bite of cake.). This verifies to them that their equation is incorrect.
Elena: Solo si tenemos que cambiar el formula, el equation, ¿no? (The only thing we have to change is the formula, the equation, no?)	Elena agrees that the equation is incorrect.

Although the students were not able to find the proper equation to span their IN/OUT table, their interactions demonstrate a comfort with the mathematical discourse and practice within and across L1 and L2. In this excerpt, we can see that the students made many connections to a variety of resources, such as previously shared mathematical ideas, with all the students using both L1 and L2, symbolic algebraic representations, and visual-graphic texts from the graphing calculator screen.

Discussion

The students worked on this exponential growth problem over a period of three days (not the whole math period). What emerges from examining these vignettes is a sense of how well these students interacted with one another and with the mathematics that they were exploring. Their dialogue and mutual negotiation of mathematical ideas were at the center of their mathematical activity and resulted in many instances of mathematical meaning making. Positioning these students as competent problem solvers gave them the opportunity to make mathematical meaning and to engage in the process of problem solving. These students were not on the periphery of their mathematical investigations but rather substantial participants, drawing on one another, different representations, and oral and symbolic language, including gestures, as resources.

The context of the study was a twelfth-grade mainstream classroom where instruction was all in English, yet Spanish continued to be central to the learning process among the students. Even though the students were in an advanced mathematics class, they continually and fluidly moved back and forth verbally between English and Spanish while making meaning of the task at hand. At each turn in their mathematical activity, the students listened to one another, offered alternate solutions, and resolved many problems and issues fundamental to their understanding of the Alice problem.

Moreover, these vignettes also demonstrate how students used nonverbal representations that facilitated further mathematical discussions. In the first vignette, students moved from reading the mathematical text to discussing among themselves and eventually creating numerical tables and symbolic representations to express their mathematical understanding. Making meaning of abstract mathematical ideas required the students to move among written and spoken language, visual-graphic texts, the textbook, and other visual-graphic tools, such as the graphing calculator.

Case 5

Advocating for ELLs' Education Rights in the Mathematics Classroom

by Matthew S. Winsor

Consider the following questions before you read the vignette that follows:

- How familiar are you with policies and procedures used in your school to place ELLs in mathematics courses?

- What are some things that you consider when you get a new ELL in your classroom?

- Who in your school is an advocate for ELLs?

The school where I worked had an unofficial policy of placing all students who were not fluent in English in my ELL pre-algebra class. Because I was the only bilingual mathematics teacher (English and Spanish), it seemed logical to place all new ELL students in my class. This unofficial policy would prove to be ineffective, however.

One year, Marisol (a pseudonym) was placed in my first-period pre-algebra class. I taught in English but would work with students in both English and Spanish as I circulated around the class. I encouraged my students to use as much English as they were able when communicating in class. It was acceptable for students to say only the mathematical terms in English and everything else in Spanish if they were new to learning English.

Marisol, who was a senior, had been in the United States for only a few months and did not speak any English. I welcomed Marisol into my class and integrated her into one of the groups. Marisol participated in the day's activities, finishing well ahead of her group. The next day, Marisol also finished the mathematics work as if she had already studied the subject. I was pleased that Marisol was working with the other students and completing the mathematics that I had assigned. On the third day that Marisol was in class, she approached me at the beginning of class. She said that the class work was too easy and that she had studied this mathematics when she was 11. I asked Marisol to describe what she had been doing in her mathematics class back in Mexico. She reported that she had been in pre-calculus and had come to the United States to go to school so that she could learn English. Marisol planned to return to Mexico after her year at my school. I asked her a few mathematics questions about pre-calculus and was satisfied that Marisol did belong in a pre-calculus class. I went to Marisol's guidance counselor and reported that Marisol needed to be in pre-calculus. The counselor was hesitant because Marisol spoke only Spanish; in the counselor's view, she might not succeed in pre-calculus because of language issues. I assured the guidance counselor that I would help Marisol if language issues arose. Marisol needed—and deserved—to be in a pre-calculus class. I kept in contact with Marisol and her teacher. Marisol did well in her pre-calculus class. Marisol would occasionally drop by and see me for help. She was very motivated to learn English, so she excelled in both math and learning English.

After the incident with my student who needed to be in pre-calculus, the counselor realized that she needed my help. From that point on, I was a part of the placement process. Usually, I would talk to the students about their classes in Mexico, have them complete some mathematics problems, and then make a recommendation. The counselor was very supportive in the process. She simply had never thought that perhaps an ELL student might need a higher math course than pre-algebra. She was more focused on students' language needs than on their mathematical needs.

This case reminds us as educators that the ELLs whom we receive in our mathematics classrooms may have experienced mathematics content that is at a higher level than the mathematics that we are teaching. The misplacement of ELLs may be due to counselors or teachers who mistakenly think that ELLs cannot be placed in more advanced mathematics courses because of language issues (Celedón-Pattichis 2004). As educators, we need to consider what our role is in assessing ELLs' mathematical knowledge and subsequently placing them in appropriate mathematics courses.

Case 6

Issues of Identity and Power in Teaching Mathematics to Latin@ Students

by Rochelle Gutiérrez

Speaking on behalf of a group of fellow students in a high school mathematics class, a student says,

> We're all Mexican in the group. Specifically Mexican. So we usually communicate always in Spanish over there. Always talk in Spanish… We're all gonna try to stick together and communicate in Spanish. You know, we're all calm about [the math] that way. We all speak Spanish and we're comfortable. (Gutiérrez 2002, p. 1075)

In case 6, the author uses the symbol @ to represent the Spanish feminine and masculine endings *-a* and *-o*, combined in a single, gender-inclusive form, *Latin@*, and similarly, later in her piece, *Chican@*.

Would you be surprised to learn that these remarks are from an A student in a calculus class conducted in English? The course is not a bilingual class, and the teacher does not speak Spanish. Rather, the teacher has created a culture in which students feel comfortable speaking Spanish, and some students choose to do so. This student is also in an honors English class, where he analyzes the nuanced meanings of texts. So, in this case, the student has no *need* to use Spanish. Instead, using Spanish is a way of bonding with others in his class.

When you hear students speak Spanish, do you assume that is their "dominant," or "stronger," language and that they are weak in English? It is easy to slip into this way of thinking, especially if you are not multilingual yourself. Yet, people who grow up speaking more than one language know that speakers use language not just on the basis of proficiency, but as an expression of their identity. It is a reflection of who we are, where we come from, and who we are trying to become.

All too often, we have descriptions of the "problems" of English language learners in mathematics without attention to strategies or frames of reference for assigning competence to these students or building on their cultural or linguistic resources. In this final case in chapter 6, the perspectives of effective teachers and their Latin@ students are drawn from research conducted over the past fifteen years in high schools throughout the United States and in Mexico. They are presented in an effort to shine light on some of the things that teachers in various working contexts might consider when they are working with Latin@ students or other ELLs.

Language as Identity

Effective teachers of Latin@ students know that individuals can be bilingual to varying degrees and that language plays many roles in the mathematics classroom. On the one hand, mathematics is its own language, thereby making *all* students language learners. Moreover, students who speak Spanish at home and with friends may not have facility with academic Spanish or mathematical terminology in Spanish. For example, terms like *pendiente* (slope) are specific to mathematics and do not map onto the everyday speech of Spanish speakers. So, although a person speaks Spanish with others, unless that person has formally learned mathematics in Spanish (e.g., in another country), he or she is not likely to have the vocabulary to conduct mathematical conversations completely in Spanish. This may lead some students to "code switch" (alternate between Spanish and English) and others to use Spanish only in specific settings.

In high school settings, it is common for English learners to have made a transition to English-only environments, thereby leaving their teachers potentially unaware that a student speaks another language. The transition to an English-only context also leaves the student with the added challenge of negotiating a context where it may be more comfortable to "think" in Spanish before articulating a strategy, since Spanish is not customarily sanctioned in the mathematics classroom.

Teachers who teach Latin@ students effectively seek a deeper understanding of the role of language in relation to students' identities in the mathematics classroom. These teachers pay attention to the types of situations in which their students use Spanish and also with whom they use Spanish. This knowledge helps teachers begin to develop more nuanced perspectives on their students and realize that (1) "bilingual" (just like "high performing") is not a static category in the mathematics classroom and (2) not all Latin@

students are the same. Developing this deep understanding of one's students as individuals goes a long way toward creating relationships built on trust. It also raises issues for teachers who want to support their Latin@ students but who do not speak Spanish themselves, or who have not learned mathematics in Spanish.

Some questions you might pose to yourself include the following:

- When I think of language, do I tend to frame issues in terms of proficiency (someone is using a language because they have to)? Do I presume because of a Spanish surname that a student speaks Spanish? Do I see that some students may be proficient in English but may choose or want to use Spanish to maintain or express their cultural identities?

- How do I feel about my students speaking Spanish in the mathematics classroom? If I do not speak Spanish myself, do I implicitly discourage it because it makes me feel uncomfortable (e.g., I don't know what my students are saying or even whether they are talking about mathematics)?

- When students use Spanish in my class, do I presume that they are talking about social issues? Or do I look to other cues, like body language, gestures, and drawings on their papers, to help me understand whether students' conversations are about mathematics?

- Do I note when and with whom my students are using Spanish? Do I take this information into consideration when I place my students in groups or teams?

Getting to Know Your Students

Effective teachers of Latin@ students get to know their students in deep ways that allow students to express their identities (e.g., culture, language, interests, experiences, goals). Rather than expecting students to park their identities at the door, so to speak, these teachers invite students to do projects that allow them to show expertise in areas where they have experience (e.g., travel, a hobby). Most teachers want to support their students' identities but do not know how or unknowingly build on "essentialist" notions of Latin@ students. That is, they learn something from reading about or interacting with an individual, and then they presume that it is the case for others in the same demographic group. For example, if a teacher learns that a Latin@ student from one family participates in chores in a particular way (e.g., folding clothes with a mother), the teacher might assume that all Latin@ students do this in their homes and may choose to build an activity around symmetries or fractions involved in folding clothes.

In some ways, this approach can be good in that the particular student whose experiences the teacher has learned about might be positioned as an "expert" for the activity. However, if the teacher presumes that the activity will be meaningful to *all* Latin@ students, such an approach could convey the idea that she has not bothered to get to know the students beyond a quick sampling.

Similar factors come into play when teachers are thinking about historical connections. Effective teachers of Latin@ students carefully reflect on the individual students in their classes when considering whether or how to introduce a concept like the Mayan vigesimal system of counting (base 20). Again, this decision could be a good one, since such an approach can affirm a student's identity. However, students who are Puerto Rican, Dominican, Cuban, or Salvadoran, or who have other lines of ancestry that do not derive from Mayans of Mexico, may not find a particular sense of valorization in this approach. The same lack of affirmation may be felt by Chican@ students or Mexican students who are second or third generation and whose experiences do not necessarily resonate with anything that the Mayans might have invented. By allowing students to choose project topics or offer examples from their lives outside of school, teachers can avoid the danger of essentializing cultures. In this way, students are allowed more of a voice in the classroom and an experience that more meaningfully affirms and expands their identities.

Today, in terms of equity, saying that you want to "get to know your students" is in some ways analogous to saying a decade ago that you "have high expectations for your students." In other words, these phrases have become such universally accepted statements that they are almost meaningless. What teacher would say she does *not* have high expectations for her students? Similarly, what teacher would say that he does *not* want to get to know his students? A key difference between mathematics teachers who are effective with Latin@ students and those who are not is often the *reason why* they want to get to know their students and *what they do* with that knowledge once they acquire it.

Some things you might ask yourself when you are developing relationships with your students include the following:

- How do I know about the lives of my students? Do I attend their extracurricular events (e.g., sports, theatre, community functions)? Do I get invited to these events? Should I attend even if not invited?

- Do I make attempts to speak to my students' families? When I do so, do I then position the students as experts at something (e.g., how they help others in small groups, the unique ways in which they approach problems)? In my conversations with families, do I look for opportunities to find out where else (besides the mathematics classroom) my students are experts? Do I use this information in the mathematics classroom (e.g., by referring to a context with which they are familiar or in which they can be deferred to for expertise)?

- Do I want to understand my students' hobbies, habits, interests, and cultures because I believe that this knowledge will help me "hook" students into doing school mathematics better (e.g., come up with a mathematics activity that may relate to their backgrounds)? Are there limits to this way of thinking about my students (e.g., does the context allow for a rigorous exploration of the mathematical concept that I am intending for students to understand)?

- Do I want to know my students better, not just for the sake of mathematics, but because I want to develop relationships that show that I am invested in them as people who have a future that I want to support (regardless of how that relates to school mathematics)?

- When I learn something about one of my students, do I presume that his or her classmates will share that perspective, experience, or interest? How do I verify whether that is the case?

- Do I open myself up, allowing myself to be vulnerable, by sharing aspects of my personal life and identity before expecting students to do the same?

- Do I sometimes fall into the trap of thinking that I know my students well because I have learned a bit about them or because they seem to like me?

Definitions of Success

We all want our students to be successful in the mathematics classroom. Yet, we are at a moment in history when notions of success are hotly debated. Some might define success as high scores on standardized tests or As earned in a mathematics class. In fact, many teachers and policymakers today define success as closing the so-called achievement gap. Certainly, doing well on tests and courses has significant consequences for students in choosing mathematics-based careers or seeking to attend college. Yet, Latin@ families have historically shunned the idea that white student achievement levels are markers of "excellence." Instead, they have tended to rely on broader standards for themselves and their children—defining success with an eye toward not only doing well in school, but also maintaining cultural values and a critical attitude, often valuing ties to the community over individual success. Some families may also be interested in their children learning to use mathematics to measure, and thus critique, social inequities.

Some questions that you might ask yourself when thinking about success include the following:

- According to whose point of view am I defining success? Do my students wonder, "Do I get to become a better *me*? Or do I have to become *you* in order to be seen as successful in the mathematics classroom?" (Think of *you* as referring to you yourself, teachers in general, or any individuals in positions of power with respect to your students.)

- What are some of the ways that my colleagues and school administrators define success for our students? Do I agree with their definitions? Do these definitions take into consideration the identities that students bring with them to school and the identities that they are building? Or do they assume that students will accommodate themselves to school practices?

- If others in my school define success primarily in relation to "closing the achievement gap," do I challenge them to think more deeply about the implications for Latin@ students who are seen as "failing" with respect to the language associated with "achievement gap"?

- Does our mathematics faculty have an implicit goal of motivating our Latin@ students to become more like white middle-class students? Do we tend to talk about Latin@ students *in comparison with* other kinds of students? Can we talk about Latin@ students as a category worthy of attention in and of itself? Do we look for ways in which Latin@ students can set the bar for the learning of other students?

Beyond the kinds of things that may arise in teaching Latin@ students who have extensive experience in the United States are the particular kinds of things that we need to be concerned about with students who are recent immigrants or who are regular border crossers—alternating between attending schools in the United States and attending schools in another country. Some of these students spend only short periods of time in other countries while others might spend a year or more elsewhere, as a result of family or economic situations.

Many teachers are unaware of the mathematical teaching practices or standards in other countries. This lack of knowledge, combined with the general message in the media about Latin American students as academically inferior and Asian students as academically superior, may lead some teachers to discount the education resources of Latin American countries. Yet, effective teachers of Latin@ students probe deeply for ways in which they can develop their understanding of other countries and the opportunities that they offer, and the practices that they use, in education.

Crossing Borders

Students who have attended school in Mexico (and many other Latin American countries) have extensive experience in taking notes and maintaining a *cuaderno* (notebook). Many students hang onto their *cuadernos* later in life, since they represent so much work. These individuals have put a great deal of energy, labor, and dedication into taking notes while participating in the discipline of mathematics. In addition, the *cuadernos* serve as references in future mathematics courses. For the most part, these notebooks contain very neat writing, and the writers often use colored pens for different meanings (e.g., black ink for a major topic or theorem, blue ink for examples, red ink for postulates). In most U.S. mathematics classrooms, note taking (a skill that involves knowing, e.g., when to take notes, how to take them, what to do with them after taking them) is somewhat vague, varies from class to class, or is something that only the best students do regularly. Yet, taking notes and maintaining a *cuaderno* in mathematics is a very structured and rigorous process for most Mexican students. In mathematics classrooms in Mexico, all students purchase a notebook with prenumbered pages, consisting entirely of grid paper (as opposed to lined or blank paper), so that drawings can be constructed correctly. Pages are never torn out, so students exercise extra care in writing in their notebooks. Some students decide to keep two notebooks (using one to take notes in during class, and letting the other serve as a copy that they can transfer their work into at home to make it neater).

If you have students who have immigrated to the United States from Mexico (or another Latin American country), you can use your knowledge of the notebook in several ways to assign competence to the students. You might do the following:

1. Regardless of what school records or test scores show, conduct an intake interview. Ask the students if they can show you a notebook that represents the mathematics from their home country. You may be surprised to find that the content covered in other nations is more rigorous or introduced earlier than that covered in the United States.

2. Look for different algorithms that your students use during work time or on homework. Discuss those algorithms to see if they are common in their home country. Then you might ask the students if they would be willing to share their way of doing things with the class. This not only would show that you value

other ways of doing mathematics but also would position the students as experts in something that the rest of the class did not know.

3. Assign the students competence by asking them to share their *cuadernos* and note-taking skills or strategies with others, thereby positioning the students as role models from whom others can learn.

Below are some resources that you may find useful:

- Gutiérrez, Rochelle. "Beyond Essentialism: The Complexity of Language in Teaching Latina/o Students Mathematics." *American Educational Research Journal* 39 (Winter 2002): 1047–88.

- Gutiérrez, Rochelle. "A 'Gap Gazing' Fetish in Mathematics Education? Problematizing Research on the Achievement Gap." *Journal for Research in Mathematics Education* 39 (July 2008): 357–64.

- Gutiérrez, Rochelle. "Framing Equity: Helping Students 'Play the Game' and 'Change the Game.'" *Teaching for Excellence and Equity in Mathematics* 1 (Fall 2009): 4-8.

In general, effective mathematics teachers of Latin@ students think about teaching and learning as much more than a cognitive process that emphasizes quantitative student outcomes. They consider how the kinds of activities introduced and relationships built in the mathematics classroom influence the kinds of identities that their students develop and the kinds of learning trajectories that they experience. As you reflect on some of the ideas presented in this case, you might think about how issues of identity and power play out for Latin@ students in *your* context and what role *you* aim to play in helping them negotiate those issues to be successful on their own—as well as on others'—terms.

References for Chapter 6

Barnett-Clark, Carne, and Alma Ramirez. "Language Pitfalls and Pathways to Mathematics." In *Perspectives on the Teaching of Mathematics*, Sixty-sixth Yearbook of the National Council of Teachers of Mathematics (NCTM), edited by Rheta N. Rubenstein, pp. 56–66. Reston, Va.: NCTM, 2004.

Carr, John, Catherine Carroll, Sarah Cremer, Mardi Gale, Rachel Lagunoff, and Ursula Sexton. *Making Mathematics Accessible to English Learners: A Guidebook for Teachers, Grades 9–12*. San Francisco: WestEd, 2009.

Celedón-Pattichis, Sylvia. "Rethinking Policies and Procedures for Placing English Language Learners in Mathematics." *NABE Journal of Research and Practice* 2 (Winter 2004): 176–92.

Coggins, Debra, Drew Kravin, Grace Dávila Coates, and Maria Dreux Carroll. *English Language Learners in the Mathematics Classroom*. Thousand Oaks, Calif.: Corwin, 2007.

Cohen, Elizabeth G. "Restructuring the Classroom: Conditions for Productive Small Groups." *Review of Educational Research* 64 (Spring 1994): 1–35.

Common Core State Standards Initiative (CCSSI). *Common Core State Standards for Mathematics. Common Core State Standards (College- and Career-Readiness Standards and K–12 Standards in English Language Arts and Math)*. Washington, D.C.: National Governors Association Center for Best Practices and the Council of Chief State School Officers, 2010. http://www.corestandards.org.

Echevarría, Jana, Mary Ellen Vogt, and Deborah J. Short. *Making Content Comprehensible for English Language Learners: The SIOP Model*. Upper Saddle River, N.J.: Pearson, 2004.

Fendel, Dan, Diane Resek, and Lynne Alper. *Interactive Mathematics Program: Integrated High School Mathematics—Year 1*. Emeryville, Calif.: Key Curriculum Press, 1996.

Fendel, Dan, Diane Resek, Lynne Alper, and Sherry Fraser. *Interactive Mathematics Program: Integrated High School Mathematics—Year 4*. Emeryville, Calif.: Key Curriculum Press, 2000.

———. *Interactive Mathematics Program: Integrated High School Mathematics—Year 2*. Emeryville, Calif.: Key Curriculum Press, 2004.

Gutiérrez, Kris D., Patricia Baquedano-López, Héctor H. Alvarez, and Ming M. Chiu. "Building a Culture of Collaboration through Hybrid Language Practices." *Theory into Practice* 38, no. 2 (1999): 87-92.

Gutiérrez, Rochelle. "Beyond Essentialism: The Complexity of Language in Teaching Mathematics to Latina/o Students." *American Educational Research Journal* 39, no. 4 (2002): 1047–88.

Interactive Mathematics Program (IMP). *IMP Year 1, the Overland Trail Unit, Teacher's Guide*. Emeryville, Calif.: Key Curriculum Press, 2009.

Kitchen, Richard S., Julie DePree, Sylvia Celedón-Pattichis, and Jonathan Brinkerhoff. *Mathematics Education at Highly Effective Schools That Serve the Poor: Strategies for Change*. Mahwah, N.J.: Lawrence Erlbaum, 2007.

Morales, Hector, Jr. "A Naturalistic Study of Mathematical Meaning-Making by High School Latino Students." PhD diss., University of Illinois at Chicago, 2004.

National Council of Teachers of Mathematics (NCTM). *Principles and Standards for School Mathematics*. Reston, Va.: NCTM, 2000.

National Research Council (NRC). *Adding It Up: Helping Children Learn Mathematics*. Jeremy Kilpatrick, Jane Swafford, and Bradford Findell, eds. Mathematics Learning Study Committee, Center for Education, Division of Behavioral and Social Sciences and Education. Washington, D.C.: National Academy Press, 2001.

Chapter 7

Parents and Children Come Together: Latino and Latina Parents Speak Up about Mathematics Teaching and Learning

by Marta Civil and José María Menéndez

- Parents' Classroom Visit (form for parents' use)

Consider the advice offered by Marisol, a long-time participant in projects for Latina and Latino parents and mathematics:

> In a classroom there were children from different parts of Latin America, and one mother goes and asks the teacher, "How is my child? How is my child doing?" "Oh, ma'am. Perfect. He understands very well. He is very disciplined. He rarely talks. He is a model child." But, you know what? With all that, I want to tell you that it's very important, when you have a student who is an immigrant, for you to look closely, to talk with him or her, to communicate in his or her cultural and family context, because the perfect child who didn't talk, who didn't participate, who was very disciplined, was all because he didn't understand a bit of English. (Marisol, Parent Panel, CEMELA School, June 2008)

This quotation reflects some of the advice that Marisol gave at an intensive professional development event for graduate students and postdoctoral fellows at a CEMELA (Center for the Mathematics Education of Latinos/as) school. (Marisol's remarks and all the quotations that follow from other parents have been translated from Spanish, and some have been edited for readability.)

Marisol's observation captures a fundamental message that we want to convey through this chapter to teachers, school personnel, and educators in general: We need to learn about students' cultural, social, and language backgrounds. As Delgado-Gaitan (2004), whose work centers on Latino and Latina parents, notes, "Both elementary and secondary educators need to remember that regardless of culture, educational attainment, and socio economic standing, all families have strengths, and educators can tap that potential to maximize student achievement" (p. 16). This idea of learning about and building on

CEMELA (Center for the Mathematics Education of Latinos/as) is a Center for Learning and Teaching supported by the National Science Foundation, grant number ESI-0424983. Any opinions, findings, and conclusions or recommendations expressed in this document are those of the authors and do not necessarily reflect the views of the National Science Foundation.

students' and their families' experiences and strengths is the central tenet of the Funds of Knowledge for Teaching project (González, Moll, and Amanti 2005), which the first author worked to extend to the teaching and learning of mathematics (Civil 2007). We need to know what kinds of mathematical experiences students bring to school and how to build on those, even though they may be different from the ones we know. As Marisol said several years earlier, "Teachers need to understand that parents and children come together."

In this chapter, we draw on fifteen years of work with parents and mathematics to share some suggestions for strengthening parents-schools relations, particularly as they apply to the mathematics education of English language learners (ELLs). Our work is primarily situated in Mexican American communities and encompasses many families who are recent immigrants and for whom Spanish is their home language. We believe that the suggestions that we present here can be applied to other settings of cultural and linguistic diversity, since the premise behind our work is that language and cultural diversity is an educational asset for the mathematics education of all students.

Why Do We Need to Develop a Dialogue between Parents and Schools?

The two vignettes that follow illustrate some of the reasons why an ongoing dialogue between parents and teachers is essential. The vignettes address valorization of knowledge, the importance of building relationships as in a family, and issues related to the teaching and learning of mathematics and ELLs.

Vignette 1

Teachers' method vs. parents' method

A father reported having had a problem with his son and the way that the teacher was teaching him division as compared to how he had learned it in Mexico. He had tried to teach his son his way, and the son had said that the teacher was doing it a different way. The father had gone to see the teacher to talk about the situation. The teacher told him, "You have to learn how to divide like that because that is my method." Another teacher who witnessed the exchange and happened to be a participant in a large parental engagement project in mathematics took the father aside and validated his method while also explaining the teacher's approach to division and inviting him to attend the workshops that were part of our parental engagement project—an invitation that he accepted.

Throughout our work with parents and mathematics, we have encountered many situations like the one in vignette 1. The idea of parents having approaches to doing mathematics that are different from those that their children are learning in school is not new. Mathematics teaching has changed over the years, and now it is very likely that students are in classrooms where they learn about different algorithms for arithmetic operations, explore topics that their parents might not have studied in school (such as discrete mathematics or early algebra in the elementary school), are expected to explain their reasoning orally or in writing, work in groups and use manipulative materials, and so on. Parents may be surprised by these different approaches and wonder about them, or even go to the school to ask the teacher, as the father did in this vignette. What we want to emphasize, however, is the complexity of the situation when the parents may have been schooled in a different country (in our work, e.g., Mexico), may not speak English well or at all, or may be unfamiliar with their children's school system. Replies such as the teacher's, "You have to learn how to divide like that because that is my method," underscore issues around valorization of knowledge, which we discuss next.

In any interaction like that in vignette 1, we all bring our own values about what we count as valid mathematical knowledge, valid ways of doing mathematics, and so on. Parents bring their values, and so do teachers. When we are working with non-dominant groups (e.g., immigrant, low-income, non-English speakers, racial or ethnic minorities), the situation is particularly worrisome because it brings up issues of power. As Quintos, Bratton, and Civil (2005) assert, "The knowledge that working class and minoritized parents possess is not given the same value as that which middle class parents possess.... Alternative approaches are often not treated equally.... In this context, the parents' or home method is not given the same value as the teacher's or textbook method. Historical relations of power at the schools can not only be reproduced but also exacerbated through mathematics education" (pp. 1184, 1189).

There is a strong need for a meaningful dialogue between parents and teachers in which learning about the different methods and approaches can occur for all. For example, when students or parents possess different ways of doing arithmetic operations, teachers can use these different approaches as learning opportunities instead of dismissing them, as the first teacher in the vignette did and as did a fifth-grade teacher who told a student who shared a method that his mother had taught him, "Yes, but that's in mama's home. Let's do it the way that we do it in the school." It turns out that the method, as the boy presented it, did not quite work. Instead of dismissing it and creating a barrier between home knowledge and school knowledge, the teacher could have invited the mother to come and share her method, or she could have told the child to ask his mother again.

A sustained dialogue between parents and teachers about the teaching and learning of mathematics would allow for building connections between home and school, rather than keeping these worlds apart. This is particularly important for immigrant children (or children of immigrant parents), who are often navigating two worlds. As Suárez-Orozco and Suárez-Orozco (2001) describe, these children are caught between trying to follow and respect their parents' cultural ways, including maintaining the home language, and trying to fit into the new cultural context, including learning English and a different approach to schooling. What do we need to do so that parents will not feel a barrier developing between their children and themselves when it comes to schooling, such as one mother, Mónica, describes?

> Last night my son said to me that school from Mexico was not valued the same as school here—that is, it doesn't count. What I studied there doesn't count here, and he said, "Mom, do you know this problem?" "No, to tell you the truth, I don't," I said to him. He says, "See, that's why I said that they didn't teach you [there] what they teach me here." ... He knows that what is taught here is different from what is taught there, and so he says, "Why would I ask my mom for help if she's not going to know?" So, there is a barrier. (*Tertulia Matemática* [mathematical get-together], February 2004)

We need to create spaces where parents feel comfortable sharing their views on, and experiences of, the teaching and learning of mathematics and schooling in general. Having such a space was empowering to Carlota, a Spanish-speaking mother from Mexico who is very eloquent about the power issues that she has encountered in schools and the need to develop communication because "we are all a family." In what follows, we present two excerpts focusing on Carlota, one from a Math for Parents (MFP) session and the other one from an interview we had with her. ("Math for Parents" is a program of short courses for parents on specific domains of mathematics [MAPPS 2003].)

> I didn't know anything until I went to the meetings. I plucked up the courage, and they gave me the weapons to defend myself, but before, it was like "Oh, well… The teacher is right." …I think teachers think, "Well, the parent isn't going to say anything." (MFP, October 2008)

> We are all equal. Just because you are the teacher, you shouldn't think you don't have to accept your responsibility. I, as a parent, if you told me, "Ma'am, I already told you, and you are not helping him." Yes, that's true; I admit that sometimes I get lazy, that I don't like it. I admit it, but I want to change, and I want you [the teacher], me, and the principal to change the techniques we are using. Because we are all a family. We are here all day. They have our children all day. We are somehow related, and I think that if we break those barriers, you'll see, I think everything will work better… I concentrate on that a lot: that the foundation of everything is the communication that the school wants to do with the parents. If that family is never really built, I think that it will not be reflected on… Because if a school is doing well, it's because there is a good relationship with you. (Interview, January 2009)

Carlota points to the shared responsibility that parents and school (teachers and principals) have in the mission of educating the children. She underscores the importance of communication and relationships as the basis for building a strong family—a family that goes beyond the home (parents, siblings, and other relatives) to include the school personnel.

Differences in approaches to mathematical problems are an important reason for advocating for a stronger dialogue between parents and teachers or school administrators. Another important reason for this dialogue is to address issues of language that arise in the teaching and learning of mathematics with ELLs. The following vignette is a composite of several mothers' voices, intended to convey the emotional stress that, over the years, these and other parents have shared with us in relation to the language barrier.

Vignette 2

Language and homework

Many mothers have expressed their frustration at knowing the mathematics, yet not being able to help their children because they do not feel they know enough English to understand the problems, and their children do not know how to talk about mathematics in Spanish.

Selena: My son tells me, "Mom, I'm going to do what I can, and I'm going to read the rest to you." And he translates to me in Spanish what he can; sometimes, I understand what he's telling me in English; others, I understand nothing. That's why I'm going to English classes; I tell him, "Son, I don't understand this part," and I put a circle around it so that the teacher can see it. (Interview, November 2005)

Cándida: When the homework was all in English only, I felt really bad. I would get frustrated because I couldn't explain it to them; I would have liked to explain it to them, and I couldn't. (Interview, February 2006)

Verónica: My son doesn't feel very sure that I understand him because the problem is written in English. I don't know how to read it, and he doesn't know how to translate it well for me because he speaks Spanish and reads Spanish, but when kids learn Spanish here, their vocabulary is not as developed, and he doesn't translate like he should so that I'm able to help him. (Interview, February 2004)

Adriana: Sometimes, my daughter can't tell me. I tell her, "Tell me in English," because I have also noticed that she cannot tell me a lot of things in Spanish anymore. (Debriefing classroom visit, March 2006)

Some teachers have responded to these laments by providing the homework in Spanish as well as English (and sometimes facilitating access to the textbook in Spanish) whenever it is possible for them to do so, but even when the teachers and schools have the means, they probably are not aware that parents have these needs unless there is good communication between schools and families. Many teachers expect parents to be involved in helping their children with the mathematics homework, but they do not provide the parents with the tools to do so successfully.

In the next section, we present two approaches that we have used in our work with parents in the interest of developing this very needed dialogue about teaching and learning mathematics. First, we describe how we use mathematics short courses in combination with mathematical *tertulias* as an approach to engage parents in doing mathematics while also sharing their experiences with—and sometimes their concerns about—their children's mathematics education. Then we present some suggestions for conducting mathematics classroom visits with parents as a catalyst for further dialogue.

How Can We Develop a Dialogue between Parents and Schools?

The differences in teaching and learning mathematics between the United States and other countries are not restricted to algorithms, as illustrated in vignette 1. A standards-based curriculum makes a higher language demand on students than a traditional curriculum, since students need to understand the wording of the problems (which tend to have a richer context than those in traditional mathematics texts) and elaborate more on their thinking, thus doing more than merely performing computations. Furthermore, the implementation of the recommendations of the NCTM Standards (2000) and of the Common Core State Standards for Mathematics (CCSSM) (CCSSI 2010) involves restructuring the order and the emphasis given to the mathematics content, as well as specific mathematical practices (the Standards for Mathematical Practice in CCSSM).

Most likely, parents have not experienced this sort of restructured mathematics themselves, and maybe they are not aware of its emphases, causing a misunderstanding about what and how their children are learning in their mathematics classes in school. Although this problem may arise simply through a generation gap (all parents in the United States may be in the same predicament), it is accentuated when a language difference makes the curricular material less accessible to the parents of ELL students. In our experience, we have found the following activities to be successful at improving communication and understanding of current school mathematics.

Short courses and *tertulias*

Throughout the years, we have tried different formats for short courses, depending on the parents' needs and interests. But our approach has always centered on a few principles, the most basic of which is to provide a participatory, hands-on experience with a variety of mathematical topics (e.g., numbers and operations, geometry, probability, algebra). We introduce ideas from the schools' curricula to familiarize parents with what their children are learning, and we combine these ideas with situations that may be more accessible from the point of view of an adult learner. Some short courses included the children, at the request of the parents, who viewed the sessions as an opportunity to engage with academic content together, as a family. The sessions were conducted in Spanish, or in some cases, in a bilingual mode (Spanish and English).

An important component of these short courses is the concept of *tertulia*. We took this word from the Spanish language, thinking of the context of social gatherings where, for example, people get together to discuss literature. We think of these spaces as opportunities to engage with the parents in discussions about mathematics—its teaching and its learning. It is through these dialogues that issues of valorization of knowledge may come up, as well as different ways to do mathematics and issues related to language and the teaching and learning of mathematics, particularly in the context of ELLs.

Vignette 3

Teachers' method vs. parents' method, again

A recurrent topic in our conversations with parents who were schooled in Mexico is the difference between division as taught in Mexico and the long division algorithm usually taught in the United States. The main difference is that in Mexico the subtraction is done mentally and only the result is shown. Mexican parents often comment that they prefer *their* method because it is more efficient (faster) since they do not have to write as much, and it promotes mental agility since they have to do the subtraction in their head. An exchange between two mothers on this topic follows:

Marisol: When I looked at how my son was dividing, he subtracted and subtracted and that he wrote all the equation complete, I said, "This teacher wants to make things complicated. No, son, not that way! This way!" And he learned faster with this procedure [*the traditional representation of division in Mexico*]. I say that the first barrier is visual; we as parents don't speak English, we don't understand

English. Numbers don't need language—only, of course, that the child tells you what you need to do. But if visually you see such a mess [*referring to the traditional representation of division in the United States*]…

Verónica: I tried to do the same with my child with divisions, that he didn't write everything, but he says, "No, no, mom, the teacher is going to think that I did it on the computer." "You don't need to write the subtraction, son," I say, "You only put what is left." "No, no, my teacher is going to think that I did it on the computer; I have to do it like that." "OK, you think that, but I want to teach you how we learned." And I did teach him, but he still uses his method, and that way he feels safe that he is doing his homework as they told him to. The same thing with writing above what they borrow and crossing it out, I tell him, "I remember our homework did not have to have any cross-outs," whereas his does. (*Tertulia Matemática,* October 2003)

When we have shared the representation of division in Mexican schools with in-service and preservice teachers in the United States, the general reaction is one of surprise. Some have expressed confusion, as they are not quite sure how to make sense of it. Of particular concern are reactions that appear to indicate that if students do not write out the whole subtraction, something is missing. Yet, many people in other countries (not just Mexico) divide by doing the subtraction in their head. Again, we are pointing to the need for more communication so that respect for different approaches can develop. In the preceding exchange between the two mothers, Verónica points to the situation that children find themselves in when trying to negotiate the home method and the school method. We do not know for a fact that her son's teacher would really think that by not writing down the subtraction the student did it on the computer. But we would not be surprised to hear that this was the case, given the reactions that we have had from preservice and in-service teachers, some of whom have told us that they would think the student had cheated if he or she did not show the subtraction.

In that same exchange, Marisol brings up a language issue that needs to be addressed. Marisol is not alone in believing that somehow language may not be much of a factor in mathematics because "numbers don't need language," as she says. Other parents have shared similar thinking, in comments along the lines of, "Numbers are numbers; whether in English or Spanish, two plus two is four." However, as we know, and particularly with standards-based materials, language plays a key role in mathematics, and it is an issue that needs to be examined further when working with parents of ELLs. But to conclude this discussion on the representation of division, we share one activity that we implemented in a short course with parents, teachers, and children. We asked some of the mothers to explain how they divide; then the facilitator did the same division by using the traditional U.S. long-division algorithm. The first author shared the way that she had learned how to divide in Spain, and finally two sixth-grade students shared the scaffold method that they were using in their classroom. This sharing of methods led to a lively discussion in which different participants could learn about the various approaches as well as discuss the advantages and disadvantages that they saw in each approach. This was not about trying to establish which method is better but instead about valuing the different experiences that each of us had. Figure 7.1 shows a screenshot of the four approaches that we discussed.

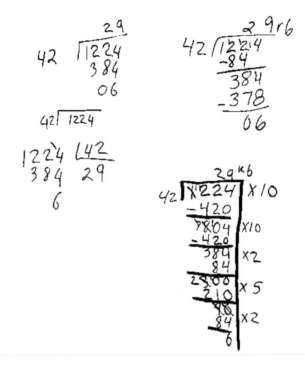

Fig. 7.1. Four approaches to division

As we said earlier, in the short courses and *tertulias*, parents had a chance to become familiar with some of the tasks and approaches used in their children's classrooms as well as to engage in exploring mathematics as adult learners. Classroom visits allowed parents to witness what and how their children are being taught. These visits are what we describe next.

Classroom visits

The main goal of structured visits to mathematics classrooms is for the parents to see firsthand how mathematics is being taught to their children. Over the years, we have worked with several teachers with whom we have developed close relationships. Thus, when we have asked any of them if we could visit their classroom with a group of parents, they have always been very open to this idea.

First, we gather with the parents before going to the classroom, to share with them a form to help guide the classroom visit (see fig. 7.2; also available at www.nctm.org /more4u). This form focuses on the physical aspects of the classroom (decoration with mathematics themes and sitting arrangement), interactions among students and between students and teacher, students' participation, tools in use during the class (textbook, worksheets, manipulatives, calculators, etc.), and the kind of problems or questions posed in class.

CENTER FOR THE MATHEMATICS EDUCATION OF LATINOS/AS

CEMELA

The University of Arizona • University of California, Santa Cruz • University of Illinois at Chicago • The University of New Mexico

Parents' Classroom Visit

Your name: _____   Date of observation: _____

School where observation is made: _____

Teacher's name: _____

Grade: _____   Topic: _____

1. What does the classroom look like? Are there any mathematics posters on the walls or bulletin boards? If so, please describe.

2. How would you describe the interactions teacher-student(s) and student-student?

3. How would you describe the participation in this class? (For example, are there some students who participate more than others? Describe.)

4. What tools are students using in this class? (textbook, worksheets, manipulatives (specify), calculators, etc.)

5. What kinds of problems / questions were asked during class? (closed, open questions, known answer?)

Fig. 7.2. A form for parents' use in classroom visits

Second, we go to the classroom, to sit during the class period from beginning to end, when possible. Depending on the classroom, the parents, and the teacher, some parents may walk around and interact with the students as they are working on problems.

Third, after we leave the classroom, we regroup to debrief the parents on the experience that they have just had. During this meeting, we guide the conversation, prompting parents to compare their expectations with what they encountered, as well as their observations with their own experiences as students. We also ask parents to share their perceptions about the teacher's goals, the mathematics content, and students' behavior (e.g., ways of participation), and we encourage them to comment on the teacher's approach to teaching mathematics, including things that they liked and things that concerned them.

Most of the parents with whom we have worked have been relatively recent immigrants, and thus, their experience is more comparable with that of children who have received mathematics instruction in other languages, in their countries of origin, and who do not yet know enough English to fully follow oral instructions and explanations. So, how do these experiences inform us of good teaching practices for ELLs? Parents report on things that teachers did that helped them to follow the class—for example, using drawings and sketches, doing hands-on activities, and showing examples on the board (and not erasing them right away). From observing student-student and teacher-student interactions, parents see the value of allowing students to discuss the problems in their native language and giving them time to develop their ideas in English (understanding that the students are indecisive or insecure about participating in class not because they do not know how to do the problem but because they have to express their ideas in English).

The excerpt that follows is from a debriefing in which two mothers shared observations from a visit to a second-grade classroom. The main topic of the lesson was doing subtraction by adding up. So, for example, to subtract $37 - 8$, students might go from 8 to 10 (+ 2), then from 10 to 30 (+ 20), and then from 30 to 37 (+ 7), for a result of $2 + 20 + 7$, or 29. The teacher encouraged the students to think of these *jumps* from one number to another as the leaps of a frog. This way of thinking about subtraction was new to one of the mothers who observed the class:

> *Adriana:* Because sometimes... You know when it's addition or subtraction, but you don't know the movement. That thing about the little frog and that... At the beginning, when I would look at it, I would say, "Well, what are they...? How did they do it?" And I would get stuck there. If I fared well, I would understand. If not, I would tell my daughter, "Well, do it yourself." [*Laughter*] But I would feel how the girl would say, "Well, my mom doesn't know," so I decided to take the time to come to the classes. (Debriefing classroom visit, March 2006)

Later in the conversation, Adriana indicates that she finds the method with the frog somewhat convoluted in terms of the number of steps that it takes to get the answer:

> *Adriana:* For example, right now, to me, they could have done that problem

*easier, and not so much… [Moves her hand as if taking many steps].
And, for example, well, you just subtract and do the subtraction, and
that's it, but they, they extended it a lot. (Debriefing classroom visit,
March 2006)*

Adriana then explains how she would have done the subtraction by using a traditional approach. She comments that she teaches that approach to her daughter but that she also wants to learn the method that they are teaching her in school because her daughter might say, "I know what the answer is, but I have to do it the way the teacher says." Later on in the debriefing, Adriana comments again on the teacher's method, which is not as quick as her own method of subtracting, but she notes that the teacher is "teaching where the numbers come from."

Classroom visits, coupled with opportunities for parents to participate in short courses and *tertulias,* as in the case of Adriana, provide a powerful avenue for developing communication with families about the teaching and learning of mathematics. Adriana, as other parents have also done, raises some questions about what to her appears to be an inefficient approach to subtraction, involving many steps. Yet, at the same time, she shares her desire to learn how her daughter is learning, and the short courses provide her with that opportunity. We view these experiences as a way to discuss our beliefs and values about what we count as doing mathematics.

Conclusion

In this chapter, we have presented vignettes that permit us to hear parents' voices as they share with us their thoughts related to the teaching and learning of mathematics. Some of these thoughts underscore issues related to power and valorization of knowledge and point to the need for schools to develop strong communication with parents—particularly immigrant parents and other non-dominant parents, who are often left out of the instructional discussion regarding mathematics. These parents have important contributions to make by sharing their own approaches to doing mathematics, their knowledge about their children as learners, and their experiences with language and mathematics (see also "Mathematical Notation Comparisons between U.S. and Latino Students" and "Mathematical Notations and Procedures of Recent Immigrant Students" in the materials accompanying chapter 2 at www.nctm.org/more4u). Short courses and *tertulias* and classroom visits are two approaches that we suggest as ways to explore mathematics together and learn from one another, to engage in dialogue about the teaching and learning of mathematics, and ultimately to break down the barriers that often exist between parents and teachers or school administrators—because, as Carlota reminds us, "We are all a family."

References

Civil, Marta. "Building on Community Knowledge: An Avenue to Equity in Mathematics Education." In *Improving Access to Mathematics: Diversity and Equity in the Classroom,* edited by Na'ilah Suad Nasir and Paul Cobb, pp. 105–117. New York: Teachers College Press, 2007.

Common Core State Standards Initiative (CCSSI). *Common Core State Standards for Mathematics. Common Core State Standards (College- and Career-Readiness Standards and K-12 Standards in*

English Language Arts and Math). Washington, D.C.: National Governors Association Center for Best Practices and the Council of Chief State School Officers, 2010. http://www.corestandards.org.

Delgado-Gaitan, Concha. *Involving Latino Families in Schools: Raising Student Achievement through Home-School Partnerships*. Thousand Oaks, Calif.: Corwin, 2004.

González, Norma, Luis Moll, and Cathy Amanti. *Funds of Knowledge: Theorizing Practices in Households, Communities, and Classrooms*. Mahwah, N.J.: Lawrence Erlbaum, 2005.

Math and Parent Partnerships in the Southwest (MAPPS). *Math for Parents Mini-Courses*. Tucson, Ariz: Math and Parent Partnerships, Department of Mathematics, University of Arizona, 2003.

National Council of Teachers of Mathematics (NCTM). *Principles and Standards for School Mathematics*. Reston, Va.: NCTM, 2000.

Quintos, Beatriz, Jill Bratton, and Marta Civil. "Engaging with Parents on a Critical Dialogue about Mathematics Education." In *Proceedings of the Fourth Congress of the European Society for Research in Mathematics Education*, edited by Mariana Bosch, pp. 1182–92. Sant Feliu de Guíxols, Spain: FUNDEMI IQS, Universitat Ramon Llull, 2005.

Suárez-Orozco, Carola, and Marcelo M. Suárez-Orozco. *Children of Immigration*. Cambridge, Mass.: Harvard University Press, 2001.

Chapter 8

Cases of Practice: Assessing ELLs in Mathematics

This chapter presents three case studies that focus on the points made in chapter 2 about the assessment of ELLs. In case 1, Richard Kitchen, Laura Burr, and Libni B. Castellón describe the stages involved in using a discursive assessment protocol in a sixth-grade course taught by the first author and using the Connected Mathematics Project (CMP) curriculum. In this case study, the authors show the need to provide multiple opportunities for bilingual students to express their mathematical thinking involving fractions.

Similarly, in case 2, Anthony Fernandes uses an interview format to present a vignette that indicates the need to understand gestures that a sixth-grade student uses to make sense of a perimeter and area mathematics task.

In case 3, María Martiniello and Mikyung Kim Wolf examine how text complexity and background knowledge may pose challenges to ELLs. The authors include think-aloud interviews and use fourth- and eighth-grade test items to illustrate these points.

Case 1

Providing Multiple Opportunities for ELLs to Communicate Their Mathematical Ideas

by Richard Kitchen, Laura Burr, and Libni B. Castellón

In the vignette that follows, Zenia, an English language learner (ELL), uses mathematical representations to explain complex mathematical ideas. Zenia was one of four ELLs who participated in a research study to document the progression of the students' mathematical thinking through a series of rational number tasks. All the students were in a sixth-grade class taught by the first author at the time that the study was undertaken, and all were Latinos or Latinas who spoke Spanish as their primary language.

In spring 2008, we began conducting intensive one-on-one clinical interviews with the four ELLs, using a formative assessment format that we refer to as the "discursive assessment protocol." In addition to calling on students to express solutions in writing, the discursive assessment protocol includes stages in which students are encouraged to think out loud. We set out to understand whether the discursive assessment protocol fostered equitable and accessible bilingual learning opportunities for the participants.

The research reported in case 1 was supported by the Center for the Mathematics Education of Latinos (CEMELA), funded by the National Science Foundation, under grant ESI-0424983, as a Center for Learning and Teaching, 2004–2009.

Zenia was trying to solve the Bicycle task:

Andrés drove his bike $39\frac{1}{6}$ meters, and Ned drove his bike $28\frac{5}{9}$ meters. How many more meters did Andrés drive than Ned?

We knew that designing the task so that the fraction in the smaller mixed number was larger than the fraction in the larger mixed number would make the task more challenging for the participating ELLs. What solution strategy do you suppose that a sixth-grade student would pursue to solve this task? One solution strategy that a student could use would be simply to convert the mixed numbers into improper fractions and subtract. Do you suppose that having a larger fraction in the smaller mixed number would make the student more or less likely to consider alternative solution strategies?

Vignette

Zenia's progress through the protocol

In stage 1 of the discursive assessment protocol, Zenia was asked to estimate the answer for the Bicycle problem. After much thought, Zenia said the answer would be less than 10 but then changed her mind, deciding that it would be a little less than 11 instead. To arrive at the solution, she explained, she thought that $39 - 28$ equals 11, but she knew that the answer would be less than 11 because $\frac{5}{9}$, which is close to one-half, is bigger than $\frac{1}{6}$, and, she said, when you subtract $\frac{5}{9}$ from $\frac{1}{6}$, the solution will be a negative number greater than -1.

In stage 2 of the discursive assessment protocol, when students use pencil and paper for problem solving, Zenia invoked the traditional algorithm in her written response: she changed mixed numbers to improper fractions, found equivalent fractions that had a common denominator, and then subtracted the two fractions, as follows:

$$39\frac{1}{6} = \frac{234}{6} \times \frac{9}{9} = \frac{2106}{54}$$

$$28\frac{5}{9} = \frac{252}{9} \times \frac{6}{6} = \frac{1512}{54}$$

$$\frac{2106}{54} - \frac{1512}{54} = \frac{594}{54} = 11$$

As you may have noticed, Zenia failed to add the numerators of the fractional portions of the mixed numbers to the numerators of the improper fractions.

Stage 3 of the protocol is an interactive interview based on the student's written response in stage 2. Zenia started to demonstrate how she had changed the mixed numbers to improper fractions and found that she had made an error. She noted that she needed to add the numerators of the fractional portions of the mixed numbers after multiplying each denominator by the whole number. She modified the calculations that she had performed on paper during stage 2 on a small whiteboard, as follows:

$$39\frac{1}{6} = \frac{235}{6} \times \frac{9}{9} = \frac{2115}{54}$$

$$28\frac{5}{9} = \frac{257}{9} \times \frac{6}{6} = \frac{1542}{54}$$

$$\frac{2115}{54} - \frac{1542}{54} = \frac{573}{54}$$

At this point, Zenia said she would change her answer to a mixed number by dividing 573 by 54. To do this, she showed how she had applied the long division algorithm, with the aid of a whiteboard. At first, Zenia determined the answer to be 1.6 because she neglected to write a 0 after the 1 in the quotient. When the interviewer asked her to approximate how many times 54 went into 573, Zenia responded, "About 10." She then recognized and corrected her mistake and obtained the quotient 10.6 by applying the traditional long division algorithm, as follows:

$$
\begin{array}{r}
10.6 \\
54\overline{)573.0} \\
-54 \\
\hline
33 \\
-0 \\
\hline
330 \\
-324 \\
\hline
6
\end{array}
$$

Note here that Zenia's reliance on the long division algorithm resulted in her obtaining an approximation with a decimal solution instead of determining the more precise solution of $10^{33}/_{54}$, or $10^{11}/_{18}$.

The interviewer continued by asking Zenia whether she could have used a different number instead of 54 as a common denominator, and Zenia suggested 36. It is important to note that the interviewer purposely used the mathematics register in her question (i.e., formal mathematical terms and language), asking Zenia whether she could have selected another "common denominator" to solve the task. After being prompted to look for an even lower common denominator, Zenia identified 18. She used this common denominator to solve the problem in another way in stage 4.

At stage 4 of the discursive assessment protocol, the goal is to create a scenario in which students cannot simply demonstrate their solution in writing but must explain their mathematical thinking verbally. Stage 4 consisted of a simulated telephone interview, with the interviewer sitting with her back to Zenia to replicate the missing visual dimension of a telephone call. After Zenia had explained the problem solution that she had used in stage 3, the interviewer asked her whether there might be another way to solve the problem. At this point, Zenia reverted to the strategy that she had alluded to during stage 1, when she worked with the whole number and fractions independently to estimate a solution. First, Zenia stated that she could subtract 28 from 39 to get 11. She then said that subtracting $^5/_9$ from $^1/_6$ would give her "a negative number." Zenia continued by explaining that she would then "subtract the negative number from the whole number."

With prompting from the interviewer, who continued to sit with her back turned, Zenia proceeded to solve the task on a whiteboard on her lap. After a short time had elapsed, the interviewer reminded Zenia to explain her work since the interviewer could not see what Zenia was doing. After explaining that she had subtracted 28 from 39 to get 11, Zenia said she was multiplying $\frac{1}{6}$ by "3 over 3," and "That's going to give me $\frac{3}{18}$." She continued, "And then I'm going to multiply $\frac{5}{9}$ times 2 over 2, and that gives me $\frac{10}{18}$. Then I need to subtract $\frac{3}{18}$ minus $\frac{10}{18}$, equals negative $\frac{7}{18}$." She continued, stating that she needed to take "negative $\frac{7}{18}$ minus 11," but then self-corrected and said "11 minus $\frac{7}{18}$ equals 10 and $\frac{11}{18}$." The interviewer asked how she arrived at her solution, and Zenia said, "I took away 10 from 11 and put them as a whole number, and so 1 is 18 over 18 and then I subtracted 7, and it gave me 11 over 18ths, and then I just put it with the whole number [10]," implying that her solution to the task was 10 and $\frac{11}{18}$. Notice here that even though Zenia struggled at times to explain her solution strategy, she clearly understood how to implement this alternative solution strategy, using $1 = \frac{18}{18}$ as a means to obtain $\frac{11}{18}$ as the fractional component of her final answer.

Research Methods and School Setting

We collected videotape data on Zenia and the other three research participants as they estimated, calculated, and explained their solutions to tasks involving fractions, mixed numbers, percents, and proportional reasoning. We designed rational number tasks that were similar to those in the students' regular mathematics textbook, and we contextualized the tasks in cultural settings that were familiar to the students. In addition, we used names of actual students in the class in the tasks. Task scenarios included students' purchasing grapes from a local market, riding bicycles in their neighborhood, or helping parents purchase gasoline to go on a trip to visit a grandmother.

All four research participants had attended a local elementary school with a strong dual language program and spoke English at a "Very Good User" level, as described by the International English Language Testing System (IELTS) (Baker 2006, p. 29). The four students attended a small, progressive Christian middle school in a large city in the Southwest. At the time of the study, all the school's students lived in poverty, and 94 percent were people of color. The school had opened in fall 2007, and its design was based on findings from a study that offered insights into how to structure an urban school to serve poor and diverse student populations productively (Kitchen et al. 2007). All students were integrated into the regular academic trajectory, a college preparatory track. Parents and individuals living both within and outside the school's community served as volunteers to support the school's high academic expectations.

The Discursive Assessment Protocol

The design of the discursive assessment protocol, or research protocol, built on and was an extension of a clinical interview protocol used by the lead author in a previous study (see Kitchen and Wilson 2004; Kulm, Wilson, and Kitchen 2005). The discursive assessment protocol was designed specifically for use with individual ELLs or groups of ELLs in mathematics but can also be used with the general student population. Preliminary research indicates that the use of the discursive assessment protocol leads to the development of positive teacher-student relationships that promote students' taking academic risks and sharing their mathematical thinking with their peers and teachers (Kitchen, Burr, and Castellón 2010; Castellón, Burr, and Kitchen 2011). As students' persistence increases, their self-efficacy or mathematical identity is enhanced. Students' positive sense of self-efficacy is reinforcing, cyclical in nature, and leads to continued academic risk taking and highly engaged learning over time. Overall, ELLs responded to the discursive assessment protocol in very positive, innovative, and empowered ways.

Our description of the discursive assessment protocol indicates accommodations that are specific to ELLs, but alternative accommodations are certainly possible for students with special needs or for other student populations. The unique feature of the discursive assessment protocol is that it offers students multiple opportunities for problem solving in differing learning contexts. In addition to calling on students to express solutions in writing, the research protocol includes stages in which students are encouraged to think out loud. The research protocol consists of four stages—making estimations, writing solutions, explaining solutions, and simulating a telephone interview.

In the estimation stage of the discursive assessment protocol (stage 1), the two interviewers, A and B, present students with a mathematics task written in English. If possible, ELLs are given the option of having the task translated into their native language. After being read the task by interviewer A, the student estimates a solution without having the benefit of any tools (e.g., ruler, paper and pencil, calculator). The student is also not permitted to write down ideas while approximating. Throughout this initial stage, either interviewer can ask clarifying questions based on students' responses.

In the second stage, students go to a different room where, working independently, they develop written solutions to all the tasks for which they had developed estimates previously. During the explanation stage (stage 3), students are asked by interviewer A to explain reasoning used to solve each task. Students are encouraged to write on a dry-erase board or interactive whiteboard to demonstrate their mathematical thinking. Interviewer A also asks clarifying questions, revoices students' explanations, or makes reference to aspects of students' work.

In the phone simulation stage (stage 4), students have one final chance to modify task solutions on the basis of feedback previously received and any new insights that they may have. During this stage, students are asked to explain their mathematical thinking to interviewer B in a simulated telephone interview. For ELLs, it is helpful if interviewer B speaks the same primary language as the students; the goal, whenever possible, is to provide students with the choice of discussing their mathematical thinking on the phone in either their first language or English. Because Interviewer B spoke Spanish, Zenia could have used Spanish during this stage, but she elected to speak English. Although the interviewer in stage 4 cannot see what students have written (it is a simulated telephone interview), students may use a dry-erase board or interactive whiteboard as a means to recall the process that they used to solve the task previously or develop a new solution. Interviewer B cannot view any of the students' written work during this stage, since the goal is to motivate students to provide verbal descriptions of their mathematical reasoning to solve the task. As in stage 3, interviewer B can ask clarifying questions, revoice explanations, or refer to written solutions completed by students during stage 2.

During stages 3 and 4, students are allowed to review and refer to the written solutions that they produced during stage 2. It is interesting to note that students often modify their earlier solutions as they interact with the interviewers during stages 3 and 4.

Throughout, interviewers communicate the expectation that students will thoroughly explain how they obtained answers during each stage of the process. On occasion, interviewers ask questions to help students to clarify their thinking and encourage them to persist with problem-solving strategies. It is also not uncommon for the interviewers to provide a "scaffolded" lesson or mini-lesson to assist students in making connections, justifying a generalization, expounding further on their reasoning, or even abandoning an unproductive problem-solving strategy.

Looking Back: Communicating Mathematical Ideas

Zenia's interest in the Bicycle task demonstrates the importance of selecting tasks that are relevant and of interest to students. Moreover, the level of complexity of the task was appropriate. The task was challenging for Zenia, but she also demonstrated that she was capable of solving it in more than one way. In the solution that she demonstrated in stages 2 and 3, Zenia primarily showed in writing (both on paper and on a small whiteboard) how to obtain the solution by converting the mixed numbers into improper fractions and then subtracting. Given the opportunity to revisit the work that she had completed during stage 2, Zenia found and corrected an error that she had previously made while solving the task during stage 3. In stage 4, after being encouraged to solve the task by using an alternative approach, Zenia pursued a strategy that she had hinted at while estimating the solution during stage 1. In this innovative strategy, Zenia subtracted the wholes and fractional parts of the given mixed numbers separately to derive a solution. During the final stage, Zenia developed an efficient strategy to solve the Bicycle problem when she converted one whole to $^{18}/_{18}$ and then obtained a solution without getting lost in complex calculations.

The discursive assessment protocol is a multi-stage formative assessment tool that provided an opportunity (in stage 4) for Zenia to more fully develop a solution that she had originally communicated (in stage 1). During stage 1, Zenia verbally communicated how she approached the task of estimating the difference between Andrés's and Ned's distances. In stage 4, with some encouragement, Zenia was willing to revisit her original thinking and develop a relatively sophisticated strategy for arriving at the exact difference. In general, the discursive assessment protocol promotes academic discourse as teachers learn how to construct questions for individual students or groups of students as a means for students to both clarify and develop their mathematical thinking (Kitchen, Burr, and Castellón 2010; Castellón, Burr, and Kitchen 2011). We believe that this is particularly valuable for ELLs, as demonstrated by Zenia. Providing her with multiple opportunities to communicate, revisit, and refine her mathematical thinking, coupled with interviewers' high expectations and encouragement, resulted in Zenia's expressing knowledge and demonstrating skills needed to solve the task in more than one way.

If Zenia had simply been asked to solve this task with paper and pencil, the robust mathematical knowledge that she demonstrated during the interview would not have been revealed. It is interesting to note that she abandoned her estimation strategy (operate on the whole numbers and fractions independently to arrive at a solution) during stages 2 and 3 and initially during stage 4. Only through some prompting from an interviewer did Zenia return to this strategy, which she was able to formalize and correctly apply to obtain the solution. We hypothesize that the reason that Zenia moved away from her estimation strategy to the more traditional algorithmic approach to solve the problem was that she attached high status to this strategy. Most likely, because of the formal instruction received in the past, Zenia had developed the sense that converting the mixed numbers into improper fractions with common denominators and then operating on the numbers was the approach most valued by her teachers and her textbook authors.

On a summative assessment (e.g., a quiz), Zenia might not have received full credit for the solution that she provided in stage 2, since she made calculation errors as she attempted to solve the task by using learned algorithms. Although she did not immediately arrive at a correct solution, Zenia demonstrated throughout all four stages that there was much that she *did* know. For instance, she demonstrated knowledge of the mathematical register (Moschkovich 1999a), verbalizing such important ideas as "whole number" and "common denominator." Zenia was also able to convert mixed numbers to improper fractions and an improper fraction to a decimal, and she seemed to invent a strategy to subtract a fraction from a whole. Although on occasion Zenia could not precisely verbalize the strategies that she was using to solve the task, by having multiple opportunities to revisit her mathematical ideas, she discovered errors that she had made and refined her solution strategies. It is also imperative to view Zenia's work through an equity lens, highlighting what she knew, as opposed to viewing her work through a deficit lens, highlighting what she did not know (Moll and Ruiz 2002). By providing ELLs such as Zenia with multiple opportunities to revisit and refine ideas, we are simultaneously validating their mathematical ideas and ways of expressing those ideas while actualizing their mathematical potentialities by supporting them as they continue to develop and apply the mathematical register in new contexts.

Accurately assessing what a student knows is very difficult, and the techniques that are most effective are the most time intensive. This is particularly true when the student is an ELL and the teacher does not speak the same language as the ELL. We are pursuing this line of research with the goal of developing efficient applications of the discursive assessment protocol that will be of use to classroom teachers. For instance, we have initiated studies in which a classroom teacher uses the research protocol with small cooperative groups in which some or all of the participants are ELLs. We are encouraged by this work because we have found that the use of the discursive assessment protocol with Zenia and other ELLs cultivates a culturally affirming and empowering learning environment (for more specifics, see Kitchen, Burr, and Castellón [2010]).

Case 2

Attending to Student Gestures

by Anthony Fernandes

A task-based interview engaged students in discussing four measurement problems, one of which was the Trapezoid problem:

The research reported in case 2 was supported by the National Science Foundation, under grant ESI-0424983, awarded to the Center for Mathematics Education of Latino/as (CEMELA). The views expressed here are those of the author and do not necessarily reflect the views of the funding agency.

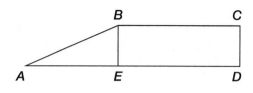

The area of rectangle *BCDE* shown above is 60 square inches. If the length of *AE* is 10 inches and the length of *ED* is 15 inches, what is the area of trapezoid *ABCD*, in square inches?

Rita's gestures related to her understanding of area

Rita (not her real name), a sixth-grade Latina student, discussed the Trapezoid problem in a task-based interview conducted by Carol, a university researcher. The entire interview was video recorded, and this case focuses on two episodes during the interview, in which Rita makes use of gestures related to the concepts of area and perimeter.

Episode 1: Gestures related to the concept of area

The first episode on which the case focuses occurs at the beginning of the interview, when Rita tells Carol that she does not understand the Trapezoid problem, and Carol proceeds to uncover what Rita does knows about it, with the intention of building on this knowledge to assist Rita in solving the problem.

Carol: OK, tell me, you know, tell me what part you don't get, or... and tell me what parts you get. So, like, read the first sentence for me, and then tell me what you think of it.

Rita: [*Reading the problem out loud*] The area of rectangle *BCDE* shown above is 60 square inches.

Carol: OK, so... What does that mean? Can you tell me something about this shape [*moves her hand to indicate the drawn shape*], and tell me what they are talking about?

Rita: [*After a slight pause*] That all of this [*points to the base with the pencil; see fig. 8.1*] this [*changes to indicate rectangle BCDE; see fig. 8.2*]...

Carol: [*Interjecting*] OK.

Rita: [*Continuing to speak*] ...rectangle is 60.

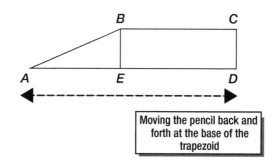

Fig. 8.1. Rita indicates the base (segment *AD*) with her pencil.

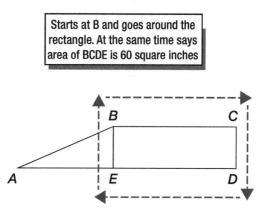

Fig. 8.2. Rita indicates rectangle *BCDE* with her pencil.

Carol: OK, so can you put the 60 somewhere in the figure, and... to... to keep in mind this information.

Rita: Right here [*points to BC with the pencil; see fig. 8.3*].

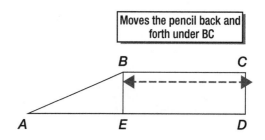

Fig. 8.3. Rita indicates segment *BC* with her pencil.

Carol: OK, just put it where you think it goes.

[Rita writes 60 inside the rectangle just below BC.]

The gestures that Rita uses in the first episode raise questions immediately about her understanding of area since none of her gestures show a space-covering motion. At first, she points to the base of the trapezoid in reference to the area of rectangle *BCDE*, and then she changes to the gesture that goes around *BCDE*. Both of these are gestures that indicate either length or perimeter, with no attempt to display space. When Carol tries to get a confirmation of Rita's understanding of area by asking her to write the 60 somewhere in the figure, Rita points to segment *BC* and writes 60 below it. Even though Rita writes the 60 *inside* the rectangle, her gesture to segment *BC* indicates length rather than the space inside the rectangle. Note that this is usually the way in which length of a segment is labeled in geometric figures.

Episode 2: Gestures related to the process of determining area

The second episode on which we focus occurs later in the interview, when Rita exhibits confusion about the operations to perform to find the area and perimeter. Carol seeks to address this confusion separately from the Trapezoid problem:

Carol: Let me ask you a different question. If I draw a rectangle [*draws a rectangle on the paper*], what do you do to find the area of a rectangle? How do you find the area of a rectangle?

Rita: Add the length of sides [*points to all four sides of the rectangle*].

Carol: OK, so make up some numbers [*hand hovering over the paper*]… Let's forget this problem [*hand moves to block the Trapezoid problem from sight*]. Put some numbers [*refers to the newly drawn rectangle*].

[Rita starts writing 5, 5, 15, 15 on the four sides, with 5 as the width and 15 as the base.]

Carol: OK, so how will you find the area of this rectangle?

Rita: Add 'em together [*referring to the numbers around the rectangle recently drawn*].

Carol: OK, how will you find the perimeter of this rectangle?

Rita: Times… 5 times 15.

Carol: OK [*flips to the Triangle and Square problem, shown in fig. 8.4; earlier, Rita had solved this problem successfully on her own, without any assistance*]. Here, when you did perimeter, what did you do?

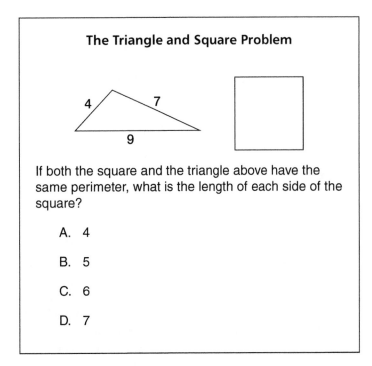

The Triangle and Square Problem

If both the square and the triangle above have the same perimeter, what is the length of each side of the square?

    A. 4

    B. 5

    C. 6

    D. 7

Fig. 8.4. The Triangle and Square problem, given to Rita earlier

Rita:	Add these [*points to the 9, 7, and 4 on the sides of the triangle*].
Carol:	OK [*flips back to the Trapezoid problem*], so here when you do perimeter, what do you do?
Rita:	Oh, times [*points to the 5 and the 15*].
Carol:	So, can you tell me? I mean, I am getting a little bit confused here with the perimeter and the area… Can you refresh my memory about perimeter and area and how you find one and the other? What they are, and what they mean. You have a rectangle that measures 5 and 15 for the sides. What is the perimeter of this rectangle… What am I looking at?

[*Carol pauses; 16 seconds elapse.*]

Carol:	If you were to explain to a fourth grader what perimeter is, how would you explain it?
Rita:	The inside of any shape [*simultaneously outlines a square or rectangle on the table with the pencil that she had in her hand; see fig. 8.5*].

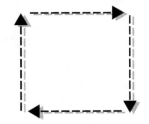

Fig. 8.5. Rita outlines a square or rectangle with her pencil.

Carol: OK, so [*flips back to the Triangle and Square problem*]... Here we were talking about perimeter. Did you do the inside or the outside?

Rita: The inside [*outlines the square or rectangle on the table, using her pencil, as in fig. 8.5, and then hesitates*]... No...

[*Rita pauses; 8 seconds elapse.*]

Carol: What is area?

Rita: Oh, the inside [*simultaneously outlines a square or rectangle on the table with the pencil, as in fig. 8.5*], and the perimeter is the outside [*shifts hand from the table to the paper that was in front of her and moves her pencil around the outside of the square provided in the Triangle and Square problem; see fig. 8.4*].

Rita uses the same gestures to indicate the area and the perimeter of the rectangle. When referring to area, she says "inside" but outlines straight line segments to indicate a square or rectangle. When discussing perimeter, Rita goes back to the square that was provided in the Triangle and Square problem and outlines straight line segments that were literally on the *outside* of the square. Rita probably interpreted the "inside of the shape" (when referring to area) to mean just inside the boundary of the object but still measuring length instead of space, and the "outside of the shape" (when referring to perimeter) to mean measuring lengths outside the boundary of the shape. At no point did her gestures for area seem to indicate the enclosed space in an object.

Context of the Vignette

The vignette presented above was taken from a larger project that involved task-based interviews with a group of twenty-five Mexican American students attending schools in working-class neighborhoods in the Southwest. The group, consisting of students from grades 4 through 8, was presented with four National Assessment for Educational Progress (NAEP) measurement problems at various levels of difficulty (easy, medium, and hard, as defined by NAEP). The interviews were usually conducted by a researcher and were videotaped. The students were presented with the problem and given some time to work on it independently before interacting with the interviewer. The overall focus of the study was to gain a better understanding of how this group of students approached the NAEP measurement problems and the challenges that they faced in communicating their solutions. In this interview, Rita, an ELL, had solved the first two problems—the Triangle and Square problem and the Area Comparison problem—independently and was able to communicate her solutions successfully to Carol.

Discussion: Rita's Use of Language and Gestures

Examining the two episodes presented above from the vignette, we observe that Rita could use the necessary language, like using the word *inside* when discussing area and the word *outside* when referring to perimeter, but her gestures indicated that she attached different meanings to these terms from those assumed by the interviewer. It is possible that notation like "*BCDE*" in the Trapezoid problem was unfamiliar to Rita, and that she assumed that

BCDE indicated the line segments *BC*, *CD*, *DE*, and *EA*, taken in this order, and referred to the area of the rectangle in this problem. From the vignette, we infer that gestures play an important role, along with speech, in revealing the student's thinking.

Implications for Assessment

Assessment is a key aspect of instruction that allows teachers to gauge students' understanding of the material and then use this knowledge to guide future instruction. Informal assessments, such as interactions with the students during class and in interviews, can provide valuable information about students' understanding, supporting the Assessment Principle as outlined in *Principles and Standards for School Mathematics* (NCTM 2000). As teachers evaluate their students' thinking in verbal interactions with those students, the teachers may have a tendency to rely mainly on the speech produced by the students. However, English language learners such as Rita, who are still learning the academic language, may find it challenging to express themselves fully through English speech and may thus rely on additional resources, such as their native language and gestures (Moschkovich 1999b, 2002). Teachers should pay attention to the gestures that the students make, especially in instances where the gestures deviate from the concept being discussed in speech, as in the case of Rita, who was making gestures for perimeter when talking about area. These differences could indicate a possible misconception that propagates in the students' thinking.

When working with all students, but especially ELLs, teachers can use appropriate gestures in addition to their verbal explanations to ensure proper comprehension. Engaging students in concrete activities such as shading regions of different shapes to understand the meaning of "inside of the shape" when referring to area can provide a platform on which the teacher and the students can work on their gestures during interactions. For example, gesturing a space-filling motion for area and distinguishing this from the gestures used for perimeter can help ELLs grasp the proper meanings of the terms *inside* and *outside*. By expanding students' inputs to include gestures, teachers can increase their understanding of student thinking, and this knowledge can inform future instructional design.

Case 3

Exploring ELLs' Understanding of Word Problems in Mathematics Assessments—The Role of Text Complexity and Student Background Knowledge

by María Martiniello and Mikyung Kim Wolf

When Rosa, an English language learner (ELL), answered the following assessment question, she gave a correct answer based on her interpretation of the word problem. However, what challenges might the words in the problem have posed for Rosa in interpreting the question as intended?

The pictograph below shows the amount of money each fourth-grade class raised for an animal shelter.

Amount Raised by Each Class

Class	Amount Raised
Ms. Smith	$ $ $ $ $ $
Mr. Powell	$ $ $ $
Ms. Carly	$ $ $ $ $ $ $ $
Mr. Roper	$ $ $ $ $ $

If Mr. Powell's class raised $20 and Mr. Roper's class raised $30, how much money does one $ represent?

In case 3, we discuss possible challenges that ELLs face in tackling word problems in mathematics assessments. ELLs display a broad range of mathematics knowledge and ability in the classroom, but in state and national assessments of mathematics, ELLs are among the lowest-scoring groups. For example, on the 2009 National Assessment of Educational Progress (NAEP), 72 percent of eighth-grade ELLs scored below "basic" in mathematics, as compared with 26 percent of non-ELL students (National Center for Education Statistics 2009), and on the 2010 California state accountability assessment in general mathematics, only 12 percent of eighth-grade ELLs scored at the "proficient" level, as compared with 27 percent of English-only eighth graders (California Department of Education 2010).

As researchers strive to ensure that assessments given to ELLs are valid and fair, we seek to understand whether this pattern of low performance by ELLs on mathematics assessments is associated with any of the following student characteristics:

1. Mathematics knowledge and skills (related to opportunity to learn and accessibility of mathematics instruction)

2. Understanding of the test language (related to the interaction between the complexity of the text and the ELLs' level of English language proficiency)

3. Familiarity with sociocultural references (related to the overlap between the students' background knowledge and the sociocultural practices, beliefs, or objects depicted in these assessments).

Disentangling these three factors, we believe, is not only important for assessment specialists but also can be very helpful to classroom teachers as they strive to improve ELLs' performance in such assessments. Mathematics teachers learn to focus on the first factor: students' content knowledge. In their practice, mathematics teachers constantly gauge where students are, what students need to learn, and what teaching activities will help students acquire the desired mathematical skills. Less often, mathematics teachers focus on the second and third factors: how English language proficiency (ELP) and background knowledge affect their students' mathematics performance.

In case 3, we share some of the lessons that we have learned in analyzing large-scale mathematics assessments and conducting think-aloud interviews with ELL students responding to test items. Through think-aloud interviews, we were able to learn more about ELL students' problem-solving processes as well as comprehension processes associated with the language and cultural references presented in word problems. We will discuss three examples of word problems that require students to apply mathematical concepts or procedures to scenarios depicting real-world situations. These items, from fourth- and eighth-grade mathematics assessments, were identified as posing greater difficulty for ELLs than for non-ELLs with equivalent mathematics proficiency.

For each example, we will first present the word problem. We will describe potential challenges for ELLs that arise from the text complexity and from the use of cultural references that require background knowledge to understand the item scenario. We will then illustrate some of these challenges with transcriptions of ELLs' think-aloud responses to these word problems. Last, we will suggest ways in which teachers can use the information provided in the think-aloud responses to inform their teaching.

Assessment Item 1: Polysemy and Background Knowledge Issues

Understanding story problems that involve polysemous words and cultural references can be particularly challenging for ELLs in taking standardized mathematics assessments in English (Martiniello 2008, 2010). Polysemous words are words with different meanings or connotations, depending on the context provided by the text or discourse. We find many examples of words with multiple meanings in everyday language and mathematical discourse (e.g., *table* meaning a piece of furniture, *table* meaning a display of data). At the beginning of case 3, we showed the assessment item that follows, but we repeat it below in full, with the accompanying multiple-choice answers, for the reader's convenience as we discuss the potential difficulties related to polysemous vocabulary and background knowledge required to understand the context or scenario depicted in the problem.

The pictograph below shows the amount of money each fourth-grade class raised for an animal shelter.

Amount Raised by Each Class

Class	Amount Raised
Ms. Smith	$ $ $ $ $ $
Mr. Powell	$ $ $ $
Ms. Carly	$ $ $ $ $ $ $ $
Mr. Roper	$ $ $ $ $ $

If Mr. Powell's class raised $20 and Mr. Roper's class raised $30, how much money does one $ represent?

A. $1

B. $4

C. $5

D. $20

Challenges to ELLs

In this word problem, the sociocultural context and complex text language can pose difficulties for ELLs. We will describe these areas of difficulty briefly, and then we will illustrate the challenge posed to ELLs by words with multiple meanings.

Syntax

The language in the item stem has complex syntactic features that are likely to hamper text comprehension for ELLs as well as for struggling readers. Its two sentences are long and dense, including a reduced relative clause (omitting the relative pronoun: "the amount of money *that* each fourth-grade class raised") and multiple conditional clauses.

Vocabulary

Along with high-frequency words (e.g., "fourth," "grade," "class," "money," "animal"), which are likely to be known by ELLs at beginning-intermediate levels of ELP, this word problem contains words used less frequently. These words, including "pictograph," "represent," "raised," and "shelter," may pose difficulty for ELLs at all levels of ELP. The words "pictograph" and "represent" are discipline-specific and general academic words, respectively. As such, teachers are likely to target the use of these words in classroom discourse.

In the item's scenario, the verb "raised" indicates the (past) action of collecting funds to support an animal shelter. The polysemous word "raise" occurs frequently in conversational and written English and may be known by ELLs at intermediate levels of ELP. In their classrooms, ELLs may be asked to "raise your hands," or "raise the volume." In settings outside their classrooms, they may hear the expression "raising the rent," or "receiving a raise." Making sense of words like "raise," which carry multiple meanings or connotations depending on the context, presents a double challenge. The reader must be knowledgeable about the particular meaning or connotation used or must be aware of cues in the context that allow him or her to infer the particular meaning.

Context

Although situated in a school setting, the problem scenario may be unfamiliar to some ELLs, as it involves a particular sociocultural practice, raising funds for a cause—in this case, the protection of animals—which might not be part of all ELLs' cultural or social background. The think-aloud interview below illustrates these challenges.

Interview on assessment item 1

Rosa is a Spanish-speaking fourth grader at intermediate-advanced levels of English language proficiency. Rosa completed first and second grade with honors in her native Puerto Rico. Her family moved to the United States eighteen months earlier, and Rosa is now enrolled in a fourth-grade dual language program.

To gauge her decoding skills and reading fluency, we asked Rosa to read aloud the item text in English and explain what the item required her to do. Rosa had no problem decoding the text of the word problem. She spoke primarily in Spanish during the interview, switching to English sporadically. Below is the transcription of Rosa's responses.

Translations from Spanish to English appear in parentheses. When the student uses words in English, they appear in quotation marks.

Student: Este "pictograph" es como una foto que te están enseñando abajo.

(This "pictograph" is like a picture that is shown below.)

Cuánto es la, cuánto es la… uhm… dinero cada cuarto grado [*pause*]

(How much is, how much is the … uhm… money each fourth grade)

Uhm… aumentar, aumentar para el "animal shelter" [*pause*]

(Uhm… increase, increase for the "animal shelter")

Student: Aumentar, "raised," es tener más, (To increase, "raised," is to have more)

Como… yo tengo ahora 5 dólares y después tengo 10 dólares,

(Like… now I have 5 dollars, and later I have 10 dollars.)

Cuánto dinero I "raised"? 5 dólares, puedo aumentar 5 para tener 10.

(How much money did I raise? 5 dollars, I can increase by 5 to have 10.)

"If Mr. Powell class raised 20, how much money does 1 cash sign represent?"

Unlike ELLs at beginner levels of ELP, Rosa could comprehend the item's complex syntactic structures. But not surprisingly, Rosa was not able to infer the particular meaning of the verb "raised" associated with the sociocultural practice of fund-raising. Rosa understood "raised" as "increased." Although "increase" is a common meaning of the verb "raise," it is not the intended meaning in the particular context of this word problem. Rosa's interpretation of "raised" as "increased" resulted in the misunderstanding of both the word problem scenario and the required task.

Polysemous words can be very challenging for ELLs. These students are likely to know only one of the multiple meanings of a polysemous word—usually the most familiar one, as in Rosa's case.

Polysemy: What can teachers do?

Several approaches offer teachers possibilities for reducing the challenges that polysemous words present to ELLs:

- For a given topic or lesson, identify polysemous words that students will encounter in the mathematical discourse used in the classroom or textbook and provide explicit instruction in the meaning of polysemous words depending on the context.

- When teaching a mathematical concept, ensure that ELLs understand the particular meaning of the polysemous words used, especially if ELLs are likely to be familiar with meanings that are different from those used in their classroom or textbook.

- Use polysemous words that are part of your classroom discourse as opportunities to teach ELLs about language. Progressively expose ELLs to different connotations of the polysemous words, and help them infer a word's meaning on the basis of the context.

Sometimes the context in which polysemous words are used assumes familiarity with social and cultural references, as the next item illustrates.

Assessment Item 2: Background Knowledge Issues

The following example provides an opportunity to consider the importance of gauging and building background knowledge about social, historical, or cultural references for ELL students:

Of the following, which is the closest approximation of a 15 percent tip on a restaurant check of $24.99?

A. $2.50

B. $3.00

C. $3.75

D. $4.50

When Jacob, a former ELL student, answered this assessment question, he chose option A, $2.50. Jacob provided his reasoning to support his answer. How do you think Jacob's prior experiences and background knowledge influenced his interpretation of the problem and strategy to solve it?

Challenges to ELLs

A challenge for ELLs is understanding the sociocultural references and the polysemous vocabulary in this word problem. These two areas of challenge are very closely related in this example, since the sociocultural referent provides the context needed to infer the intended meanings of the polysemous words.

Vocabulary

To understand this problem scenario containing the polysemous words "check" and "tip," ELLs must know first that a "restaurant check" is not the same as a "bank check" but is instead the bill for the amount of the meal, and second that the word "tip" in this context is a gratuity given to waiters or waitresses for their service.

Context

In the school context, ELLs at beginning-intermediate levels of ELP might have learned the meaning of the noun "tip" as used in phrases such as "the tip of your nose." Some ELLs may be familiar with the meaning of "tip" in a restaurant situation if they have received instruction about this word's multiple meanings in context or if the experience of dining at a restaurant is relevant to their lives.

Background knowledge

Tipping behavior is very specific to social and cultural groups. This word problem assumes that readers know that a "tip" is a gratuity offered to those who provide a service and that the amount of the tip is customarily a percentage of the amount of the bill—in this case, 15 percent. Thus, there is an implicit assumption that tipping in restaurants is a common practice and that the tip varies, depending on the total bill.

Interview on assessment item 2

Jacob is a Spanish-speaking eighth-grader with advanced ELP. Born in Mexico, Jacob moved to the United States with his family at age 5. He entered first grade speaking only Spanish. He was classified as an ELL for most of his schooling until the eighth grade, when Jacob was redesignated as proficient in English. His interview was conducted in English.

Student: Of the following, which is the closest approximation of a fifteen percent tip on a restaurant check? Of two four. Twenty-four ninety-nine... And I also remember when we go to restaurants, and the check is like that, and my mom gives two fifty. So, yeah. That's also how I remembered it.

Interviewer: OK. Your mom gives two fifty? And what percent is that?

Student: Fifteen? I don't know.

Interviewer: OK. So what answer did you get?

Student: I put two fifty... I got two fifty because I thought about how much my mom gave.

Interviewer: And so, what do you think the problem is about? Like, if you wanted to describe the problem in your own words.

Student: Like, for people to know, like, how much, like, so they won't give too much or they won't give too little of tips.

Interviewer: Of tips?

Student: Yeah.

Interviewer: OK, so what do you think the problem is asking you to do?

Student: Like how many, fifteen percent tip on a restaurant check you're supposed to give for twenty-four dollars and ninety-nine cents?

Jacob understood the meaning of "tip" and "restaurant check" but could not make sense of them as part of a mathematical problem related to percents. In his experience, his mother gives $2.50 as a gratuity to waiters for their service in restaurants. For Jacob,

$2.50 is a fair amount, "not too much, not too little." As we mentioned previously, tipping in restaurants is a highly situational and sociocultural practice. In some countries, tipping waiters and waitresses is not expected. In other countries, small tips are given as tokens of appreciation, but the tip amount is not in direct proportion to the total check amount. In the United States, it is customary to tip waiters and waitresses for their service. The amount of the tip is somewhat discretionary, but it is usually a percentage of the total amount of the bill, and it often depends on the quality of the service.

In this case, Jacob is familiar with the concept of "tip" because he has seen his mother tip in restaurants. But Jacob seems to conceive of the tip as a constant amount and not a variable amount that depends on the total bill. Most of the time, his mother gives $2.50—"not too much, not too little." Jacob disregards the reference to 15 percent and provides his best answer of $2.50, based on his background knowledge.

Background knowledge: What can teachers do?

Textbooks and assessment problems often require particular sociocultural background knowledge. The following approaches can reduce the challenge that ELLs face:

- Check and, if needed, build students' background knowledge about social and cultural references contained in textbooks and assessment problems. Do not assume that ELLs have had the prior experiences needed to understand the problem scenarios.

- Devote time to building background knowledge for ELLs. This process can be time-consuming and frustrating for teachers who want to spend most of their time teaching mathematical content. But ELLs need extra time to build the background knowledge that non-ELLs bring to school by virtue of speaking English at home and growing up in a particular environment.

- Use word problems as opportunities for students to talk about and discuss mathematical ideas in relation to their cultural traditions and practices.

- When introducing a topic, such as percents, for example, determine what your students know. Ask them, for instance, whether or where they have seen percents in their lives. Then you can start working with word problems that are relevant to the backgrounds of your ELLs.

- After your students have the necessary conceptual understanding and the procedural fluency, move to examples with novel situations. Create opportunities to encourage your ELLs to develop connections and communication as described in the Process Standards (NCTM 2000).

Assessment Item 3: Reading Comprehension Issues

When George, a recently arrived ELL from a Spanish-speaking background, answered the following assessment item, he was able to read the text aloud in English, but his answer was incorrect:

A group of students has a total of 29 pencils, and everyone has at least one pencil. Six students have 1 pencil each, five students have 3 pencils each, and the rest of the students have 2 pencils each. How many students have only 2 pencils?

    A.   4

    B.   6

    C.   8

    D.   9

Because George could read all the English words in the item, his teacher concluded that George lacked the mathematical knowledge required to answer this question. What additional information would you gather to prove or disprove this conclusion?

Challenges to ELLs

In this assessment problem, neither vocabulary nor background knowledge is likely to be a major source of difficulty for ELLs, with the possible exception of students with low ELP or with little or interrupted formal schooling. But the problem text is relatively long and dense in information. This presents two important challenges to ELLs. One is making sense of the text in the item's multiple sentences. This relates to the students' reading comprehension in English. The other is modeling the situation mathematically, translating the text into a mathematical model or writing an equation that allows students to solve the problem (CCSSI 2010). These challenges are not unique to ELLs but are more pronounced for this population.

Context

In this case, the scenario presented in the item is likely to be relevant to most ELLs and connected to their background knowledge, since the problem is situated in the classroom.

Vocabulary

Most of the words in the problem are from a school-based vocabulary or lexicon and are likely to be learned when ELLs enter school (e.g., "students," "pencils").

Syntax, discourse, and cognitive load

The word problem contains multiple sentences, each including relevant mathematical information that needs to be represented and processed before students can solve the problem. Lexical cohesion, which includes a chain of related words to refer to the same thing, requires the students to recognize relationships between words in this item. This increases the item's cognitive load and demand on working memory.

Interview on assessment item 3

As we indicated earlier, George is a recently arrived ELL, and he has a beginning-intermediate level of ELP. Born and raised in Mexico, George received most of his formal education in Spanish. George has attended a school in the United States for over a year and is now in the eighth grade. His interview was conducted in English.

Student: [*Reads the English text aloud*] A group of students has a total of twenty-nine pencils, and everyone has at least one pencil. Six students have one pencil each, five students have three pencils each, and the rest of the students have two pencils each. How many students have only two pencils?

Student: Um, I'm going to add the one where it says six students have one pencil and then the three, and I'll probably get four... And then I'll add the two.

Interviewer: OK, why is that? Because the question is asking what?

Student: Um. How many students have only two pencils?

Interviewer: OK, so why don't you go ahead and do that and just explain to me as you're doing it?

Student: I'm going to add 3, 2, and 1, and I'll get 6. That's how I did it.

In his think-aloud interview, George was able to read aloud all the words in the item. He could also identify the sentence posing the item question, distinguishing it amid the long scenario. George scribbled on his booklet all the numbers appearing in this sentence (i.e., 3, 2, 1); he did not include the numerals written in words (i.e., "six", "five"). However, he could neither comprehend the lengthy text that he was reading nor could he negotiate its mathematical meaning. George resorted to working with the numbers within the text: 3, 2, and 1. He added these numbers. The sum of the addition—6—was given as one of the options (B), and George selected it as his response.

Reading comprehension: What can teachers do?

Teachers can use the following approaches to alleviate the challenges in reading comprehension that textbooks and assessment problems present to ELLs:

- Assess students' comprehension of the text in test items and textbook problems. Do not assume that correctly decoding words means that the student understands and makes meaning of the text. Reading aloud or being able to repeat the phrases in the text does not equal comprehension. Inquire further; ask students to rephrase the scenario in their own words.

- Explain the meaning of phrases such as "a total of," "at least," and "the rest of" as used in this item and more generally as part of mathematical discourse. Ask students to communicate (orally and in writing) by using these phrases.

- Give opportunities for students to work in small groups to make meaning of the problem.

- Use students' native language, if possible, and encourage students to use their native language to help them make sense of the text.

- Guide your ELLs in unpacking the meaning of complex text in each of an item's sentences. Whenever possible, guide them in using models or diagrams that interpret the sentences mathematically. Make it a regular practice in the classroom to unpack problems so that students learn to do this on their own when faced with assessment problems.

- Encourage the use of non-linguistic forms of representation to communicate the mathematical meaning embodied in the text (Martiniello 2009). Help students become fluent in (a) moving across different forms of representation and (b) translating text into mathematical models (see chapter 12).

Summary

In case 3, we have discussed some of the comprehension challenges that ELLs encounter in word problems in mathematics assessments. Our examples illustrate how ELLs at various levels of ELP might struggle with some aspects of—

- text complexity (difficult vocabulary with multiple meanings, or long and complex sentences); and

- unfamiliar sociocultural references (references that are not relevant to the students' background knowledge or prior experiences).

We have made some suggestions for teachers to consider in helping their ELL students improve their English language proficiency, comprehension skills, or background knowledge while engaging in mathematical discourse involving word problems. Although being mindful of teaching both language and content is challenging to mathematics teachers, in work with ELLs it is of paramount importance to target both mathematical understanding and language comprehension, tailoring instruction to the students' levels of English language proficiency. ELL students should have as many opportunities as possible to communicate their understanding of mathematics word problems verbally. If the students are struggling to express themselves in English, teachers might ask them to represent their understanding in different ways (e.g., their native language, symbols, drawings). In our research, we have explored these understandings through think-aloud interviews of ELLs responding to word problems. Through continuous discussions and communication activities, teachers can not only identify and address challenges that ELL students face but also generate multiple opportunities for students to build their background knowledge, master complex language skills, and engage in rich mathematical discourse.

References for Chapter 8

Baker, Colin. *Foundations of Bilingual Education and Bilingualism.* Clevedon, UK: Multilingual Matters, 2006.

California Department of Education. *Standardized Testing and Reporting (STAR) Results: 2010 STAR Test Results.* http://star.cde.ca.gov/star2010/aboutSTAR_reports.asp.

Castellón, Libni B., Laura Burr, and Richard S. Kitchen. "English Language Learners' Conceptual Understanding of Fractions: An Interactive Interview Approach as a Means to Learn with Understanding." In *Latinos and Mathematics Education: Research on Learning and Teaching in Classrooms and Communities,* edited by Kip Téllez, Judit N. Moschkovich, and Marta Civil, pp. 259–82. Charlotte, N.C.: Information Age Publishing, 2011.

Common Core State Standards Initiative (CCSSI). *Common Core State Standards for Mathematics. Common Core State Standards (College- and Career-Readiness Standards and K–12 Standards in English Language Arts and Math).* Washington, D.C.: National Governors Association

Center for Best Practices and the Council of Chief State School Officers, 2010. http://www.corestandards.org.

Kitchen, Richard S., Laura Burr, and Libni B. Castellón. "Cultivating a Culturally Affirming and Empowering Learning Environment for Latino/a Youth through Formative Assessment." In *Assessing English Language Learners in Mathematics* (A Research Monograph of TODOS: Mathematics for All), edited by Richard S. Kitchen and Edward Silver, pp. 59–82. Washington, D.C.: National Education Association, 2010.

Kitchen, Richard S., Julie DePree, Sylvia Celedón-Pattichis, and Jonathan Brinkerhoff. *Mathematics Education at Highly Effective Schools That Serve the Poor: Strategies for Change.* Mahwah, N.J.: Lawrence Erlbaum, 2007.

Kitchen, Richard S., and Linda D. Wilson. "Lessons Learned from Students about Assessment and Instruction." *Teaching Children Mathematics* 10 (April 2004): 394–99.

Kulm, Gerald, Linda D. Wilson, and Richard S. Kitchen. "Alignment of Content and Effectiveness of Mathematics Assessment Items." *Educational Assessment Journal* 10 (November 2005): 333–56.

Martiniello, María. "Language and the Performance of English Language Learners in Math Word Problems." *Harvard Educational Review* 78 (Summer 2008): 333–68.

———. "Linguistic Complexity, Schematic Representations, and Differential Item Functioning for English Language Learners in Math Tests." *Educational Assessment* 14 (December 2009): 160–79.

———. "Linguistic Complexity in Mathematics Assessments and the Performance of English Language Learners." In *Assessing English Language Learners in Mathematics,* a Research Monograph of TODOS: Mathematics for All, edited by Richard S. Kitchen and Edward Silver, pp. 1–17. Washington, D.C.: National Education Association, 2010.

Moll, Luis C., and Richard Ruiz. "The Schooling of Latino Children." In *Latinos: Remaking America,* edited by Marcelo M. Suárez-Orozco and Mariela M. Páez, pp. 362–74. Berkeley, Calif.: University of California Press, 2002.

Moschkovich, Judit. "Supporting the Participation of English Language Learners in Mathematical Discussions." *For the Learning of Mathematics* 19 (March 1999a): 11–19.

———. "Understanding the Needs of Latino Students in Reform-Oriented Mathematics Classrooms". In *Changing the Faces of Mathematics: Perspectives on Latinos,* edited by Walter Secada, pp. 5–12. Reston, Va.: National Council of Teachers of Mathematics, 1999b.

———. "A Situated and Sociocultural Perspective on Bilingual Mathematics Learners." *Mathematical Thinking and Learning* 4 (2002): 189–212.

National Center for Education Statistics. *The Nation's Report Card: Mathematics 2009. National Assessment of Educational Progress at Grades 4 and 8.* NCED 2010-451. Washington, D.C.: Institute of Education Sciences, U.S. Department of Education. http://nces.ed.gov/nationsreportcard /pdf/main2009/2010451.pdf.

National Council of Teachers of Mathematics (NCTM). *Principles and Standards for School Mathematics.* Reston, Va.: NCTM, 2000.

Chapter 9

Knowledge for Teaching English Language Learners Mathematics: A Dilemma

by Mark Driscoll, Daniel Heck, and Kristen Malzahn

more4U

- Lesson Planning Guide (table)
- Lesson Implementation Guide (table)
- Lesson Reflection Template

For many teachers of mathematics, deciding how much speaking and writing to elicit from English language learners (ELLs) in the classroom is a delicate matter. After all, goes one line of thinking, these young people are struggling enough to acclimate to a new place, new culture, and new language. Why make their lives more challenging— even uncomfortable? Furthermore, goes another line of thinking, mathematics is *mathematics*, not language arts! This chapter is based on two premises:

1. If teachers accede to this hesitation and do not work to engage ELLs in active learning of mathematics in the classroom, ELLs will suffer in the short term and in the long term.

2. Teachers can engage ELLs in active participation in learning mathematics in ways that will ensure that they feel not only comfortable, but empowered and competent as well.

This chapter begins with a vignette from an actual seventh-grade mathematics classroom lesson. The lesson revolved around an area task that the teacher used to challenge the students to reason about area, extending their thinking beyond the rote use of area formulas. In a meeting with her mathematics coach before the lesson, the teacher said that she also wanted to be more effective in enabling her ELLs to be more actively engaged in speaking, writing, and drawing. When asked why she hadn't been more proactive with the English language learners in the past, she said she was reluctant to "pressure them and make them uncomfortable." The session with the mathematics coach ended with the teacher's commitment to engage the ELLs more actively.

This chapter reports research from the project Fostering Mathematics Success of English Language Learners (FMSELL), funded by the National Science Foundation under grant DRL-0821950. Opinions expressed in the chapter are those of the authors and are not necessarily the opinions of the National Science Foundation.

Vignette

A seventh-grade lesson

The teacher divided the class into small groups and gave each student a card with an irregular polygonal figure drawn on a grid. In each small group, no two students had the same figure. The task required students to come up with three different ways to calculate the area of the figure on the card and then share their thinking with others in the group. As the vignette begins, the teacher has approached a group of four students, all designated as English learners (Chinese/Mandarin), and all at "beginner" or "early intermediate" levels of English proficiency.

Teacher: OK, so what are we doing here? It looks like you have a strategy there, Ian. You're finding the area. What did you start to do here?

Ian: Count the box that was inside.

Teacher: Yeah, you counted the squares that were inside, good. Keep doing that. See what you come up with—that's a good strategy. Lin, what are you doing?

Lin: Cutting parts.

Teacher: As if you could cut that off and paste it down there. Jen, what are you up to?

Jen: Don't know [*examines the triangle shown in fig. 9.1*].

Teacher: You're not sure? What are you looking for?

Jen: Area.

Fig. 9.1. The triangle that Jen considers

Teacher: OK, how are you going to find the area?... What does "area" mean?

Jen: It's the boxes inside the...

Teacher: The squares inside the triangle, the square units, OK. Could you approximate, and guess—like, count? Or what are some other strategies we might know? Do you remember doing stuff like this before? What were some other strategies? I see... Did you draw a line here and a line here? [*Points to places on Jen's paper; see fig. 9.2.*]

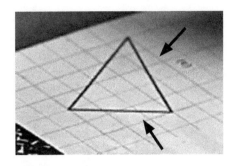

Fig. 9.2. The arrows indicate where Jen appears to have erased lines.

Teacher: Is that what I see, and you erased them? Yeah, I caught you erasing them. That was a good strategy. I think you should go back, and you should try that strategy—that's a good one. Wayne, what are you doing?

Wayne: [*Working with the polygon shown in fig. 9.3*] Cut it into a triangle so it's easier to find area.

Fig. 9.3. Wayne decomposes a polygon into triangles.

Teacher: Okay, you're cutting it into different triangles to find the area. Interesting. So, like, you're saying it's easier to find the area. So, what would be the area of this triangle? Is that easy?

Wayne: No.

Teacher: [*Examines Wayne's work, as shown in fig. 9.4*] I see here... It looks like... Are you saying that this height might be four? Is that what this dotted line was? Interesting, how did you decide that it was about four?

Fig. 9.4. The teacher examines Wayne's work; the arrow indicates the student's dotted line.

Wayne: Because I think each square has one centimeter.

Teacher: Each square has about a centimeter? And then…

Wayne: And this four square across… I think it's four centimeters.

Teacher: So you think it's four. So, one, two,… OK. And you decided that this was three? Is that from here to here? Interesting. Can I ask you something? What is this measurement right here? [*She draws a line segment, as indicated in fig. 9.5.*] From here to here.

Fig. 9.5. The teacher adds a line segment to the student's work.

[*The interaction between the teacher and the group continues for several more minutes, with the teacher giving particular attention to encouraging the students to interact with each other.*]

As brief as this lesson segment is, it still conveys the complexity of teaching mathematics when eliciting and enhancing student thinking are central goals, particularly when there are ELLs in the classroom. Reflect on your own experience as you consider the following questions that the vignette might raise:

- When students are working in small groups, what kinds of supports can maximize ELLs' access and help them engage productively in challenging mathematics activities?
- What kinds of features might you look for in mathematics tasks that enable ELLs to express their mathematical thinking and reasoning?
- In designing small-group work, what design decisions might enhance ELLs' development of academic language and create mathematical discourse opportunities for them?

These questions represent aspects of principles that guide our work with mathematics teachers of ELLs.

Three Guiding Principles

The rapid growth in the number of ELLs in schools across the continent has intensified the importance of tackling a core question: What knowledge do teachers of mathematics need to support the learning of English language learners? This question is essential for teachers of ELLs to resolve, given the persistent dearth of learning opportunities for ELLs in mathematics classrooms. In efforts to meet the challenge for ELLs, states and districts have focused on *adding to* teachers' knowledge repertoires, extending these into areas that go well beyond the teaching of mathematics (e.g., understanding policy implications and expectations, using language development frameworks, adopting cultural relevance perspectives and activities, implementing principles of effective scaffolding). Without a doubt, this extended knowledge is necessary, but we believe that it is equally necessary for mathematics teachers to be able to see and make sense of ELLs' needs through the lens of the knowledge that they already have as teachers of mathematics. In other words, instructional resources to support ELLs' learning may be embedded in the tenets of effective mathematics teaching and simply need to be tapped.

In our professional development work with mathematics coaches and teachers in New York City and at various sites in California and Massachusetts over the past few years, we have incorporated three key principles of effective instruction, which we believe are important to securing equal opportunities for ELLs to learn mathematics:

1. **Challenging Mathematical Tasks Principle.** It is both possible and important to engage ELLs at *all* levels of language proficiency in mathematical work that challenges them on a regular basis to reason mathematically and solve problems. *For example, teachers may question students to extend their thinking and to promote sense making and reasoning. They may prompt students who are working in pairs to engage with each other in making convincing mathematical explanations.* Our use of "challenging mathematical tasks" refers to tasks that are comparable to the "high cognitive demand tasks" described by the QUASAR Project (Silver and Stein 1996)—that is, tasks that take students beyond only memorizing and using procedures without recognizing connections to doing mathematics or using

procedures with an awareness of connections to their underlying mathematical meaning.

2. **Multimodal Representation Principle.** Classroom environments that make ample use of multiple modes—pictures, diagrams, presentations, written explanations, and gestures—afford ELLs the means first to understand the mathematics with which they are engaged, and second to express the thinking behind their reasoning and problem solving. *For example, teachers can help students learn to diagram mathematically and encourage them to use diagrams in solving problems.*

3. **Academic Language Principle.** In the mathematics classroom, ELLs can learn to express their mathematical thinking and reasoning in precise academic English; they can learn to engage productively in mathematical discourse with other students. *For example, teachers can explicitly model the use of academic language, clear mathematical explanations, and sentence structures used to express mathematical reasoning (such as "if… then….").* When we say "academic language," we refer to language that falls into two categories: (1) technical, discipline-specific words and phrases used in content-area texts, including, in the area of mathematics, *hypotenuse, prime number,* and *if and only if,* and (2) all-purpose academic words, used across content areas, such as *procedure, analyze,* and *structure.* In both categories, students build on their own everyday language, with the teacher's help, to extend their proficiency.

In addition to our professional development work with mathematics coaches and teachers, these three principles are guiding our NSF-funded research project, Fostering Mathematics Success of English Language Learners (FMSELL). The FMSELL project is a study investigating the use of the Fostering Geometric Thinking Toolkit with mathematics teachers of ELLs and its impacts on mathematics teaching and learning. These principles appear to resonate with mathematics educators who are invested in helping ELLs and who recognize that mathematical exercises relying mostly on the recall and implementation of formulas and procedures do not require much reasoning. These educators understand that such exercises do not demand much of solvers when they attempt to describe their thinking—and that a steady diet of such exercises robs ELLs of opportunities to learn mathematics.

Challenging mathematical tasks, on the other hand, require solvers to engage in mathematical reasoning and problem solving, but conveying that thinking to others can often be difficult. That is where academic language and multimodal representation enter the picture. Clear communication about reasoning and problem solving relies on academic language for the precision required in mathematics. In addition, precise language shapes thinking. Academic language is something that many students struggle with, especially ELLs. Multimodal representation of ideas can provide support to students as they work toward using academic language in the context of challenging mathematical tasks.

The vignette at the beginning of this chapter involved a small group of students. However, the three principles apply as well to teaching whole classes; furthermore, they apply broadly in pedagogical decisions affecting *all* students, not just ELLs. That said, we emphasize that they have major relevance in the teaching of ELLs. For example, in conjunction with the challenging mathematical tasks and multimodal representation principles, research unequivocally supports a recommendation to *teach all students to use diagrams to represent and solve problems* (Hurley and Novick 2006; Jitendra et al. 2009; Mayer et al. 1999; Ng and Lee 2009). Although this research is not concentrated on ELLs, it suggests the value of using multimodal representation to support ELLs in becoming proficient in mathematical problem solving. As the article by Ng and Lee suggests, the mathematical diagram, chosen carefully, can serve as an intermediate step between the textual and symbolic phases of solving a word problem, revealing to the solver the *mathematical structure* of the problem. For ELLs, this intermediate step can also serve as a supplementary tool for engaging with the text of the problem. Once that door of access and understanding is open, students can further develop academic language—the third principle—and use it to engage in meaningful mathematical discourse.

For all the excitement greeting the Common Core State Standards (CCSSI 2010)—particularly the Standards for Mathematical Practice—it will be challenging to ensure that ELLs have easy access to the mathematical processes recommended in the practice standards, since meeting these standards obliges mathematics teachers to find ways to help ELLs make sense of problems, construct viable arguments and critique the reasoning of others, use appropriate tools strategically, and so on. Our three principles offer a way for mathematics teachers of ELLs to provide access and to be strategic at all levels of student need.

The range of challenges across classrooms with ELLs is remarkable in its complexity. The teacher who has four ELL newcomers to the United States in her class, each speaking a different language, has very different challenges from the teacher who has twenty ELLs in his class, all of whom speak Spanish, and who span various levels of English proficiency. We maintain that the three principles are germane to both teachers, though the application is likely to differ in the two situations. They can guide lesson planning, implementation, and reflection for the full range of classrooms containing English language learners. And the relevance of the principles rests on ample evidence in the research literature.

Relevance of the Three Principles

Since 1980, the number of U.S. children living in households where the native language is not English has more than doubled, from 9 percent to 19 percent (Firestone, Martinez, and Polovsky 2006). The total number of students labeled as ELL is about 10 percent of the student population, or 4.7 million (U.S. Department of Education 2010). On the mathematics part of the 2009 NAEP, 72 percent of eighth-grade ELLs scored below "basic," compared to 26 percent of non-ELLs—a huge gap (NCES 2009). Data from state-level testing are equally troubling. For example, in Massachusetts, 40 percent of eighth graders overall score at "proficient and above" in the state mathematics assessment; only 13 percent of ELL eighth graders score at that level (Rennie Center 2007). In such assessment settings, validity of interpretation is an issue for ELLs (Abedi 2004; Martiniello 2008; Solano-Flores and Trumbull 2003). For example, ELLs who perform poorly are at heightened risk of being diagnosed inappropriately as learning disabled (August et al. 2005).

The crisis for English language learners in mathematics is likely to be linked to the lack of opportunities to learn and show competency in classroom interactions, since "ethnic minority students have less exposure to content and their instruction tends to cover less content relative to non-minority students" (Herman and Abedi 2004, p. 5;

Masini 2001). Because of current testing demands, many schools are tempted to address ELLs' needs by separating language work from mathematics work, with "short-term, expedient coping strategies" (Firestone, Martinez, and Polovsky 2006, p. 54). Often, this failure to integrate language and content development results in a lack of active engagement by ELLs in the mathematical work being done in their classrooms (Brenner 1998). Particularly important in middle grades and higher are opportunities to learn and practice mathematical reasoning and problem-solving skills. The literature underscores the importance of teachers providing regular opportunities for mathematical work that is cognitively challenging—for all students, but especially for ELLs (Henningsen and Stein 1997; Silver and Stein 1996).

Opportunities for ELLs to learn mathematics seem tightly linked to integrating language and content during lessons (August et al. 2005; Brenner 1998; Calderon 2007; Garrison, Amaral, and Ponce 2006; Lager 2006; Lyster 2007; Secada and De La Cruz 1996; Snow 2007; Snow, Lawrence, and White 2009; Thornburg and Karp 1992). Sustained academic vocabulary work with ELLs, *in the context of mathematical work*, is essential—to develop understanding of words referring to thinking and communicating (e.g., *analysis, deny*); words common across subjects, but with different meanings depending on subject (e.g., *base, element*); and words that have common meanings that differ from discipline-specific meanings (e.g., *prove, property*). Also, ELLs need to participate regularly, both orally and in writing, by "explaining solution processes, describing conjectures, proving conclusions and presenting arguments" (Moschkovich 1999, p. 11). Mathematics has its own register—that is, its own ways of employing language to construct and communicate knowledge. Features of the mathematics register include technical vocabulary (e.g., *hypotenuse*), dense noun phrases (for example, from Schleppegrell [2007, p. 143], "the volume of a rectangular prism with sides 8, 10, and 12 cm"), precision in definition, and particular norms for convincing argument (e.g., frequent use of "'if... then...'" sentences).

Thus, for ELLs, opportunities to learn mathematics require their *active classroom participation*—through engagement with cognitively demanding tasks and frequent use of academic language. Linguists and cognitive specialists recognize that language enables students to bring order and meaning to their classroom experiences and should be practiced by second-language students "not only as a communicative tool but also as a cognitive tool for interacting with the teacher, with one another, and with content knowledge itself" (Lyster 2007, p. 22). As evidenced in the literature, a third feature fits with, and even bridges, language-content integration and opportunities for cognitively challenging work for ELLs—namely, the creation of learning environments that use multimodal mathematical representation to reinforce the learning of mathematical concepts, processes, language, and norms of mathematical communication (Chval and Khisty 2001; Goldenberg 1991; Goldin-Meadow 2000; Khisty and Chval 2002; Moschkovich 2002). Teachers' use of multimodal representation seems essential in helping ELLs learn mathematical reasoning and problem-solving skills as well as the academic language to express their reasoning.

Looking for Evidence of the Three Principles

We believe the three principles can and should guide the full cycle of instruction involving ELLs, from *lesson planning* to *lesson implementation* to *post-lesson reflection*. To demonstrate concretely, we will use the vignette of the lesson segment captured from video and portrayed at the start of this chapter.

Lesson planning

With help from her mathematics coach, the teacher crafted a lesson plan, the first part of which is shown in figure 9.6.

Mathematical goals:	Students will develop several strategies for reasoning about and calculating area for irregular polygons on a grid.
Language goals:	Students will appropriately use mathematical vocabulary, both written and verbally, such as *vertex, vertices, area, base, height, reflection, coordinates, isosceles, scalene, acute, obtuse, right triangles, square units*. Students will explain their strategies for calculating area so that other students can understand.
Small-group activity:	Each student at a table will get a different polygon on a grid.

Students will: *Describe at least three different ways to find the area of their polygon.*

Next, students will work with a partner to compare strategies and polygons and determine if their strategies work for their partner's polygon. *Will your strategies work for your partner's polygon?* |

Fig. 9.6. A portion of the teacher's lesson plan

Two features of the lesson plan are worth noting in light of the three guiding principles. First, the teacher chose to engage students in *geometric reasoning and problem solving*, and second, she planned the lesson in ways that ensured the prominence of *language goals*.

We believe that the first feature—the teacher's decision to engage the students in geometric reasoning and problem solving—is noteworthy in two respects: (1) such efforts are not widespread in middle-grades instruction, and their scarcity is reflected in the weak performance of U.S. students in international comparisons; and (2) in our experience, geometry opens doors of opportunity for ELLs to demonstrate their thinking through drawing, gesturing, verbal description, and written or symbolic representation.

Just as important, the multimodal representation offers rich data for teachers to use in formative assessment.

The second notable feature of the lesson plan is the teacher's construction of it in ways that ensure that language goals will be prominent. Particularly in classes where ELLs constitute a relatively small percentage of students, language can easily lose its importance in lesson planning—and therefore in lesson implementation.

The first principle—challenging mathematical tasks—guided the lesson plan in that the teacher wanted students to engage in a problem-solving activity and to display multiple strategies. The second principle—multimodal representation—also guided the lesson not only in the choice of geometry as content, but also in the teacher's decision to have each student work with a single shape and apply multiple drawings and gestures to calculating the area.

Finally, there is evidence that the third principle—academic language—guided the lesson plan. The teacher not only anticipated words that she wanted to highlight but also structured the small-group work so that each student in a group had a unique shape and so was obliged to explain how he or she thought about and calculated the area of that shape.

Lesson implementation

The vignette provides a useful lens on possibilities for using the three principles to guide instruction of ELLs. In fairness to the teacher and students, it is important to recall that (a) the vignette represents a brief section of the opening part of the lesson; and (b) in any case, the vignette is not offered as an exemplar, but rather as a context in which the influence of the three principles on the teacher's decisions can be identified. Nonetheless, we maintain that features of the teacher's actions are consistent with chapter 2's recommendations on ways that teachers can support ELLs to become active participants in mathematics discourse communities.

The first principle appears to influence the teacher's decision to let the ELLs engage in the task on their own, as well as her decision to persist in eliciting and advancing student thinking by asking such questions as, "What are you looking for?" and "So what would be the area of this triangle?" The teacher's effort to elicit thinking continued when she switched into assessment mode, trying to elicit prior knowledge and possible misunderstandings by asking such questions as, "What is area?" and "How did you decide it was about four?"

The influence of the second principle appears evident in the teacher's use of the diagrams to engage the students in thought and discourse. Also, she gestured toward the dotted segment, and then drew her own segment on the student's picture, to help him check his conclusion that the height was 4 units.

Furthermore, the teacher realized that another student's (Jen's) diagram showed signs that she had tried the strategy of embedding her triangle in a rectangle—something the teacher pointed out and encouraged her to pursue further. Several minutes after the portion of the lesson captured in the vignette, the teacher returned to the student to see how her drawing and thinking had progressed. She found more pictorial evidence of thinking (see fig. 9.7), which led to further efforts to help the student describe verbally what the picture represented.

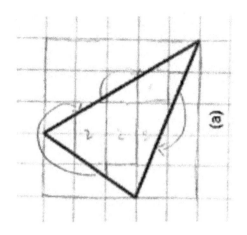

Fig. 9.7. Jen's embedding of the triangle in a rectangle

The influence of the third principle—academic language—appears to show in the two times when the teacher *rephrased* "boxes" as "squares" and "square units." This instructional strategy is particularly valuable when ELLs are involved in high-demand cognitive work, as in this case. (Alternatively, when their thinking is more procedure- or memory-based, the teacher may choose not to rephrase but instead to ask the student to recall the more precise mathematical term.) The teacher *modeled* academic language in, for example, her use of such words as *strategy* and *approximate*. And she also modeled an important mathematical self-monitoring question when she asked Jen, "What are you looking for?"

Lesson reflection

In the post-lesson debrief, the teacher revisited the small-group interactions with her mathematics coach:

Teacher: Both Jen and Ian were so… well, shy, but also, Ian… I was trying to encourage him with one of his strategies and telling him it was good, and then when I looked over again after talking to the other two boys, he had erased the whole thing.

Coach: Mmm-hmm.

Teacher: And then Jen, too… I could tell that she tried too—she does well in math, I know she has ability, but she had drawn the rectangle around her original figure and then erased it.

Coach: [*Checking her observation notes*] So, you came over to that group initially when you were working on this, and said, "What are we doing here? Lin, what are you doing?" And Lin said something; I didn't hear it. You said, "Jen, what are you up to?" I don't think she said anything, and then you said, "What are you looking for?" because she was doing something on her paper. And she said, "Area," to you. And you said, "How are you going to find area?" And you said, "Well, what does 'area' mean?" And she said, "The boxes inside the triangle."

Teacher: She had some understanding. Right.

Coach: She was talking with you. So you said, you know, she was counting them, and you said, "Can you approximate the count?" And then you noticed that she had drawn something around, and you said, "Did you draw that square around? That was a good strategy; you should go back to it." And then you kind of left her alone, and she continued to work. But you asked her, like, five questions, you kept pushing. And last time you were here, you regretted not asking any questions of ELLs—

Teacher: I know, but she looked like she was going to cry. I felt like I was torturing her… And I don't know, if she was with other people, I don't think she would have talked any more.

Coach: Right, so it's this balance of… It's trying to create a comfortable environment in which kids will speak. Because they're not speaking in here.

Teacher: They're not.

Coach: They're not using these words ever.

Teacher: I know.

Coach: They're not using the math language outside of these seventy minutes. If she doesn't speak, if she doesn't say these words when she's with you, or when she's in this room, she's not saying them.

Teacher: Right, right. I secretly think she has them. Do you know what I mean? I don't think Ian has them, and I don't think Lin has them, but I think that Jen has more of it. That in different circumstances, or if she could express it in a different way, different time, or in writing, do you know what I mean? I might be wrong, but in her writing, she's able to put more words, academic language, on paper than Lin or Ian can.

Coach: So, there's a couple things. One is, can—does she understand the words? And can she communicate them? So maybe she's more comfortable writing them than speaking them. The one issue is, does she understand it? Does she understand the math, and does she have the language to support it in writing? And then there's this other issue—there's this other capacity that she needs to develop, is to be able to speak it.

In this interaction, we see an appreciation that the ELLs were doing challenging mathematical work, and a recognition that no small part of the challenge that they felt was to communicate the strategies guiding their work. The interaction also reveals a commitment on the part of the mathematics coach and the teacher to move away from the option of protecting the feelings of ELLs by doing nothing and to look for other options to minimize discomfort while enhancing their mathematical work and communication—for example, in this case, by using writing as a prelude to speaking. Allowing ELLs to be quiet and invisible often results in their being disengaged, and that should not happen. They can do challenging mathematical work, use multiple modes to represent their thinking, and develop the academic language to communicate their thinking precisely.

Putting the Principles into Action

The first way to make the three principles relevant in teacher practice is to use them explicitly in lesson planning. The teacher in the vignette was part of a project in which the teachers and mathematics coaches did just that, with a sequence of planning questions with the principles acting as threads running through them. Figure 9.8 shows a table with the kinds of questions that were part of this teacher's planning. Note how at each stage of the lesson—opening, core, and summary—the questions relate to all three principles. The point is not to answer every question for every lesson—that would be an onerous task. Teachers should ask each question fairly regularly, however, and they can use the list as an occasional tool to reflect on practice globally—taking note, for example, of any questions that they *never* ask, and why.

LESSON OPENING	*How will I assess and activate students' prior knowledge and prepare them to engage in the task(s) of the lesson without lowering the demand?* *How will I introduce the mathematical ideas and challenges in the lesson without lowering the demand?* *What will I hear (language) or see (gestures, drawings, etc.) that will indicate students understand the task(s)?* *Will students work on the task(s) individually or in pairs/small groups? Will students be partnered in a specific way? If so, in what way?* *What resources and tools will be available for students to use?* *How will students record and report their work?*
LESSON CORE	*What will I do if a student does not know how to begin to solve the task(s)? How will I support students without lowering the demand?* *What questions will I ask to uncover, assess, focus, and advance students' understanding of key mathematical ideas and academic language?* *What opportunities are here for students to use mathematical diagrams, physical models, or technology? What kind of diagrams?* *What will I hear or see that tells me students are thinking about key math ideas?* *What academic language will I listen for students to use?* *What academic language will I model? How/when will I model it?*
LESSON SUMMARY	*What mathematical and language understandings do I want students to take away from this lesson?* *What mathematical ideas do I want shared and discussed? How will they be shared and discussed? What order of sharing will promote connections and develop students' understanding?* *How will I know if they "got it"? What will I see or hear in student discussions of the mathematics or in their work that indicates they understand the mathematical ideas?*

Fig. 9.8. Lesson planning guide: planning questions with the three principles running through them as guiding threads

In the lesson implementation stage, particular teacher actions are representative of each of the three principles, as detailed in the table shown in figure 9.9. Our FMSELL project uses a classroom observation protocol based on this table for research. The protocol calls on observers to note examples of these kinds of teacher actions from the lesson (this table of teacher actions is also available at www.nctm.org/more4u).

Guiding Principles	Teacher Actions
Challenging Mathematical Tasks	• Scaffolding tasks to maintain a high level of cognitive demand while building on students' prior knowledge • Questioning students to extend their thinking and promote sense making • Modeling convincing mathematical arguments, clear explanations, a variety of solution strategies, and the process of making conjectures and generalizations • Prompting students to ask questions, consider different solutions, conjecture, and generalize • Encouraging students to share their solutions by using justifications, convincing mathematical arguments, and clear explanations • Other
Multimodal Representation	• Highlighting the variety of ways (e.g., diagrams, drawings, gestures, technology, concrete objects, mathematical symbols) that mathematical ideas are communicated during lessons • Helping students learn to diagram mathematically and encouraging them to use diagrams • Providing specific tools that allow students opportunities to communicate mathematical ideas in multiple ways • Prompting students to represent a concept or solution by using one or more modes in addition to language—gestures, writing or drawing, technology, concrete objects, mathematical symbols • Making explicit connections between different ways that mathematical ideas are represented or communicated (e.g., verbal descriptions, gestures, writing or drawings, technology, concrete objects, mathematical symbols) • Other
Academic Language	• Modeling mathematical language and clear explanations • Highlighting and clarifying relevant terms that come up in the lesson • Prompting students to use mathematically accurate language • Providing students ample opportunity to communicate (e.g., read, write, speak) about mathematics • Grouping students to promote mathematical discussions (e.g., pairing ELLs with non-ELLs, including peers who can communicate in ELLs' primary language) • Connecting mathematical symbols to mathematical language • Rephrasing a student's everyday language with proper mathematical language • Requesting student clarification of statements • Other

Fig. 9.9. Lesson implementation guide: teacher actions that support the three principles

Finally, it is important for the teacher—perhaps with the help of a mathematics coach—to reflect back on the lesson just taught, giving particular attention to the three principles, and giving special attention to their roles in ELLs' engagement with the mathematical tasks. Guiding the reflection process should be *evidence* of student mathematical thinking, such as written student work, and evidence of the use (or lack of use) of academic language. Figure 9.10 shows some of the elements of students' work that teachers might consider in relation to each of the three principles.

Goal(s) of the lesson:
How do I know if the students "got it"? What did I see or hear in student discussions of the mathematics or in their work that indicated that they understood the mathematical ideas?

Challenging Mathematical Tasks: Student Actions	Multimodal Representation: Student Actions	Academic Language: Student Actions
• Thinking about or reflecting on the meaning of the mathematics content • Making conjectures, generating generalizations, and comparing alternative solutions • Providing a variety of mathematical solutions and explanations (e.g., counter-examples, non-examples) • Providing explanations of other students' thinking, including reasons why solutions are correct or incorrect • Other	• Using multiple representations (e.g., diagramming, drawings, gestures, technology, concrete objects, mathematical symbols) to support their mathematical thinking • Translating visual representations into verbal descriptions • Discussing the relationships among different representations • Other	• Communicating (e.g., reading, writing, speaking) about mathematics • Stating mathematical language in their own words, using everyday or primary language • Using mathematically accurate language • Engaging in student-to-student or student-to-teacher mathematical discussions • Other

Upon reflection, what aspects of the lesson seemed to support students' learning of the mathematics and academic language? In what ways?

Upon reflection, what aspects of the lesson did not support students' learning of the mathematics and academic language? Why? What design decisions or implementation moves can I make differently next time?

Fig. 9.10. Lesson reflection template: looking for *evidence* of students' mathematical thinking, in relation to the three principles

Conclusion

"Challenging mathematical tasks, multimodal representation, and academic language? That's just good instruction!" We have heard this reaction more than once when presenting our framework comprising the three principles. We agree with this opinion—up to a point. Without a doubt, the principles do represent features of mathematics pedagogy that should inform all lessons and include all students. And without a doubt, the principles speak only to part of effective mathematics pedagogy for ELLs. However, a broad and depressing amount of evidence indicates that ELLs do not generally share in the bounty offered by these three pedagogical principles. Too often, they sit quietly in class with little opportunity to engage (Brenner 1998; Herman and Abedi 2004).

The vignette presented earlier illustrated, in brief, a teacher's efforts to counter the common phenomenon of disengaged ELLs and to support their active engagement. Drawing from her experience, we then listed three questions for readers to reflect on, which foreshadowed the three principles:

1. When students are working in small groups, what kinds of supports can maximize ELLs' access and help them engage productively in challenging mathematics activities?

2. What kinds of features might you look for in mathematics tasks that enable ELLs to express their mathematical thinking and reasoning?

3. In designing small-group work, what design decisions might enhance ELLs' development of academic language and create mathematical discourse opportunities for them?

There are, of course, no absolute, surefire answers to these questions. That said, let's consider how the teacher's planning and actions in the vignette offer one set of answers to the questions and then consider other options.

Consider the teacher's planning of the lesson in relation to the first question. After viewing the video of this lesson clip, teachers and mathematics coaches have mentioned to us that they valued the teacher's structuring of the small-group task. This is, they appreciated the fact that she gave students time to work individually (in this case, a consequence of each student in a group having a unique polygon to work on), and then expected them, after some time, to relate their strategies to others in the group—thus creating an opportunity for productive mathematical discourse. Furthermore, the teacher led students to consider generalizing through the simply worded prompt, "Will your strategies work for your partner's polygon?" In her own post-lesson reflection, the teacher conjectured that the ELLs might benefit from a prompt that had them *write* about their strategies, before explaining them out loud.

In response to the second question, the teacher chose a mathematical context—calculating area of polygons on a grid—that clearly invited geometric drawings, gestures, and visual indicators, such as arrows. As a consequence, the students' work made numerous pieces of evidence of their thinking available to the teacher *before* the students were expected to verbalize their strategies. Clearly, one helpful feature of a task is the extent to which it invites the student to use multiple modes of representation of thinking. Similarly, one might seek tasks for which all students in the class have the capacity to use mathematical diagrams in solving. For example, a teacher might choose a word problem such as the following as a task for a lesson:

Rosa traveled 200 miles in 4 hours. How long did it take her to travel 150 miles?

It is one thing to relegate students (including ELLs) to translating the words into computational symbols. It is another to be able to remind them to use diagrams that they know how to use, such as that shown in figure 9.11.

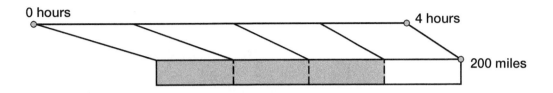

Fig. 9.11. Translating a word problem into a diagram

Finally, in response to the third question, the teacher's lesson plan prepared her to emphasize important words and terms, like *area, square units, base,* and *height.* She also was deliberate about using academic words such as *strategy* and *approximate.* The lesson design also called for students to share strategies in pairs, a technique that maximizes the chances that all ELLs will be actively engaged in mathematical explanation. Another device that the teacher used on other occasions was student-completed sentence frames that reflect mathematically powerful language. For example, "When I dilated the triangle with a 2-dilation, _____ changed and _____ stayed the same." The teacher chose the sentence frames to represent key elements of productive mathematical discourse.

In her own reflections, the teacher assessed her efforts as far from perfect, yet we would argue that she did take steps that all mathematics teachers of ELLs should be taking: providing ELLs with challenging mathematical tasks on a regular basis, increasing the accessibility of the challenging tasks by creating an environment rich in multimodal representation, and integrating academic language development into ELLs' mathematical work. Having them *produce* in mathematics lessons is the key to making them productive mathematics learners and participants in mathematical discourse communities.

References

Abedi, Jamal. "The No Child Left Behind Act and English Language Learners: Assessment and Accountability Issues." *Educational Researcher* 33 (January 2004): 4–14.

August, Diane, Maria Carlo, Cheryl Dressler, and Catherine Snow. "The Critical Role of Vocabulary Development for English Language Learners." *Learning Disabilities Research & Practice* 20 (February 2005): 50–57.

Brenner, Mary E. "Development of Mathematical Communication in Problem Solving Groups by Language Minority Students." *Bilingual Research Journal* 22 (Spring/Fall 1998): 103–28.

Calderon, Margarita. *Teaching Reading to English Language Learners, Grades 6–12: A Framework for Improving Achievement in the Content Areas.* Thousand Oaks, Calif.: Corwin, 2007.

Chval, Kathryn B., and Lena L. Khisty. "Bilingual Latino Students, Writing and Mathematics: A Case Study of Successful Teaching and Learning." In *Multilingualism in Mathematics Classrooms: Global Perspectives,* edited by Richard Barwell, pp. 128–44. Clevedon, UK: Multilingual Matters, 2009.

Common Core State Standards Initiative (CCSSI). *Common Core State Standards for Mathematics. Common Core State Standards (College- and Career-Readiness Standards and K–12 Standards in English Language Arts and Math).* Washington, D.C.: National Governors Association Center for Best Practices and the Council of Chief State School Officers, 2010. http://www.corestandards.org.

Firestone, William A., M. Cecilia Martinez, and Terri Polovsky. "Teaching Mathematics and Science to English Language Learners: The Experience of Four New Jersey Elementary Schools." *New Jersey Math Science Partnership* (2006). http://hub.mspnet.org/index.cfm/13070.

Garrison, Leslie, Olga Amaral, and Gregorio Ponce. "UnLATCHing Mathematics Instruction for English Learners." *Journal of Mathematics Education Leadership* 9, no. 1 (2006): 14–24.

Goldenberg, Claude. *Instructional Conversations and Their Classroom Application.* Educational Practice Report 2. Washington, D.C.: Center for Applied Linguistics, 1991. http://repositories.cdlib.org/crede/ncrcdslleducational/EPR02.

Goldin-Meadow, Susan. "Beyond Words: The Importance of Gesture to Researchers and Learners." *Child Development* 71 (January/February 2000): 231–39.

Henningsen, Marjorie, and Mary K. Stein. "Mathematical Tasks and Student Cognition: Classroom-Based Factors That Support and Inhibit High-Level Mathematical Thinking and Reasoning." *Journal for Research in Mathematics Education* 28 (November 1997): 524–49.

Herman, Joan L., and Jamal Abedi. *Issues in Assessing English Language Learners' Opportunity to Learn Mathematics.* Center for the Study of Evaluation Report No. 633. Los Angeles: University of California at Los Angeles, 2004.

Hurley, Sean M., and Laura R. Novick. "Context and Structure: The Nature of Students' Knowledge about Three Spatial Diagram Representations." *Thinking & Reasoning* 12, no. 3 (2006): 281–308.

Jitendra, Asha K., Jon R. Star, Kristin Starosta, Jayne M. Leh, Sheetal Sood, Grace Caskie, Cheyenne L. Hughes, and Toshi R. Mack. "Improving Seventh Grade Students' Learning of Ratio and Proportion: The Role of Schema-Based Instruction." *Contemporary Educational Psychology* 34 (July 2009): 250–64.

Khisty, Lena L., and Kathryn Chval. "Pedagogic Discourse and Equity in Mathematics: When Teachers' Talk Matters." *Mathematics Education Research Journal* 14 (December 2002): 154–68.

Lager, Carl. "Types of Mathematics-Language Reading Interactions That Unnecessarily Hinder Algebra Learning and Assessment." *Reading Psychology* 27 (April/June 2006): 165–204.

Lyster, Roy. *Learning and Teaching Languages through Content: A Counterbalanced Approach.* Amsterdam: John Benjamins, 2007.

Martiniello, María. "Language and the Performance of English-Language Learners in Math Word Problems." *Harvard Educational Review* 78 (Summer 2008): 333–68.

Masini, Blase E. "Race Differences in Exposure to Algebra and Geometry among U.S. Eighth-Grade Students." Paper presented at the annual meeting of the American Educational Research Association, Seattle, Wash., April 2001.

Mayer, Richard E., Roxanna Moreno, Michelle Boire, and Shannon Vagge. "Maximizing Constructivist Learning from Multimedia Communications by Minimizing Cognitive Load." *Journal of Educational Psychology* 91, no 4 (1999): 638–43.

Moschkovich, Judit. "Supporting the Participation of English Language Learners in Mathematical Discussions." *For the Learning of Mathematics* 19 (March 1999): 11–19.

————. "A Situated and Sociocultural Perspective on Bilingual Mathematics Learners." *Mathematical Thinking and Learning* 4, nos. 2 and 3 (2002): 189–212.

National Center for Education Statistics (NCES). *The Nation's Report Card: Mathematics 2009.* NCES 2010-451. Washington, D.C.: U.S. Department of Education, 2009.

Ng, Swee Fong, and Kerry Lee. "The Model Method: Singapore Children's Tool for Representing and Solving Algebraic Word Problems." *Journal for Research in Mathematics Education* 40 (May 2009): 282–313.

Rennie Center for Education Research and Policy (Rennie Center). *Seeking Effective Policies and Practices for English Language Learners.* Cambridge, Mass.: Rennie Center, 2007.

Schleppegrell, Mary J. "The Linguistic Challenges of Mathematics Teaching and Learning: A Research Review." *Reading & Writing Quarterly* 23 (April 2007): 139–59.

Secada, Walter G., and Yolanda De La Cruz. "Teaching Mathematics for Understanding to Bilingual Students." In *Children of la Frontera: Binational Efforts to Serve Mexican Migrant and Immigrant Students*, edited by Judith LeBlanc Flores, pp. 285–308. Charleston, W.Va.: ERIC Clearinghouse on Rural Education and Small Schools, 1996. ERIC Document Reproduction Service No. ED393646.

Silver, Edward A., and Mary K. Stein. "The QUASAR Project: The 'Revolution of the Possible' in Mathematics Instructional Reform in Urban Middle Schools." *Urban Education* 30 (January 1996): 476–522.

Snow, Catherine. "Learning All-Purpose Academic Words." Webinar, September 6, 2007.

Snow, Catherine, Joshua Lawrence, and Claire White. "Generating Knowledge of Academic Language among Urban Middle School Students." *Journal of Research on Educational Effectiveness* 2, no. 4 (2009): 325–44.

Solano-Flores, Guillermo, and Elise Trumbull. "Examining Language in Context: The Need for New Research and Practice Paradigms in the Testing of English-Language Learners." *Educational Researcher* 32 (March 2003): 3–13.

Thornburg, Devin G., and Karen S. Karp. "Lessons Learned: Mathematics + Science + Higher-Order Thinking × Second-Language Learning = ?" *Journal of Educational Issues with Language Minority Students* 10 (1992): 159–84.

U.S. Department of Education. *Title III Accountability: Behind the Numbers, Evaluation Brief: The English Language Acquisition, Language Enhancement, and Academic Achievement Act.* Washington, D.C.: U.S. Department of Education, Office of Planning Evaluation, and Policy Development, Policy and Program Studies Service, 2010.

Chapter 10

What's Language Got to Do with It? Identifying Language Demands in Mathematics Instruction for English Language Learners

by Julia M. Aguirre and George C. Bunch

more4U

- Language Demand in Mathematics Lessons (LDML) Tool (matrix)
- Completed LDML Tool (completed sample matrix)

Contrary to popular belief, mathematics is not "language free." Although numbers and symbols play a central role in mathematics teaching and learning, students must also use language to engage in mathematics lessons. Most K–12 mathematics education standards in the United States now emphasize cognitively demanding tasks, problem solving, and "math talk," increasing the language demands facing students and calling for an explicit focus on communication and representation (CCSSI 2010; NCTM 2000; Parrish 2010; Stein et al. 2000; Thompson and Chappell 2007). Although language plays a significant role for all students who are learning mathematics, students whose mathematics instruction occurs in a language other than that spoken at home face particular challenges. In the United States, where the language of instruction is overwhelmingly English, these students include those who have immigrated with their families, the children of immigrants, indigenous North Americans (e.g., First Nations, Yup'ik Eskimo, Native Hawaiians), and students from U.S. territories (e.g., Puerto Rico, Samoa, Guam) where languages other than English are common but where students study in English-medium classrooms, either in these territories or on moving to the mainland United States. English language learners (ELLs), those who were never designated as ELLs, and those who are reclassified as proficient in English at some point during their schooling may all be in need of support to have access to mainstream mathematics instruction in English. We use the term *ELL* with the understanding that the approaches that we advocate may be appropriate for this broader group of students as well.

Language plays a powerful and complex role in classroom learning and teaching. Many practicing and preservice teachers have had neither linguistics training nor professional development opportunities aimed at teaching mathematics to ELLs. We have found that a productive first step toward understanding what language has to do with

This chapter is based on work supported by the National Science Foundation, award number ESI-0424983—Center for the Mathematics Education of Latinos/as (CEMELA). Any opinions, findings, and conclusions or recommendations expressed in this chapter are those of the authors and do not necessarily reflect the views of the National Science Foundation. We would like to thank the editors for their helpful comments.

mathematics instruction is to ask teachers to begin thinking about the classroom language demands facing ELLs—and for that matter, all students—in terms of five specific language modalities: *reading, listening, speaking, writing,* and *representing.* Such an analysis by teachers can complement other efforts to help teachers understand the important roles of language in mathematics instruction and support their students' use and development of a wide range of mathematical discourse (Moschkovich 2007, 2010).

In this chapter, we discuss in more detail the five modalities related to language demands in mathematics lessons. Then we introduce the Language Demand in Mathematics Lessons (LDML) tool to help teachers identify specific language demands of their mathematics lessons. The LDML tool has a dual purpose, for planning and analyzing mathematics instruction. Next, we invite the reader to practice using the LDML tool by watching a public-access video clip of an upper elementary mathematics lesson on data analysis. We then provide our own reflections on the language demands present in the mathematics lesson as one example of how the LDML tool can be used. The chapter concludes with some ideas on how teachers might use the information about language demands as a first step toward providing specific instructional supports for ELLs in mathematics instruction and work with the tool in future mathematics instruction venues, including collaborative lesson planning and professional development.

Identifying Mathematics Language Demands

Because of the traditional emphasis in mathematics on numbers and symbols, it is tempting to think of it as a domain with limited language demands and therefore easily accessible to children who might be learning the content in a second language. However, research has demonstrated that learning and teaching mathematics are linguistically complex, with multiple language modalities in play beyond equations and recall of specialized vocabulary (Moschkovich 2000, 2002, 2007, 2010; Gutiérrez, Sengupta-Irving, and Dieckmann 2010; Khisty 2010; Schleppegrell 2010).

Figure 10.1 shows the five main language modalities of mathematics (reading, writing, listening, speaking, and representing). It is important to understand that students do not use or develop language in any modality in isolation. The figure is designed to introduce the modalities and illustrate their relationship with one another to help teachers begin to understand the multitude of ways in which language is used in their classrooms.

Representing is positioned in the center of figure 10.1 because of its centrality in mathematics teaching and learning (Goldin 2003). There is a fundamental link between how mathematical ideas are represented and how one makes meaning of and uses those mathematical ideas (CCSSI 2010; NCTM 2000). According to *Principles and Standards for School Mathematics* (NCTM 2000), the term *representation* has multiple meanings that are important in mathematics teaching and learning:

> The term *representation* refers both to process and to product—in other words, to the act of capturing a mathematical concept or relationship in some form and to the form itself.... Moreover, the term applies to processes and products that are observable externally as well as "internally" in the minds of people doing mathematics. All these meanings of representations are important to consider in school mathematics. (p. 67)

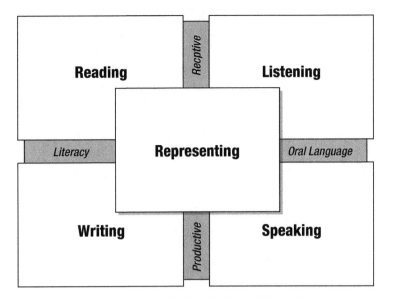

Fig. 10.1. Language demands in mathematics lessons

Thus, children must create, understand, and use representations to make sense of and communicate about mathematical ideas. To communicate about representations, the other modalities are often required. Representing is linked to specific oral and written mathematical conventions, such as argumentation, justification, and proof. It can mediate how an idea is heard (listening) as well as affect what is being said (speaking). It includes diagrams, models, symbols, texts, and graphs. And it also involves how those representing forms convey mathematical ideas to a person individually and in dialogue with others.

Figure 10.1 positions the more "traditional" language modalities (reading, writing, listening, and speaking) in a manner that emphasizes two different ways in which they are related to each other. Reading and listening are placed next to each other horizontally, at the top of the diagram, because they both involve *receptive* language skills. In mathematics classrooms, students are called upon to read a variety of "texts," including written instructions in textbooks and on worksheets, written explanations of mathematical concepts, question stems and multiple choice answers on assignments and assessments, and word problems (Barwell 2009; Thompson and Chappell 2007). In addition, listening is what students in many classrooms are expected to do much of the time. In whole-class settings, students must listen to teachers' introductions to lessons, explanations of mathematical concepts or procedures, instructions for activities and assignments, and responses to students' questions, comments, and contributions. Depending on their level of English proficiency, some ELLs might have trouble understanding the teacher's use of "everyday" (nonspecialized) English, and it is likely that many ELLs (and some non-ELLs) will have difficulty comprehending the use of specialized mathematical discourse.

Likewise, the two *productive* language modalities, writing and speaking, are aligned horizontally with each other at the bottom of the diagram in figure 10.1. Current mathematics standards focus on the importance of communicating mathematical thinking, particularly in writing (CCSSI 2010; NCTM 2000). In mathematics classrooms, tasks might include asking students to write a journal reflection about what they learned in their mathematics lesson, construct a portfolio to display samples of mathematics work, create word problems for class distribution, or write a data analysis report using a specific representation (e.g., Venn diagram, line graph) to explain a survey finding (Burns 2004, 2005; Garrison 1999; Thompson and Chappell 2007). These writing tasks provide an opportunity for teachers to assess students' growing mathematical understanding and create challenges for students, who must communicate their understandings by using linguistic forms that may be unfamiliar or emergent. In addition, teachers increasingly include speaking demands in mathematics lessons, creating opportunities to evaluate students' mathematical understanding on the basis of their ability to articulate their mathematical thinking as they generate conjectures, justify solutions, and debate conditions, making students' speaking skills even more important in the mathematics classroom.

Thus, being able to receive, process, and comprehend information, either when listening to oral input or when reading, involves a number of active cognitive processes. Speaking and writing are also active processes but involve different skills. Depending on their experience in using English, ELLs may be stronger in either receptive or productive skills. Typically, ELLs are able to comprehend oral and written language at higher levels than they are able to produce it, but this may not be the case for some recent arrivals who have had significant writing instruction in English in their home countries yet limited exposure to listening to the language.

Looking at figure 10.1 differently, we note that reading and writing are positioned together at the left of the diagram to emphasize that they both involve written literacy skills. These two modalities stand in contrast to the oral modalities of listening and speaking, which are aligned together on the right half of the diagram. All human beings, barring extreme isolation and abuse as children, fully develop the oral language skills of speaking and listening to engage in a variety of communicative purposes. Reading and writing, by contrast, are specialized technologies, which historically have been used by only a subset of speakers of any given language—in fact, many of the world's languages do not even have a written form.

As in the productive and receptive categories, ELLs from different backgrounds will have different strengths in oral language skills and literacy skills. Some ELLs may arrive in the United States with strong literacy skills in their first language that contribute to their acquisition of literacy in English, yet these students may have little experience with using the language for oral communication. In contrast, other students develop English listening and speaking skills that outpace their development of reading and writing skills. Teachers need to recognize the different challenges that students from different backgrounds face so that they can provide different kinds of supports and opportunities for them to improve in the modalities in which they have less experience.

In practice, all five modalities are called for in multiple and interacting ways in most mathematics classrooms. Designing mathematics instruction for ELLs requires extensive consideration of the multiple and complex roles of language. By identifying language demands connected with the five modalities, teachers can begin to decide how best to support their ELLs in planning and implementing, as well as reflecting on, mathematics instruction.

Using the LDML Tool

To provide a more detailed understanding of the five language modalities and the multiple and complex ways in which they create language demands in mathematics lessons, we have developed the Language Demand in Mathematics Lessons (LDML) tool, shown in figure 10.2 (and also found at www.nctm.org/more4u). This lesson design tool draws teachers' attention to these language demands while they are planning, implementing, and reflecting on their mathematics lessons. We have used earlier versions of this tool in our own work with preservice and in-service teachers of mathematics in California and Washington. We have organized the LDML tool as a matrix that allows teachers to record the various language demands in all the different phases of a lesson.

Lesson Phase	Reading	Writing	Speaking	Listening	Representing
Phase 1: Before/Launch					
Phase 2: During/Explore					
Phase 3: After/Summarize					

Fig. 10.2. Language Demand in Mathematics Lessons (LDML) tool

The lesson phase descriptors in the LDML tool are modified from a variety of sources, including Van de Walle, Karp, and Bay-Williams (2010) and Lappen and colleagues (2006). We recognize that lesson design can be a highly individualized part of teachers' work, but we have used these basic lesson design features effectively in our own professional development work with preservice and in-service teachers of mathematics.

On the left side of the tool, we have chosen to highlight three possible phases of a mathematics lesson:

Phase 1: Before/Launch—The activity or tasks designed to introduce the main concept of the lesson, activate prior knowledge, and establish lesson expectations or pre-assess students' knowledge about the concept or procedure.

Phase 2: During/Explore—The main activities or tasks of the lesson, in which all students explore and practice the concept or procedure in depth.

Phase 3: After/Summarize—The concluding part of the lesson, which encourages students to summarize what they have learned, discuss important mathematical ideas or strategies of the lesson, and perhaps complete an exit task (e.g., extra problem, journal reflection).

Each subsequent column provides a space to record specific examples of each language demand within the mathematics lesson. When read horizontally, the LDML tool provides helpful information about the language demands occurring in each phase of the lesson. When completed, the matrix can also be read vertically, to provide a visual organizer that can give teachers an understanding of the language demands involved throughout the entire lesson, including the type and frequency of language demands in each modality. Some sample instructional questions to consider when using the tool during instructional design follow:

- Do one or two language demands dominate my lesson plan?
- What does this information tell me about how I can support my ELL students?
- Are language demands in one of the modes absent in a specific phase or the entire lesson?
- If my lesson plan has no writing demands, how will the absence of writing affect my ELLs' mathematics learning?

Responses to these kinds of questions can further focus teachers' attention on planning for language opportunities and challenges for ELLs before implementing a lesson or in reflecting on a lesson after it has occurred, to inform future instruction.

We encourage teachers to use this tool to modify their lessons to promote additional opportunities for students to use various modalities in the lesson, to provide specific supports for the modalities present—especially those that might be particularly challenging to ELLs—and to target specific modalities to emphasize in future lessons. The versatility of this LDML tool is that it can be used to design and analyze a lesson plan, a set of lessons, or a unit to give teachers a sense of the language demands that might have an impact on the students'—especially ELLs'—learning of the mathematics concept.

To demonstrate how the LDML tool might work to identify language demands of a mathematics lesson, we provide an example using video footage from an actual mathematics classroom. We invite the reader to access the video clip called "Questioning Data," Video Lesson 32 from Teaching Math: A Video Library, K–4 (http://www .learner.org/resources/series32.html; videos were made possible by funding from the Annenberg Foundation). This lesson begins with a discussion of a local newspaper article describing mall owners' desire to institute a dress code for shoppers and a survey that students conducted related to the article. Next, students work in small groups to interpret graphs from various newspapers or to organize data from surveys that they designed about topics of personal interest. The lesson ends with a group discussion of students' interpretations and questions. The lesson occurs in a fourth- to sixth-grade urban classroom that is racially and ethnically diverse, with predominantly Latino students and some white and African American students.

We selected this particular mathematics lesson video clip because it follows the general three-phase lesson framework of launch, explore, and summarize. It also focuses on a mathematics topic that demands mathematical organization, interpretation, and representation (i.e., data analysis), it spans upper elementary and middle school, and it presents a classroom that is racially diverse, with a sizeable Latino student population. Although we do not know the English language proficiency of students, we want to illustrate ways to identify language demands in a mathematics lesson and the extent to which the language demands might be both challenging and beneficial for ELLs as they attempt to learn the mathematics at the heart of the lesson.

While viewing the video clip, look for evidence of reading, writing, speaking, listening, and representing in the mathematics lesson, using the LDML tool, located at www. nctm.org/more4u, as a recording sheet. After you have viewed the clip and recorded your observations about the language demands in the lesson, consider our own analysis of the video clip, also provided at www.nctm.org.more4u. We encourage you to follow the LDML and our analysis as practice for thinking about language demands in mathematics instruction and how this kind of analysis might be extended into your future design of mathematics instruction.

Post-Viewing LDML Analysis

In our analysis, we identify and discuss the language demands of the lesson "Questioning Data" according to the different categories of the LDML. We have grouped listening and speaking together and have paired reading and writing as well, while examining representing on its own.

Listening and speaking

Using the LDML tool, we identified several listening and speaking demands in the "Questioning Data" mathematics lesson. It was clear from the beginning that *listening* and comprehending oral English played a central role in this lesson. For students to understand the introduction, in which the teacher asked them to recall reading an article about mall owners considering a dress code and collecting data about student agreement with the proposed dress code, they had to listen to and understand their teacher's remarks and their fellow students' comments. To launch the current lesson, the teacher asked students what the article was about, what the class's sample had been, and what the data had shown. Students needed to understand the questions, not only to participate by volunteering and answering, but also to have a better chance of following other students' responses. Such listening comprehension was also necessary for them to get the gist of the introduction. Listening was also crucial throughout the remainder of the lesson, including the "after/summarize" phase. In her voice-over comments on the lesson, the teacher discussed how important students' reporting back to the whole class was for their ability to process the central elements of the lesson; the teacher stressed that the students' voices broadened the viewpoints expressed. Of course, these viewpoints were available only to students who could comprehend the language being used to express them.

Speaking was also a central component of the lesson. In the lesson's introduction, described above, students were asked to summarize the previous reading, describe the sample that the class had used for its survey, and discuss the results. Therefore, participating as a speaker in this segment of the lesson required students to have at least some facility with the language functions of summarizing, describing, and discussing. Even if students did not volunteer to speak during the whole-class portions of the lesson (i.e. "beginning/launch" and "after/summarize" phases of the lesson), the teacher clearly relied on students' oral explanations to help her evaluate their understanding. In fact, the teacher described giving students the opportunity to explain their thinking as a "highlight" of the class. She also consistently asked strategic questions, such as, "What can you tell me about this?" to elicit oral responses from students. According to the teacher, she was not as interested in whether students' mathematical thinking was "correct," but rather what processes they used in that thinking, and how students showed what they *do* understand. In her summative comments at the end of the video, the teacher emphasized the importance that she placed on giving students opportunities to "talk about what they are finding out," and that she took many of her "cues" from what the students did during the task. Although information about the students' and teacher's proficiency in languages other than English is not provided, the exclusive use of English in the video clip suggests that in this classroom students were expected to demonstrate all this mathematical understanding in English.

Reading and writing

This problem-based mathematics lesson incorporated several reading and writing demands. Beginning with the opening activity, *reading* was clearly demanded of students to enable them to render an opinion about a short newspaper article describing the dress code being considered at the local mall. From this reading assignment, students constructed a class survey question about their agreement with the proposed policy. This reading demand set the stage for the lesson's continuing focus on data analysis. To make sense of the *USA Today* graphs, specific category labels and graph titles required reading. Last, the lesson included a specific set of written instructions that the instructor called a "statistics menu," designed to help students structure their analysis and write their reports.

Writing to express mathematical thinking was also a central component of this mathematics lesson. After choosing a *USA Today* graph to interpret and analyze, students were asked to write about it in a number of ways, using their own words to answer the following questions:

- What is the meaning of the graph?
- Who would be the audience for the graph?
- What questions would you ask the person who made the graph?

The activity's writing requirements were designed to facilitate students' analysis of the statistics portrayed by the graphs, as well as their ability to communicate their interpretations. To accomplish the main mathematical tasks of this lesson (i.e., in the "during/explore" phase), students had to coordinate written conventions, representations, and meaning making. This coordination resulted in a written record (individual or partner report) of their mathematical understandings. This written record was then used as a resource during class discussions as well as the student-work artifact to be submitted for evaluation.

Representing

Multiple representing demands were evident in this lesson. In addition to the opening sequence, in which the teacher conducted a review of the student survey results about the mall article, the main activity of the lesson demanded selecting, understanding, organizing, interpreting, and summarizing representations of information. Using the *USA Today* graphs, students worked with partners to make sense of a graph about current events. The graphs sometimes presented mathematical dilemmas that students had to clarify, as seen, for example, in the discussion about the reasons why the percentages of people who visited the United States did not total 100.

The mathematics lesson also included students figuring out how to represent data they had collected. In the "during/explore" phase of the lesson, students needed to construct a representation that would both organize and communicate specific findings. As the video illustrates, the representing demand was complex for some students. For example, a student named Miguel constructed a Venn diagram to use for his survey question results. The teacher provided the specific mathematical term for the representation ("This is what they call a *Venn diagram*") and pointed out a problem with using this representation to illustrate his data. Focusing on the regions in Miguel's diagram ("Yes—won by luck," "No—won by luck," "don't know"), the teacher noted that the data in the overlap region marked "don't know" did not make sense in this representation. Instead of showing him a new representation, she elected to refocus his attention on the strengths of the categories and encouraged him to seek out a different representation: "You need to think of a way to represent this data without using this Venn diagram." Then, later in the class, she asked Miguel to come to another group and share his Venn diagram representation for their data set: "Let me show Miguel this. He was trying to do a diagram that I think will help you guys. She asked people if they liked Pepsi, Diet Pepsi, or both. Can you see how they could use your diagram to do that?" She asked Miguel to re-create his Venn diagram and work with this group.

The representation demands of this lesson were both a challenge and an opportunity for Miguel. Although his initial ideas to organize his data with this representation did not work, the teacher created an opportunity for him to show how his Venn diagram representation could work with another group's data. By paying close attention to the representing demands of the lesson, the teacher enabled Miguel to successfully navigate the various representation demands and be a mathematical resource for his classmates.

Language demands in all lesson phases

Our analysis reveals that this lesson included numerous language demands in all phases of the lesson. Clearly, the teacher provided multiple opportunities for her students, including ELLs, if present, to work with varying mathematics language modalities. Speaking, listening, representing, and, to a lesser degree, reading were language demands heavily emphasized in each phase of this lesson. Writing was particularly prevalent in the "during/explore" phase of the lesson and absent in the "before/launch" and "after/summarize" phases of the lesson. Some specific examples within the lesson include instances of both the students and the teacher modeling mathematical language, as well as students carefully listening to explanations and questions, conveying their understanding orally and in writing, and organizing and interpreting data through representations. Understanding the presence or absence of language demands in a lesson and how those demands are negotiated in this specific lesson provides important information for planning purposes in the next iteration of the lesson.

It is important to note that the numerous language opportunities present can also be challenging for ELLs. For example, requiring the primary use of English in particular modalities for students to participate in the learning activities and for the teacher to make sense of the students' mathematical understandings puts some ELLs at a disadvantage, especially those at the beginning stages of acquiring English. Simultaneously, however, an emphasis on various language modalities in English can be an advantage for ELLs, *if properly supported* (see chapter 2), because it facilitates students' mathematical learning and English language development. Teachers must be mindful of this dynamic tension related to increasing language demands in a mathematics lesson, reflecting on both the opportunities and the challenges that they afford for ELLs. The LDML tool can help address this tension by helping teachers identify such language demands as they design instruction.

Conclusion

Used by individual teachers or as part of collaborative efforts that involve co-planning and peer observations, the LDML tool can be helpful in all stages of mathematics instruction. The specific mathematical language demands involving reading, writing, listening, speaking, and representing identified by using the LDML tool can create both opportunities and challenges for ELLs that need careful attention during mathematics lesson planning, implementation, and reflection. It is worth reemphasizing, however, that the LDML tool is designed to assist teachers in explicitly identifying—not eliminating—language demands in mathematics instruction. To pursue a reduction or limitation of language challenges—what Zwiers (2008) has called "linguistic enabling"—would foreclose opportunities for students to develop the very kinds of language that they will need to use as they progress through the grade levels in mathematics.

Instead, the goal should be to evaluate lessons (self-created or curriculum-provided), whether in the planning stages or revision process, with respect to language demands as a step toward providing language supports for students to facilitate mathematics learning. By identifying language demands, teachers can include the linguistic scaffolding necessary for students to comprehend the instruction, participate in learning activities, demonstrate what they are learning, and begin to develop the facility with various language modalities that will serve them well in learning mathematics in and beyond school. As Walqui and van Lier (2010) point out, the goal of scaffolding is not to control what the student can or cannot do, but rather to create conditions under which learners can develop greater autonomy. Therefore, when designing supports for English language learners in mathematics instruction, teachers are advised to heed Walqui and van Lier's advice: "amplify, don't simplify."

We offer the LDML tool as an initial step toward helping teachers pay closer attention to language in mathematics instruction, work toward expanding the mathematical opportunities for ELLs to access and participate in mathematics lessons, and use multiple strategies to support and extend ELLs' mathematical learning and development of linguistic repertoires that will serve them well now and in the future.

References

Barwell, Richard. "Mathematical Word Problems and Bilingual Learners." In *Multilingualism in Mathematics Classrooms: Global Perspectives*, edited by Richard Barwell, pp. 63–77. Clevedon, UK: Multilingual Matters, 2009.

Burns, Marilyn. "Writing in Math." *Educational Leadership* 62 (October 2004): 30–33.

———. "Looking at How Students Reason." *Educational Leadership* 63 (November 2005): 26–31.

Common Core State Standards Initiative (CCSSI). *Common Core State Standards for Mathematics. Common Core State Standards (College- and Career-Readiness Standards and K–12 Standards in English Language Arts and Math)*. Washington, D.C.: National Governors Association Center for Best Practices and the Council of Chief State School Officers, 2010. http://www.corestandards.org.

Garrison, Leslie. "Portafolio de Matemática: Using Mathematics Portfolios with Latino Students." In *Changing the Faces of Mathematics: Perspectives on Latinos*, edited by Luis Ortiz-Franco, Norma G. Hernandez, and Yolanda De La Cruz, pp. 85–97. Reston, Va.: National Council of Teachers of Mathematics, 1999.

Goldin, Gerald. "Representation in School Mathematics: A Unifying Research Perspective." In *A Research Companion to "Principles and Standards for School Mathematics,"* edited by Jeremy Kilpatrick, W. Gary Martin, and Deborah Schifter, pp. 275–86. Reston, Va.: National Council of Teachers of Mathematics, 2003.

Gutiérrez, Kris, Tesha Sengupta-Irving, and Jack Dieckmann. "Developing a Mathematics Vision: Mathematics as a Discursive and Embodied Practice." In *Language and Mathematics Education: Multiple Perspectives and Directions for Research*, edited by Judit N. Moschkovich, pp. 73–112. Charlotte, N.C.: Information Age Publishing, 2010.

Khisty, Lena L. "Children Talking Mathematically in Multilingual Classrooms: Issues in the Role of Language." In *Mathematics for Tomorrow's Young Children: International Perspectives on Curriculum*, edited by Helen Mansfield, Neil A. Pateman, and Nadine Bednarz, pp. 240–45. Boston: Kluwer, 2010.

Lappan, Glenda, James T. Fey, William M. Fitzgerald, Susan N. Friel, and Elizabeth D. Phillips. *Connected Mathematics*. Boston: Pearson, 2006.

Moschkovich, Judit N. "Learning Mathematics in Two Languages: Moving from Obstacles to Resources." In *Changing the Faces of Mathematics: Perspectives on Multiculturalism and Gender Equity*, edited by Walter Secada, pp. 85–93. Reston, Va.: NCTM, 2000.

———. "A Situated and Sociocultural Perspective on Bilingual Mathematics Learners." *Mathematical Thinking and Learning* 4, nos. 2 and 3 (2002): 189–212.

———. "Examining Mathematical Discourse Practices." *For the Learning of Mathematics* 27, no. 1 (2007): 24–30.

———. *Language and Mathematics Education: Multiple Perspectives and Directions for Research*. Charlotte, N.C.: Information Age Publishing, 2010.

National Council of Teachers of Mathematics (NCTM). *Principles and Standards for School Mathematics*. Reston, Va.: NCTM, 2000.

Parrish, Sherry. *Number Talks: Helping Children Build Mental Math and Computation Strategies, Grades K–5*. Sausalito, Calif.: Math Solutions, 2010.

Stein, Mary Kay, Margaret Schwan Smith, Marjorie A. Henningsen, and Edward A. Silver. *Implementing Standards-Based Mathematics Instruction: A Casebook for Professional Development*. New York: Teachers College Press, 2000.

Schleppegrell, Mary J. "Language in Mathematics Teaching and Learning: A Research Review." In *Language and Mathematics Education: Multiple Perspectives and Directions for Research*, edited by Judit N. Moschkovich, pp. 73–112. Charlotte, N.C.: Information Age Publishing, 2010.

Thompson, Denisse R., and Michaele F. Chappell. "Communication and Representation as Elements in Mathematical Literacy." *Reading & Writing Quarterly* 23 (April 2007): 179–96.

Van de Walle, John A., Karen S. Karp, and Jennifer M. Bay-Williams. *Elementary and Middle School Mathematics: Teaching Developmentally*. 7th ed. Boston: Pearson, 2010.

Walqui, Aida, and Leo van Lier. *Scaffolding the Academic Success of Adolescent English Language Learners*. San Francisco: WestEd, 2010.

Zwiers, Jeff. *Building Academic Language: Essential Practices for Content Classrooms, Grades 5–12*. San Francisco: Jossey-Bass, 2008.

Chapter 11

The Language Demands of Word Problems for English Language Learners

by Luciana C. de Oliveira

As mathematics educators, we naturally consider the numbers that we choose to include in mathematical tasks. Do we give the same attention to the language demands of the tasks? Using two examples, this chapter presents a framework for analyzing word problems at the elementary level to call teachers' attention to the language demands on ELLs. Language-based mathematics instruction is more than just vocabulary and should draw on other aspects of school mathematics discourse.

Teachers need to enhance their ability to make content accessible to ELLs. In this chapter, the word *accessible* takes on a different connotation from the emphasis in recent literature on modifying the language of texts to help ELLs learn better from them. This chapter presents a different view of *accessible*: Making content *accessible* to ELLs means providing them *access* to the ways in which knowledge is constructed in the content areas—not by simplifying the texts, but by developing teachers' understanding about how mathematical disciplinary discourse is constructed.

Word Problems in Mathematics

Word problems present significant comprehension difficulties and are particularly challenging for ELLs (Martiniello 2008). These comprehension difficulties have to do with both lexical and sentence complexity (Abedi and Lord 2001). Lexical complexity refers to the difficulty of the vocabulary words that appear in mathematics tasks. Word problems permeate mathematics textbooks and standardized tests, and students' abilities to solve them often are seen as important measures of mathematical understanding.

One key point that must be highlighted is that particular word problems exemplify only certain features of the range of language demands that may be encountered in word problems. Other examples would bring different demands into focus. However, the word problems presented here illustrate some key language challenges with which ELLs would have to deal in performing these tasks.

The author thanks Dave Norris for his feedback on earlier drafts of this chapter.

Word problem 1

The first word problem appears as part of the Indiana Statewide Testing for Educational Progress-Plus (ISTEP+) Item Sampler, provided on the Indiana Department of Education website. ISTEP+ is the main standardized test for grades 3 through 10 in Indiana (Indiana Department of Education 2002). This test is based on Indiana's Academic Standards (Indiana Department of Education 2000). ISTEP+ covers English language arts in grades 3–10, mathematics in grades 3–10, and science in grades 5 and 7. The items in each sampler are examples of the types of problems typically found on ISTEP+ but are not practice tests. Five key academic standards for grade 2 are to be assessed in grade 3; these standards address number sense, computation, algebra and functions, geometry, measurement, and problem solving. Our first word problem appears as a sample item for the problem solving section of the test for grade 3:

> Denise is buying candy for 3 of her friends. She wants to give each friend 4 pieces of candy. If each piece of candy costs 5¢, how much money will Denise spend on candy for her friends?

This word problem can be divided into four clauses:

Clause 1: Denise is buying candy for 3 of her friends.

Clause 2: She wants to give each friend 4 pieces of candy.

Clause 3: If each piece of candy costs 5¢,

Clause 4: how much money will Denise spend on candy for her friends?

On the basis of Huang and Normandia's (2008) set of seven questions to help *students* work through word problems at the secondary level, this chapter proposes five questions to help *teachers* identify the language demands of word problems so that they can then help their students work through them:

1. What task is the student asked to perform?
2. What relevant information is presented in the word problem?
3. What mathematical concepts are presented in the information?
4. What mathematical representations and procedures can students use to solve the problem, based on the information presented and the mathematical concepts identified?
5. What additional language demands exist in this problem?

Figure 11.1 shows a framework for analyzing word problems that is built on these five questions (also available at www.nctm.org/more4u).

Framework for Analyzing Word Problems: Guiding Questions, Language Demands, and Tasks for Teachers

Guiding Questions to Ask	Language Demands to Identify	Tasks for Teachers to Perform
1. What task is the student asked to perform?	Type of questions and their structure—for example, *how many, how much*	To analyze the question by identifying what it is asking
2. What relevant information is presented in the word problem?	Overall clause construction—the verbs and *who, what, to whom*	To break down the clause by finding what information is presented
3. Which mathematical concepts are presented in the information?	Specific clause construction—numerical information presented in different parts of the clause	To connect the mathematical concepts needed by looking for specific numerical information presented in the clause
4. What mathematical representations and procedures can students use to solve the problem, based on the information presented and the mathematical concepts identified?	Question + overall clause structure + specific clause structure	To connect all previously analyzed pieces to determine a variety of mathematical representations and procedures that can be used to solve the problem
5. What additional language demands exist in this problem?	Language "chunks": nouns, verbs, prepositional phrases within clauses—not as isolated elements Connections among clauses to determine how different parts of the word problem are connected	To identify any aspect of language that seems problematic for ELLs not recognized through the previous guiding questions

Fig. 11.1. A framework for analyzing word problems

This framework is designed to guide teachers in analyzing word problems *before* they present them to students. By focusing on each question in column 1, teachers will get a better sense of the structure of a word problem and the language demands that it may present for ELLs. Each question helps teachers to focus on the mathematical concepts integrated in the word problem at the same time that they are identifying aspects of language with which ELLs may have difficulty. Column 1, "Guiding Questions," presents the questions that will guide teachers' analysis of the word problems. Column 2, "Language Demands to Identify," leads teachers in focusing specifically on the language used in the word problems as they address each guiding question. The language demands identified in this column are some examples of the demands that teachers can focus on to address the guiding questions; however, the list is not exhaustive, so teachers may find other areas that will help them address the guiding questions. Column 3, "Tasks for Teachers to Perform," explains to teachers what it is that they are doing when they are analyzing each word problem. Let's examine how teachers can analyze the language demands of word problem 1 by focusing on each guiding question.

Guiding Question 1: **_What task is the student asked to perform?_**

To help ELLs solve a word problem, teachers need to identify the task that the problem is asking students to perform. To answer this question, teachers can look at the word problem and identify the _question_ being asked. To identify the question, teachers can look at the word problem and find the question mark (?) and look closely at what that question asks students to do. (If the problem has no question mark, it may have a statement in the imperative mood, such as, "Find the perimeter, in meters, of the triangle." The imperative form _find_ implies the question, "What is the perimeter, in meters, of the triangle?")

The question in word problem 1 is, "If each piece of candy costs 5¢, how much money will Denise spend on candy for her friends?" This question asks for particular information from students. Yet, there are several language demands within this question that can be explored further.

For example, the _if_ clause, _if each piece of candy costs 5¢_, puts forth an important piece of information. Traditionally, and typically, an _if_ clause presents a condition; however, here the _if_ clause is simply presenting another important piece of information that is key for solving this problem. In mathematics, _if_ clauses generally indicate a given piece of information that is essential for solving a problem rather than a possible condition; often they are the last piece of information necessary to solve the problem. The _if_ clause in this problem is placed together with the question and can be particularly challenging for ELLs if not highlighted by the teacher. Notice too that the problem uses the symbol ¢ to refer to cents, a usage that may need to be explained to students.

The question, then, is, _how much money will Denise spend on candy for her friends?_ The expressions _how many_ and _how much_ are commonly found in word problems and request information that involves a _quantity_. We know that the question is specifically asking for a sum of money. We also know that the human participant, Denise, is the one who will be spending this money and what she will be spending it on—namely, candy. However, the construction _spend on candy_ may need to be further explained to ELLs, since the preposition _on_ in this problem does not indicate a position as it commonly does in everyday language (e.g., "the book is _on_ the table"). In the problem, the preposition _on_ goes together with the verb _spend_ in a phrase that could be a challenge and might need to be unpacked for ELLs. In addition, the phrase _for her friends_ indicates Denise's three friends, identified in the first clause of the problem as _3 of her friends_. This could be confusing because the problem subsequently refers to Denise's three friends in the phrase _for her friends_; however, the problem is really talking about only these three friends and not others. Recognizing the type of question with the construction _how much_ and the structure of the question with its potential linguistic challenges can help teachers answer Guiding Question 1, What task is the student asked to perform?

Guiding Question 2: **_What relevant information is presented in the word problem?_**

To help teachers recognize the relevant information presented in the word problem, we can identify _different important aspects of the text_, or what is being presented in terms of the content of the problem. For example, we see at the beginning of the problem a _human participant_—a person—who?—identified as _Denise_. This person is doing something—what is she doing? Denise _is buying_. What is Denise buying? _Candy_. For whom? _For 3 of_ *her friends*—also human participants, though not named. We can see in this first clause that a lot is being presented in compressed form to give students the context of the situation as quickly as possible. The verb *is buying* is important to understand because students will need to know that when you *buy* something, you *spend* money. Even though the verb *spend* does not appear in this first clause, it appears in the question, as we already recognized in responding to Guiding Question 1. Also, we already know *what* Denise is buying: *candy*. Candy may be a familiar word for students, but if it isn't, the teacher will have to provide visual representations or actual objects as necessary to help students understand the problem. Perhaps the most crucial part of this clause is *for 3 of her friends*. Note that the number 3 is very important mathematical information that students will need to solve the problem. What relevant information do we know from this first clause, then? We know who (*Denise*) is buying what (*candy*) and for whom (*for 3 of her friends*).

The second clause in the problem, *She wants to give each friend 4 pieces of candy*, also has key mathematical information that students need to recognize. First, they need to make the connection between the pronoun *she* and its referent, *Denise*. The verbal group *wants to give* shows a mental process and a desire (in *wants*), plus an action (in *to give*). We also know the receiver of the action of giving, *each friend*. But *each friend* is a complex construction for ELLs because they need to make the connection between the word *each* and the number 1—*each* is equivalent to 1. What does Denise want to give each friend? *4 pieces of candy*. Note that the number 4 is very important mathematical information that students will need to solve the problem. Furthermore, the problem uses the word *pieces* to identify more than one candy, which could also be confusing for ELLs. What relevant information do we know from this second clause, then? We know who (*she = Denise*) wants to give what (*4 pieces of candy*) to whom (*each friend*).

The last piece of information presented in the problem, already identified when we discussed Guiding Question 1, is how much each candy costs—information that is presented in *If each piece of candy costs 5¢*, which appears as part of the mathematical question. But this *if* clause is actually part of the given information that is key for answering the word problem. The table in figure 11.2 can help teachers identify these language demands.

Clauses and Relevant Information Provided in Word Problem 1

Clause	Relevant Information Provided
Denise is buying candy for 3 of her friends.	Who? = Denise What is she doing? = is buying What? = candy For whom? = 3 of her friends
She wants to give each friend 4 pieces of candy.	Who? = She [Denise] What does she want? = wants to give To whom? = each friend What? = 4 pieces of candy
If each piece of candy costs 5¢	What? = each piece of candy How much is each piece of candy? = 5¢

Fig. 11.2. Breaking down word problem 1 into clauses and relevant information

This table can help the teacher understand how a word problem is constructed and how the clauses put together all the crucial mathematical information that students will need to solve the problem. Recognizing the different parts of the clauses and breaking each clause into its different parts with their potential linguistic challenges can help teachers answer Guiding Question 2, What relevant information is presented in the word problem?

Guiding Question 3: ***Which mathematical concepts are presented in the information?***

To recognize the mathematical concepts presented in the information in a word problem, teachers can connect the information analyzed in Guiding Question 2 with the mathematics concepts needed to solve the problem. For example, our analysis of the question in word problem 1 revealed that it is asking about a *quantity*, as indicated by *how much money*. We know from our analysis what information is presented; our task as teachers now is to help students connect the mathematical concepts with the information—the language—that presents these concepts. The table in figure 11.3, based on Huang and Normandia (2008), can help teachers connect the information and the mathematical concepts presented in the problem.

Information Provided and Mathematizing the Problem Situation

Information Provided	Mathematizing the Problem Situation
Clause 1: Denise is buying candy for 3 of her friends.	Total number of friends = 3
Clause 2: She wants to give each friend 4 pieces of candy.	Number of pieces of candy = 4 Each friend = 1 Therefore, 4 pieces of candy for 1 friend
Clause 3: If each piece of candy costs 5¢	Price for each (1) piece of candy = 5¢

Fig. 11.3. A table relating the information provided in word problem 1 to a mathematizing of the situation

First, we know the total number of friends to whom Denise wants to give candy (3), identified in clause 1. Clause 2 has two important mathematical concepts, the number of pieces of candy (4) for each (1) friend. Clause 3 presents the price for each (1) piece of candy (5¢). Going back to the task that the student is asked to perform—finding *how much money Denise will spend on candy for her friends*—we now know that this involves the mathematical concept of an **unknown** that directly connects to **quantities**. Perhaps someone who can comprehend the word problem without much difficulty can directly make these connections. However, these connections need to be made explicit for ELLs *before* the students start to solve the problem. Connecting the information analyzed with the mathematics concepts needed to solve the problem can help teachers answer Guiding Question 3, Which mathematical concepts are presented in the information?

Guiding Question 4: *What mathematical representations and procedures can be used to solve the problem, based on the information presented and the mathematical concepts identified?*

To help ELLs solve the problem, teachers can connect all the different guiding questions presented to determine a variety of mathematical representations and procedures needed to solve the problem. Given the information presented in the case of word problem 1, we know that we need first to find how many total pieces of candy Denise will buy. We know that Denise has 3 friends, and each friend will receive 4 pieces. Therefore, the mathematical procedure will be as follows: 4 pieces of candy plus 4 pieces of candy plus 4 pieces of candy equals 12, which is the total number of pieces of candy Denise will need to buy. Now that we know that Denise will buy 12 pieces of candy in total, and we know that each piece of candy costs 5¢, we could use the following mathematical procedure: $5 + 5 + 5 + 5 + 5 + 5 + 5 + 5 + 5 + 5 + 5 + 5 = 60¢$. The answer to the question *how much money will Denise spend on candy for her friends?* is therefore 60 cents. We chose addition for this problem because Indiana's Academic Standards for Mathematics (Indiana Department of Education 2000) give "Addition and Subtraction" as part of the standards for grade 2. The table in figure 11.4 connects the information, the mathematical concepts presented in the problem, and the mathematical representations and procedures that can be used to solve the problem.

This table helps the teacher draw on the crucial mathematical language and ideas inherent in the construction of the word problem to plan lessons that will enhance ELLs' access to the problem. Connecting all the different guiding questions presented can help teachers answer Guiding Question 4, What mathematical representations and procedures can be used to solve the problem, based on the information presented and the mathematical concepts identified?

Guiding Question 5: *What additional language demands exist in this problem?*

To help identify any other aspect of language that might be problematic for ELLs, teachers can identify language "chunks," such as combinations of nouns, verbs, and prepositional phrases within clauses that may be difficult for ELLs to comprehend or recognize their relationships to other parts of the word problem. It is important to focus on these language combinations not as isolated elements but as real chunks to avoid focusing just on vocabulary apart from where it occurs in a clause. One of the major challenges of word problem 1 is the *reference devices* that it uses, or "words that stand for other words in a text" (Schleppegrell and de Oliveira 2006, p. 263). For example, the human participant, Denise, is first introduced as *Denise* in clause 1, and then is referred to as *She* in clause 2. The noun group *3 of her friends* is introduced in clause 1, and then these participants are picked up in clause 2 as *each friend* and in clause 4 as *her friends*. Teachers have to notice that mathematically there is no one-to-one correspondence between *each friend* and *3 of her friends*. This means that *each friend* means one friend, but *3 of her friends* and *her friends* refer to the same participants. As previously mentioned, the numeral 3, used when this participant is first introduced, may also cause confusion. We identified several other language demands as we addressed other guiding questions, all of which could be

Information Provided, Mathematical Concepts, and Mathematical Representations and Procedures in Word Problem 1

Information Provided	Mathematical Concepts	Mathematical Representations and Procedures
Clause 1: Denise is buying candy for 3 of her friends.	Total number of friends = 3	**Clause 1 Representation** Friend 1 Friend 2 Friend 3
Clause 2: She wants to give each friend 4 pieces of candy.	Number of pieces of candy = 4 Each friend = 1 Therefore, 4 pieces of candy for 1 friend	**Clause 2 Representation** 1 piece of candy Friend 1 Friend 2 Friend 3 12 pieces of candy Addition 4 + 4 + 4: 3 groups of 4 because there are 3 friends. 4 + 4 + 4 = 12 pieces of candy total that Denise will buy
Clause 3: If each piece of candy costs 5¢	1 piece of candy = 5¢	**Clause 3 Representation** Friend 1 5¢ 5¢ 5¢ 5¢ Friend 2 5¢ 5¢ 5¢ 5¢ Friend 3 5¢ 5¢ 5¢ 5¢ 12 groups of 5¢ 5 + 5 + 5 + 5 + 5 + 5 + 5 + 5 + 5 + 5 + 5 + 5 = 60¢

Fig. 11.4. A table showing the connections among the information provided, the mathematical concepts, and the mathematical representations and procedures in word problem 1

pointed out to ELLs. Identifying the language chunks that may be difficult for ELLs to comprehend can help teachers answer Guiding Question 5, What additional language demands exist in this problem?

This close look at the language of this word problem shows how teachers can analyze the construction of word problems by following the guiding questions presented. The goal of this framework is to make content accessible to ELLs by providing them with *access* to the ways in which knowledge is constructed in mathematics word problems, *as they are written.* The goal is not to simplify these word problems but to enhance teachers' understanding about how mathematical disciplinary discourse is constructed in them.

Word problem 2

Our second word problem comes from a fifth-grade mathematics textbook (Crown, Fennell, and Charles 2005). This word problem is more demanding than the first word problem because of the way in which each clause is structured and the mathematical information is presented.

> Three sisters attended a movie that cost $5 per person. Each sister spent $2 on popcorn. Their mother gave them $30 to spend for all three. How much money was left?

This word problem can be divided into 4 clauses:

Clause 1: Three sisters attended a movie that cost $5 per person.

Clause 2: Each sister spent $2 on popcorn.

Clause 3: Their mother gave them $30 to spend for all three.

Clause 4: How much money was left?

We invite you to analyze the language demands of this second word problem by using the Analyzing Word Problems Framework template, available at www.nctm.org/more4u, to focus on each guiding question. Once you have completed the analysis, compare it to the completed analysis of word problem 2, also at www.nctm.org/more4u.

Language-Based Mathematics Instruction

Language-based mathematics instruction refers to a simultaneous focus on mathematics discourse and mathematics content. To address mathematics content, teachers must attend to mathematics discourse. As Ramirez and Celedón-Pattichis explain in chapter 2 and Aguirre and Bunch explain in chapter 10, mathematics discourse should be the focus of teaching mathematics to ELLs. Mathematics discourse that goes beyond vocabulary is the basis for mathematics instruction. At its core is "understanding the mathematical meaning of concepts, knowing how to use precise mathematical language, and using terminology to explain and connect mathematical concepts" (Ramirez and Celedón-Pattichis, chapter 2, p. 20).

One of the general principles for teaching mathematics to ELLs identified in chapter 2 is the belief that "facility with the English language is acquired when ELLs learn mathematics through effective instructional practices, including support structures that scaffold students' language development… [and] make mathematics content linguistically comprehensible to them" (p. 21). This principle is addressed in this chapter by providing a framework for analyzing word problems with guiding questions that teachers can use to identify (1) the task that the student is asked to perform, (2) the relevant information presented in the word problem, (3) the mathematical concepts presented in the information, and (4) the mathematical representations and procedures that can be used to solve the problem. This framework enables teachers to focus on effective instructional practices that address language development and mathematics content. Teachers are responsible for making mathematics content "linguistically comprehensible" for ELLs. They can begin to fulfill this responsibility by identifying the language demands of word problems.

Both teachers and students of school mathematics can develop a certain linguistic awareness of some typical discourse features of mathematics. To be able to read mathematics word problems effectively, English language learners need to be able to engage with the meanings in use. Discourse structure is seldom attended to in mathematics classrooms. Content is never separate from the language through which that content manifests itself. Learning mathematics means learning the language that expresses mathematics. The language demands that this chapter addresses highlight the kind of discipline-specific academic support in language and literacy development that would enable English language learners to be more successful in their mathematics learning.

One of the main goals of this work is to enable teachers to be more proactive in helping ELLs learn the ways in which language is used to construct mathematical knowledge. Efforts to change the language of the content areas are counterproductive, as *all* students will need to deal with the specialized knowledge presented in the disciplines to participate fully in school. Learning the language of the mathematics discourse community allows individuals to have access to this community's meaning-making practices.

This chapter has demonstrated some of the language demands of mathematics discourse for English language learners. By identifying and focusing on these demands, teachers can gain a better understanding of them and address them in their curriculum and instruction. For example, teachers can select passages from mathematics textbooks and identify some of the features described in this chapter. This is a helpful activity in which teachers can engage to develop their knowledge about mathematics discourse. Teachers can then plan instruction not only to teach particular mathematical concepts but also to work on the language of mathematics with ELLs.

Accessibility is one of the major issues addressed in this chapter. Making texts more accessible means more than simplifying the language through which content manifests itself. ELLs need *access* to mathematics discourse. This is a matter of social justice. If ELLs are not given opportunities to engage and participate in experiences involving the use of appropriate mathematics discourse, they will continue to be at a disadvantage, and the so-called achievement gap between ELLs and English-only speakers will be likely to remain a reality for these students.

References

Abedi, Jamal, and Carol Lord. "The Language Factor in Mathematics Tests." *Applied Measurement in Education* 14, no. 3 (2001): 219–34.

Crown, Warren, Francis S. (Skip) Fennell, and Randall I. Charles. *Indiana Mathematics*. Glenview, Ill.: Pearson, 2005.

Huang, Jingzi, and Bruce Normandia. "Comprehending and Solving Word Problems in Mathematics: Beyond Key Words." In *Reading in Secondary Content Areas: A Language-Based Pedagogy*, edited by Zhihui Fang and Mary J. Schleppegrell, pp. 64–83. Ann Arbor: University of Michigan Press, 2008.

Indiana Department of Education. "Indiana's Academic Standards—Mathematics." Indianapolis: Indiana Department of Education, 2000. http://dc.doe.in.gov/Standards/AcademicStandards/StandardSearch.aspx.

———. "ISTEP+ Grade 3 Item Sampler." Indianapolis: Indiana Department of Education (20002). http://www.doe.in.gov/assessment/3-8_gqe_resources.html.

Martiniello, María. "Language and the Performance of English-Language Learners in Math Word Problems." *Harvard Educational Review* 78 (Summer 2008): 333–68.

Schleppegrell, Mary J., and Luciana C. de Oliveira. "An Integrated Language and Content Approach for History Teachers." *Journal of English for Academic Purposes* 5 (October 2006): 254-68.

Chapter 12

Analyzing Effective Mathematics Lessons for English Learners: A Multiple Mathematical Lens Approach

by Julia M. Aguirre, Erin E. Turner, Tonya Gau Bartell,
Corey Drake, Mary Q. Foote, and Amy Roth McDuffie

- Learning Lens (template)
- Power and Participation Lens (template)
- Task Lens (template)
- Teaching Lens (template)

A primary objective of mathematics education is to develop students' conceptual understanding and procedural fluency through mathematical problem solving (NCTM 2000). Effective mathematics lessons reflecting this approach leverage students' mathematical thinking and discourse. This increased emphasis on problem solving and mathematical discourse poses opportunities and challenges for English language learners (ELLs) and their teachers (Moschkovich 1999, 2002). Supporting teachers in recognizing, reflecting on, and addressing such opportunities and challenges in turn can support the mathematics learning of ELLs.

The purpose of this chapter is to introduce a tool for teachers to use in analyzing mathematics lessons in multiple ways to support the mathematical learning of ELLs. We invite the reader to think of this tool as a pair of glasses with specific lenses that focus attention on four distinct facets of a mathematics lesson: the task, the learning, the teaching, and the students' power and participation. Each lens is described in more detail below. Collectively, these multiple mathematical lenses facilitate analysis of the strengths and limitations of mathematical tasks, evidence of student learning, instructional strategies that effectively elicit and support ELLs' mathematical thinking, and levels of participation and dialogue. Furthermore, each lens attends to ways that teachers, students, and tasks draw on a range of mathematical knowledge bases (e.g., mathematical, cultural, community, family, linguistic, students' interests, peers) to support ELLs' mathematics learning.

This chapter is based on work from the project Teachers Empowered to Advance Change in Mathematics (TEACH MATH), supported by the National Science Foundation under grant 1020155 and involving six institutions: Iowa State University, University of Arizona, Queens College–City University of New York, University of Delaware, University of Washington–Tacoma, and Washington State University–Tri-Cities. Any opinions, findings, and conclusions or recommendations expressed in this material are those of the authors and do not necessarily reflect the views of the National Science Foundation. We would like to thank the editors for their helpful comments, as well as Tiffany Kantanyoutanant and Lucia Decosta for their editorial support in preparing the manuscript.

After we describe the Multiple Mathematical Lens (MML) tool, we invite the reader to use it to analyze video clips of four selected mathematics lessons available online. These lessons vary in mathematics topic and grade level. The chapter ends with our analysis, using the MML tool, of ways that each lesson supports ELLs' mathematics learning.

Multiple Mathematical Lenses: Task, Learning, Teaching, and Power and Participation

Researchers in the TEACH MATH (Teachers Empowered to Advance Change in Mathematics) project developed and use the MML tool to support teachers in developing understandings of how instruction can draw on multiple mathematical knowledge bases—specifically, mathematics, children's mathematical thinking, and children's community and cultural funds of knowledge—in ways that support student learning (Bartell et al. 2010; Turner, Drake, et al. 2012). *Funds of knowledge* refers to the historically accumulated knowledge, skills, and experiences that are found in students' homes and communities and that families draw on to support their work, daily activities, and well-being (González et al. 2001). This chapter describes a version of the MML activity that specifically highlights important mathematics learning and teaching issues for ELLs. The objective of the MML activity is for teachers to use the lenses as a tool to analyze a mathematics lesson and to document specific evidence (i.e., examples from the video) to support their analysis. The complete set of lenses and targeted questions is available at www.nctm.org/more4u.

Task lens

The task lens guides teachers in analyzing the effectiveness of the mathematical task or tasks of the lesson for ELLs. Targeted questions are the following:

- *What makes this a good or problematic task for ELLs?* (e.g., multiple entry points, multiple representations, varied solution strategies; cognitive demand; home language [L1]; conceptually challenging mathematics, procedural fluency with understanding, problem-solving, grade-level appropriateness)

- *What resources or knowledge does this task activate or connect to?* (e.g., mathematical, cultural, community, family, linguistic, students' interests, peers)

- *How does the task's structure create opportunities for ELLs to communicate mathematical thinking?*

Learning lens

The learning lens focuses teachers' attention on evidence of student mathematical learning, including mathematical understandings and confusions, communication of learning by ELLs, and sources of knowledge used to develop understanding. Targeted questions are the following:

- *What resources or knowledge do students draw on to understand and solve the mathematics task?* (e.g., mathematical, cultural, community, family, linguistic, students' interests, peers)

- *What specific mathematical understandings or confusions are indicated in students' work, talk, or behavior?*

- *How do ELLs communicate their mathematical understandings? How do ELLs make sense of others' mathematical ideas?* (e.g., justifications, explanations, questions or responses, written work, representations, models, gestures)

Teaching lens

The teaching lens focuses on the instructional practice and interactions in the mathematics lesson. This lens includes specific resources and strategies that the teacher uses to support ELLs' mathematical understanding, communication, and participation. Targeted questions are the following:

- *What resources and knowledge does the teacher use or draw on to support ELLs' mathematical understandings?* (e.g., mathematical, cultural, community, family, linguistic, students' interests, peers)

- *How does the teacher support opportunities for ELLs to communicate their mathematical understandings and participate in mathematical discourse?* (e.g., elicits and revoices ideas, intentionally positions a student's home language to publicly communicate mathematical ideas, affirms everyday language, recognizes gestures as tools to communicate thinking, models mathematical language)

- *How does the teacher respond to ELLs' mathematical ideas (correct answers, mistakes, confusions, partial understandings)?* (e.g., asks follow-up clarifying questions, uses students' home language and mathematical language, uses gestures or other representations, makes mathematical connections among students' strategies)

Power and participation lens

The power and participation lens focuses teachers' attention on ELLs' engagement, participation, and status in the mathematics lesson. Targeted questions are the following:

- *Who participates in this mathematics lesson? Does the classroom culture value and encourage most students, including ELLs, to speak?* (e.g., Do most students speak? Only a few students? Only the teacher?)

- *Who holds authority for knowing mathematics? The teacher? The students? Do some students' mathematical ideas have more status than others?*

- *What evidence indicates that ELLs' mathematics contributions are or are not respected and valued?* (e.g., Do ELLs share ideas publicly, only with a teacher, only in small groups with peers? Do ELLs have opportunities to use home language [L1], mathematics language, everyday language, or code switching?)

Reader Invitation and Video Descriptions

To demonstrate how the MML tool can be used in analyzing key aspects of mathematics lessons for ELLs, we invite readers to use it to analyze a set of online videos of mathematics lessons (http://www.learner.org/resources/series32.html; these open-access videos were made possible by funding from the Annenberg Foundation). We urge readers to discuss their analyses afterward with a group of colleagues.

Figure 12.1 summarizes important information for selected video mathematics lessons. It is important to note that we selected two videos, "Marshmallows" and "Valentine Exchange," which are set in bilingual classrooms with numerous English learners, and two videos, "Amazing Equations" and "Questioning Data," which are from non-bilingual classrooms, which may or may not include English learners (information about whether there were English learners in these two classrooms is not available on the host website [www.learner.org]). By strategically including both kinds of classrooms—ones where English is the sole medium of instruction and ones where teachers and students may use two or more languages—we acknowledge the range of language competencies that teachers and students may bring to mathematics lessons. Some examples include situations in which teachers may or may not speak the child's home language or in which they cannot use a student's home language in instruction. The MML tool can provide opportunities to consider how different teacher moves, tasks, student mathematical understandings, and participation structures might support the mathematics learning needs of English learners in varying instructional contexts—even those in which the language status of a student is not explicitly known.

While viewing the lessons, look for evidence (examples, teacher or student statements, powerful interactions) to support responses to each targeted question. Please note that each video represents edited portions of a *single* mathematics lesson, and as such, should not be used to draw general conclusions about a particular teacher's instruction or a particular student's learning. Instead, the videos should be viewed as opportunities to consider the complexities of mathematics teaching and learning, and to engage in close analysis of mathematics lessons that could be effective for English learners.

Descriptions of Selected Lessons

Title	Content/lesson description	Grade/school	Demographic information
Amazing Equations (video 8)	Addition/subtraction problem solving: Students investigate the concepts of addition and subtraction as they generate oral and written story problems for the number of the day. At the end of the lesson, students share their problems, including pictorial and symbolic representations, with their peers.	Grades 1 and 2; urban elementary	Racially/ethnically diverse classroom; predominantly African American, but also Latino, Asian, and white students
Marshmallows (video 10)	Whole number operations and problem solving: A bilingual (English-Spanish) second-grade class makes a bar graph based on the number of marshmallows that they estimate each person in their class would eat on a camping trip. Students then determine how many people one bag of marshmallows would feed, and how many bags to take on the trip.	Grade 2; urban elementary	Racially/ethnically/ linguistically diverse classroom; predominantly Latino students, with many English learners, some white

Fig. 12.1. A table providing profiles of four selected lessons

Descriptions of Selected Lessons

Title	Content/lesson description	Grade/ school	Demographic information
Valentine Exchange (video 42)	Patterns and problem solving: A bilingual (English-Spanish) fourth-grade class uses a Valentine's Day card exchange problem to explore mathematical relationships. Students start with a smaller version of the task and then calculate the number of cards needed if all students in the class (24) exchange valentines. Students discover patterns and are asked to explain their strategies and reasoning.	Grade 4; urban elementary	Racially/ethnically/ linguistically diverse classroom; predominantly Latino students, with many English learners, some Native American students, some white
Questioning Data (video 32)	Data analysis: The lesson begins with a discussion of a local newspaper article describing mall owners' desire to institute a dress code for shoppers and a survey that students conducted related to the article. Next, students work in small groups to interpret graphs from various newspapers or to organize data from surveys that they designed about topics of personal interest. The lesson ends with a group discussion of students' interpretations and questions.	Grades 4–6; urban elementary	Racially/ethnically diverse classroom; predominantly Latino students, with some white students, some African American students

The video numbers provided are the numbers of the videos on the website www.learner.org.

Fig. 12.1—*Continued*

Analysis of Selected Lessons Using MML Tool

Our intent in this section is to use the MML tool to focus close attention on selected aspects of each lesson that support the mathematics learning of ELLs. We invite readers to generate additional ideas and examples.

Task lens analysis

We begin by using the task lens to analyze the strengths and structures of the mathematical tasks for supporting the mathematics learning of ELL students.

High cognitive demand tasks had multiple entry points and solution strategies

Each lesson featured a mathematical task with a high cognitive demand—that is, the task required students to execute mathematical procedures in ways that evidenced connections and understanding or to "do mathematics," such as exploring relationships among representations, generating explanations, and justifying solutions (Stein et al. 2000). For example, the main problem-solving task in the "Marshmallows" lesson asked students to figure out how many children one bag of marshmallows would feed if each child ate six marshmallows, and to explain their solution. Solving this division problem required figuring out how many groups of six marshmallows were in the bag, and reasoning about any "leftover" marshmallows. For second-grade students, who probably had not been introduced to a formal procedure for division, this task presented a high cognitive demand. The task also supported a variety of possible solution strategies, such as skip counting by six, modeling the problem by partitioning off groups of six and counting the number of groups, or using number fact knowledge.

Similarly, the "Questioning Data" lesson included two multiple-strategy, high cognitive demand tasks. One task asked students to design and conduct their own survey and to select an appropriate representation to display the results. Determining how to organize and represent data is intellectually demanding. Moreover, students were given blank pieces of paper to work with (versus worksheets that included tables or charts for students to fill in), which helped to maintain the task's high cognitive demand. Additionally, by requiring students to generate their own questions and representations, the task supported multiple entry points and a range of different solutions. The second task required students to critically interpret graphs from a newspaper and to pose questions for the graph's authors. Once again, these are high cognitive demand activities. This task also afforded multiple entry points (students selected graphs on the basis of their interests) and solution strategies (depending on the aspect of a graph that students focused on, the graphs supported a range of interpretations and analyses). Access to high cognitive demand, multiple solution strategy tasks is important for all students; research has demonstrated that such tasks are beneficial to student learning (Stein et al. 2000). This is particularly true for ELLs, who frequently have limited access to rigorous, problem-solving-oriented instruction (Khisty 1995, 1997; Oakes 1990; Yoon 2008).

Tasks involved multiple languages and/or representations

Another feature of the tasks that supported ELLs' learning is that many of the tasks—as written or posed by teachers—involved multiple languages (i.e., Spanish and English), modes of discourse (e.g., informal language, academic language) or representations (e.g., pictures, objects, written and spoken words, symbols, enactments). For example, the "Amazing Equations" lesson asked first- and second-grade students to generate addition or subtraction word problems that resulted in the number 20. This activity was linked to a set of calendar-inspired mathematics lessons, which used the date—in this case, the 20th of the month—as the result (or answer). The task invited students to generate an oral story problem, record the problem on a large sheet of paper, using words, pictures, and a number sentence, and then explain the problem to teachers and peers. By design, the task involved generating multiple representations that supported a deep and connected understanding of the mathematics concepts (e.g., addition as an action that occurred in a story, addition represented by an equation, addition represented with a physical model). Although the majority of the student work highlighted in this edited video reflected less cognitively demanding number sentences (e.g., $19 + 1 = 20$, $20 - 1 = 19$), the fact that the task allowed for a range of responses (e.g., one group of students generated a story for $5 + 5 + 5 + 5 = 20$) and required students to represent their word problems in multiple ways makes it a high cognitive demand task. The task could be further strengthened by requiring students to use numbers between 40 and 300 in their stories—a change that would offer additional opportunities to explore grade-appropriate number relationships—particularly for the second graders. This enhancement, along with the emphasis on mathematical language and multiple representations, would further support ELLs' mathematical learning.

As another example, the task in the "Valentine Exchange" lesson—figuring out how many valentines would be exchanged in a class of 24 students if every student exchanged a card with every other student—was presented in two languages (Spanish and English) and supported students' use of multiple representations. With respect to the latter requirement, students enacted the problem physically or modeled the exchanges by using a range of tools (e.g., cubes, pattern blocks, pictures) and representations (e.g., charts, lists, multiplication). Tasks that encourage multiple representations can be particularly beneficial for ELLs because they offer multimodal ways to communicate mathematical thinking (through writing, numbers, pictures, models, etc.) and to make sense of the ideas of others (Maldonado et al. 2009).

Tasks leveraged familiar cultural contexts and students' home and community-based knowledge and experiences

Finally, tasks in the selected lessons connected with a range of knowledge bases and experiences, including knowledge grounded in students' homes and communities. For example, the opening task in the "Questioning Data" lesson involved interpreting the results of a survey about a new dress code at the local shopping mall. The task encouraged students to leverage knowledge and experiences from this familiar community setting both to construct the survey and to reason about the results. Students' home and community knowledge was also given importance in the "Amazing Equations" lesson. By asking students to generate their own story problems, the task invited students to draw on their interests and experiences (e.g., family events like birthday parties, out-of-school activities like riding bicycles). Similarly, the task in the "Valentine Exchange" lesson connected with a familiar cultural practice—exchanging valentine cards—and to students' recent shared experience of exchanging valentines with their classmates. The familiar context of the task encouraged students to reenact this experience to generate possible solution strategies. Supporting mathematical learning through problem-solving tasks that tap family and community funds of knowledge is especially helpful to ELLs (Civil 2007; Civil and Kahn 2001; Turner and Celedón-Pattichis 2011; Turner et al. 2009).

Learning lens analysis

Next, we use the learning lens to analyze evidence of mathematical understanding by ELLs, including ways that ELLs communicated their mathematical thinking and the resources and knowledge that ELLs drew on to make sense of and solve mathematics tasks.

ELLs communicated understanding in multiple ways, through multiple representations

In each of the selected lessons, students (including ELLs) drew on a range of resources and representations to communicate their mathematical thinking. For example, in the "Valentine Exchange" lesson, ELLs used their dominant language (in this case, Spanish) to pose questions, make comments, and share solution strategies. During the first portion of the lesson, Armando shared his solution to a smaller version of the main task (i.e., the number of valentines exchanged by three, and then four, people). He drew his strategy on the chalkboard, using both pictures and symbols to represent the exchanges, and then explained the representation in Spanish. Not only did Armando communicate his understanding, but he did so in ways that supported other students in making sense of his ideas (e.g., using multiple representations).

In the "Amazing Equations" lesson, students also communicated their mathematical reasoning in multiple ways. For example, students created a physical model of two birthday cakes with ten candles each, represented the number of candles by using a number sentence (10 + 10 = 20), and then explained their "story" orally to the teacher. During the whole-group portion of the lesson, students stated word problems orally and then interpreted a number sentence and picture representation for each story. The fact that the lesson encouraged students to communicate mathematical thinking in multiple ways suggests that this lesson would have supported ELLs' opportunities to demonstrate their understanding. In fact, research has shown that encouraging ELLs to amplify their communication with multiple resources and representations maximizes their opportunities to communicate mathematical thinking and therefore contributes to more equitable opportunities to learn (Dominguez 2005; Maldonado et al. 2009; Moschkovich 1999; Turner, Domínguez, et al. 2012).

ELLs drew on a range of resources to support understanding, including L1, peers, family, and prior knowledge and experiences

In each of the selected lessons, ELLs leveraged various experiences and resources to support them in making sense of and solving the problem-solving tasks. In the "Marshmallows" lesson, ELLs drew on family and peers as resources to engage in the main mathematical task—"If one student eats six marshmallows, how many children will one bag of marshmallows feed?" Students engaged in a mathematical dialogue with their families to determine a "reasonable amount of marshmallows one person could eat" and used that information to construct a graph. Later in the lesson, one student, Marisa, shared a possible strategy—forming groups of six marshmallows—and other students built on this idea to solve the task. Once had they formed groups of six, another student, Erika, pointed out that there were four marshmallows left over. Her comment prompted Marisa to reason that the extra marshmallows might feed a child who wanted a smaller portion (another example of using a peer as a resource). ELLs also drew on Spanish as a resource to support understanding. For example, in Erika's group, students wrote an explanation of their strategy in Spanish. When prompted by the teacher, Erika read the explanation aloud, and the teacher translated it into English. The opportunity to write and talk about the task in her first language (Spanish) may have supported Erika's understanding—and the understanding of other students in her group.

Similarly, in the "Questioning Data" lesson, students drew on a range of resources to support their engagement in and understanding of the task. For example, when two students were working together to determine an appropriate representation for their survey data, the teacher invited Miguel, a student who had previously misused a Venn diagram, to talk about how a Venn diagram might be appropriate for the two students' data. These students could then use Miguel's idea as a resource to support their own understanding. Furthermore, when students interpreted graphs from the newspaper, they drew on prior knowledge and experiences, including mathematical knowledge and out-of-school–based knowledge, to inform their interpretations. For instance, two students questioned why survey responses about overseas visitors to the United States totaled more than 100 percent, drawing on prior mathematical knowledge supporting the idea that percentages of a whole should total 100. The students then drew on other knowledge and experiences—specifically, the idea that people may have more than one reason for visiting—to explain why the total exceeded 100. Research supports the argument that historically underrepresented groups (including ELLs) benefit from instruction that draws on students' multiple knowledge bases, including their cultural, linguistic, and community-based knowledge (Civil 2002; González, Moll, and Amanti 2005; Ladson-Billings 1995; Stein et al. 2000; Turner, Celedón-Pattichis, and Marshall 2008), suggesting that ELLs would fare well in mathematics lessons like "Questioning Data."

Teaching lens analysis

We continue by using the teaching lens to analyze specific instructional practices that support the participation and mathematical learning of ELL students.

Positioning students for active participation in mathematical discourse

Each lesson offered examples of intentional teaching moves that positioned ELLs to participate actively and make valuable contributions to mathematical discussions. In the "Marshmallows" lesson, the teacher, Mrs. Torrejón, recorded students' mathematical observations about the graph. She explained, "The reason why I write notes up is because I want the children to link reading, writing, and speech always with whatever they do." For instance, one student, Jaime, observed that 6 had the most, and 8 the second most (data points). Mrs. Torrejón asked him to repeat his observations more slowly so she could write down his ideas. By eliciting students' thinking, and recording and revoicing their ideas, Mrs. Torrejón positioned students such as Jaime as valuable contributors to mathematical discourse.

Similarly, in the "Valentine Exchange" lesson, Armando, a native Spanish speaker, was invited to present his solution to the problem about how many valentines would be exchanged among four people. Previously, several students and the teacher, Ms. Olivas, had enacted the twelve exchanges. By inviting Armando to explain a different strategy, Ms. Olivas positioned him as someone with important mathematical ideas to share with the class. When asked, "How many valentines do you have, Armando? (*¿Cuántos valentinos tienes?*), he counted the exchanges aloud in Spanish, finishing with "*doce*" (twelve). Ms. Olivas restated his solution in English as she pointed to his representation:

> *Ms. Olivas:* Twelve. There were twelve valentines [*pointing to the initials that Armando used to keep track of each valentine exchanged*] that were given with four people.

By revoicing Armando's solution to the class, Ms. Olivas publicly affirmed his understanding, again positioning him as a competent mathematical learner.

These teachers demonstrated specific ways to position students to share their mathematical knowledge publicly with others. These positioning moves enabled ELLs to participate actively in mathematical discussions and highlighted their ideas as valuable contributions to the mathematical discourse of the class (Yamakawa, Forman, and Ansell 2005).

Teachers used multiple resources to support ELLs' mathematical understanding

All four lessons highlighted instances of teachers drawing on multiple resources (e.g., mathematical, family, language, peer, interests, cultural) to support students' mathematical understanding. For example, in the "Marshmallows" lesson, students prepared for a class camping trip by creating a line plot based on a mathematical conversation with family members about how many marshmallows is a reasonable number to eat. To construct the graph, the teacher, Mrs. Torrejón, tapped into students' prior mathematical knowledge by asking specific questions, such as, "Who thinks they have the least (or most) amount of marshmallows?" She explained the importance of the information:

> *Mrs. Torrejón:* Getting this information from you is going to help Mrs. Torrejón decide what numbers I'm going to need right here [*pointing to the horizontal axis*].

Next, students plotted their data and discussed the graph. Mrs. Torrejón often revoiced students' mathematical ideas and pressed for further reasoning, asking such questions as, "You would choose six; why?" Through this combination of linking to family mathematical knowledge, leveraging students' prior mathematical knowledge to co-construct a mathematical representation, and emphasizing mathematical language, the teachers ensured that ELLs' mathematical understanding was well supported.

In the "Amazing Equations" lesson, as students created their stories, the teacher, Ms. Pearson, stressed mathematical language and multiple representations—oral and written language, symbolic notation (equations), and pictures as resources to support students' understandings. For example, in the opening activity, one student, Nate, told a story about 21 dinosaurs chasing Ms. Pearson and one of the dinosaurs leaving for "Charlie's house." Nate concluded, "Then I had 20 altogether." Ms. Pearson wrote 21 and 1 vertically on the board and asked, "What kind of a problem is this?" Nate replied, "Take away." Ms. Pearson revoiced this statement to the class while writing the symbol for the operation, "We have to put our take away sign in here. Now, read Nate's equation." Ms. Pearson might have offered further support for her students' development of mathematical language by also using the more precise term *subtraction*. Moving from everyday language to more precise mathematical language while also connecting to other representations can strengthen mathematical learning for ELLs.

In contrast to providing a single support strategy (e.g., focusing only on vocabulary development), Ms. Torrejón and Ms. Pearson effectively combined several resources, including familiar contexts, student interests, and prior mathematical knowledge, as well as mathematical language and multiple representations, to support students' participation in mathematical discourse and their mathematical understanding.

Strategic questioning and references to student work to support students' mathematical thinking

Teachers in each of the lessons used strategic questioning and references to student work to elicit and clarify ELLs' mathematical thinking. In the "Questioning Data" lesson, the questioning techniques used by the teacher, Ms. Darcy, helped her identify mathematical strengths and areas of need. Some questions drew attention to the purpose of the graph (e.g., "Who would want to know this information?"). Other questions were aimed at refining ideas and clarifying confusion (e.g., "Why does that bother you that it doesn't equal 100 percent?"). Furthermore, her questions were often closely linked to students' work, as in the following:

> *Ms. Darcy:*   If I came up to you and said sometimes I drink Pepsi and sometimes I drink Diet Pepsi, where would I put my mark? [*pointing to the students' data categories*].

Research suggests that Ms. Darcy's frequent use of probing questions that were grounded in students' work would benefit ELLs and help to clarify many sources of potential confusion or misunderstanding (Khisty and Chval 2002; Maldonado et al. 2009; Moschkovich 1999).

Similarly, in the "Valentine Exchange" lesson, Ms. Olivas used strategic questioning connected to student work to support ELLs' mathematical thinking. For example, in one group interaction, she focused the boys' attention on the solution offered by one student, Winston. As she pointed to the number 24, she said, "I want you to look at what Winston has here: 24 and 24... What does the 24 mean?" Winston, a Spanish-dominant student, responded, "Twenty-four students and 24 Valentines." Ms. Olivas revoiced Winston's idea with a clarifying statement and question, "And you each had a valentine... If you started making exchanges, would there be 24 exchanges?" Winston nodded his head affirmatively while another tablemate used blocks to model the exchanges and concluded, "You get 48." Next, Blas, the third student in the group, replied, "Forty-eight is probably not the answer." Ms. Olivas posed another clarifying question to the boys, "Do you think this answer [48] is too big or too small?" Blas noted, "It is probably much larger," pointing to his tablemate's physical model to demonstrate additional exchanges that were not represented.

Ms. Olivas's strategic use of questioning, accompanied by specific references to students' mathematical representations, helped students like Winston, who was developing his English language skills (academic English and everyday English), articulate mathematical thinking and illuminate partial understandings and confusions (see chapter 2). Instead of explicitly correcting students' strategies or use of language, Ms. Olivas used probing questions and students' work to invite ELLs to reflect on and potentially revise their ideas.

Both Ms. Darcy and Ms. Olivas stressed the importance of probing students' mathematical thinking and providing opportunities for ELLs to critically analyze and reflect on their work rather than focus solely on the "correct" answer or "correct" terms (see chapter 2). These strategies challenge the conventional mathematics teaching wisdom that immediate correction of mathematical language and student mistakes is essential for supporting mathematics learning of ELLs.

Power and participation lens analysis

Last, we use the power and participation lens to analyze aspects of each lesson that supported both ELLs' participation in mathematical discourse and the status of their contributions.

Multiple participation structures facilitated ELLs' opportunities to communicate their mathematical thinking

The selected lessons illustrated multiple ways in which ELLs participated in discussions that emphasized mathematical thinking and problem solving. These participation structures included whole-class involvement in mathematics talks and debriefs, participation by individual students in directly modeling a solution, and collaborative engagement of small groups or pairs in co-constructing their solutions (see chapter 2). For example, in the "Amazing Equations" lesson, students engaged in a whole-class math discussion, followed by a small-group session where students constructed another story, using words, pictures, and equations. Some groups initially had trouble coming up with a story that reflected everyone's contributions. Ms. Pearson deliberately fostered shared mathematical authority by insisting that the group come up with one story and suggested that they try to use all group members' ideas (shoes, Butterfingers, and camcorders). At the end of the lesson, students shared their stories during a whole-class discussion. These varied participation structures are important because they provide ELLs' with multiple opportunities to share their thinking and to engage with the ideas of others (Brenner 1998; Enyedy et al. 2008).

ELLs' mathematical authority is strategically supported by teachers

In all four videos, evidence that mathematical authority was shared among multiple students, rather than concentrated in a few, was clear. Teachers facilitated this shared authority by strategically highlighting particular students' contributions and by encouraging group accountability. For example, on several occasions in the "Marshmallows" lesson, Mrs. Torrejón highlighted an important mathematical question or insight of a specific student for the group to consider:

Mrs. Torrejón: Marisa, sweetheart, share your idea with the whole group.
Mrs. Torrejón: Felicia, did you hear what your friend Valerie said over here?
Mrs. Torrejón: Savanna, why would you cut them [*leftover marshmallows*] in half?

All of these questions serve as ways to address status issues through public assignment of competence to a particular student (Boaler 2008; Cohen 1986), and as ways to create opportunities for students to share mathematical insights.

Similarly, in the "Questioning Data" lesson, Ms. Darcy strategically used Miguel's Venn diagram representation to support another group's data organization need. Earlier, Ms. Darcy talked with Miguel about his representation and noted that the data in the region of overlap, marked "don't know," did not make sense. Then, later in the class, Ms. Darcy asked Miguel to come to another group and share his Venn diagram representation for their data set. She explained to the group, "Let me show Miguel this. He was trying to do a diagram that I think will help you guys." By asking Miguel to explore whether a Venn diagram would appropriately represent this group's data, Ms. Darcy assigned competence to Miguel and distributed mathematical authority across the various students (e.g., Miguel brought knowledge about Venn diagrams, other students brought knowledge of the data set and their findings). Miguel was positioned as an important mathematical resource and was able to make a valuable contribution to support his peers' mathematical learning. In summary, Ms. Darcy facilitated opportunities to distribute mathematical knowledge through her questioning techniques, by positioning students as mathematical resources, and by her active restraint from imposing her own mathematics strategies on her students. Equitable participation was explicitly encouraged, which research shows benefits ELL students as well (Cohen 1986; Featherstone et al. 2011).

These lessons demonstrate specific ways in which equitable participation can be structured to support mathematical learning. This happens in classrooms where the mathematical authority is shared and status issues are minimized (Boaler 2008; Boaler and Staples 2008; Featherstone et al. 2011). When well supported, all students—especially ELLs—can actively participate and make valuable contributions to mathematical problem solving and discussion (Khisty and Chval 2002; Maldonado et al. 2009; Moschkovich 1999, 2002; Turner, Domínguez, et al. 2012).

Concluding Remarks and Next Steps

The Multiple Mathematical Lens tool is aimed at helping teachers consider specific dimensions of lessons that are important for the mathematics learning of ELLs. By examining a mathematics lesson from a *task lens* perspective, teachers focus attention on key design components, such as cognitive demand, multiple entry points, and multiple representations. Taking a *learning lens* perspective helps them target the multiple knowledge resources (e.g., math, language, family, peer, community) that ELLs may use to solve problems and communicate their mathematical understanding to one another and to the teacher. Examining the lesson through the *teaching lens* allows teachers to see the varied and intentional instructional strategies that extend and clarify student mathematical thinking. And using the *power and participation lens* highlights for them specific ways in which ELLs' participation in mathematical discourse can be equitably structured and their mathematical knowledge valued and shared.

We envision numerous ways in which the MML tool could be used to design and refine effective mathematics lessons for ELLs. Teachers could use the MML tool to analyze their own lesson or unit. Alternatively, it could be part of a peer observation of a lesson. Or it could be used to examine curriculum materials. It could also highlight specific areas for lesson improvement, such as in evaluating the use of multiple representations in a task, making connections to family mathematics knowledge in a lesson, or creating opportunities for ELLs to communicate their ideas in multiple ways, including in their home language.

With the increase of ELLs in our nation's schools (National Center for Education Statistics 2006), teachers need additional tools to effectively address the multiple mathematics education strengths and needs of these students. The MML tool is a straightforward method to assist in the lesson planning and reflection process. We encourage readers to use this tool in ways that will benefit their instructional practice and facilitate the mathematics learning and development of ELLs.

References

Bartell, Tonya G., Mary Q. Foote, Julia Aguirre, Amy Roth McDuffie, Corey Drake, and Erin Turner. "Preparing Pre K–8 Teachers to Connect Children's Mathematical Thinking and Community-Based Funds of Knowledge." In *Proceedings of the 32nd Annual Meeting of the North American Chapter of the International Group for the Psychology of Mathematics Education,* edited by Patricia Brosnan, Diana B. Erchick, and Lucia Flevares, pp. 1183–91. Columbus: Ohio State University, 2010.

Boaler, Jo. "Promoting 'Relational Equity' and High Mathematics Achievement through an Innovative Mixed-Ability Approach." *British Educational Research Journal* 34 (April 2008): 167–94.

Boaler, Jo, and Megan Staples. "Creating Mathematical Futures through an Equitable Teaching Approach: The Case of Railside School." *Teachers College Record* 110, no. 3 (2008): 608–45.

Brenner, Mary Elizabeth. "Development of Mathematical Communication in Problem Solving Groups by Language Minority Students." *Bilingual Research Journal* 22 (Spring/Fall 1998): 149–74.

Civil, Marta. "Culture and Mathematics: A Community Approach." *Journal of Intercultural Studies* 23, no. 2 (2002): 133–48.

———. "Building on Community Knowledge: An Avenue to Equity in Mathematics Education." In *Improving Access to Mathematics: Diversity and Equity in the Classroom,* edited by Na'ilah Suad Nasir and Paul Cobb, pp. 105–17. New York: Teachers College Press, 2007.

———. "Culture and Mathematics: A Community Approach." *Journal of Intercultural Studies* 23, no. 2 (2002): 133–48.

Civil, Marta, and Leslie H. Khan. "Mathematics Instruction Developed from a Garden Theme." *Teaching Children Mathematics* 7 (March 2001): 400–405.

Cohen, Elizabeth. *Designing Groupwork: Strategies for the Heterogeneous Classroom.* New York: Teachers College Press, 1986.

Domínguez, Higinio. "Bilingual Students' Articulation and Gesticulation of Mathematical Knowledge during Problem Solving." *Bilingual Research Journal* 29 (Summer 2005): 269–93.

Enyedy, Noel, Laurie Rubel, Viviana Castelló, Shiuli Mukhopadhyay, Indigo Esmonde, and Walter Secada. "Revoicing in a Multilingual Classroom." *Mathematical Thinking and Learning* 10 (April 2008): 134–62.

Featherstone, Helen, Sandra Crespo, Lisa Jilk, Joy Oslund, Amy Parks, and Marcy Wood. *Smarter Together: Collaboration and Equity in the Elementary Math Classroom.* Reston, Va.: NCTM, 2011.

González, N., R. Andrade, M. Civil, and L. Moll. "Bridging Funds of Distributed Knowledge: Creating Zones of Practices in Mathematics." *Journal of Education for Students Placed at Risk* 6, nos. 1 and 2 (2001): 115–32.

González, Norma, Luis Moll, and Cathy Amanti, eds. *Funds of Knowledge: Theorizing Practices in Households, Communities, and Classrooms.* Mahwah, N.J.: Lawrence Erlbaum, 2005.

Khisty, Lena L. "Making Inequality: Issues of Language and Meaning in Mathematics Teaching with Hispanic Students." In *New Directions for Equity in Mathematics Education,* edited by Walter G. Secada, Elizabeth Fennema, and Lisa Byrd Adajian, pp. 279–97. Cambridge: Cambridge University Press, 1995.

———. "Making Mathematics Accessible to Latino Students: Rethinking Instructional Practice." In *Multicultural and Gender Equity in the Mathematics Classroom: The Gift of Diversity,* 1997 Yearbook of the National Council of Teachers of Mathematics (NCTM), edited by Janet Trentacosta, pp. 92–101. Reston, Va.: NCTM, 1997.

Khisty, Lena L., and Kathryn B. Chval. "Pedagogic Discourse and Equity in Mathematics: When Teachers' Talk Matters." *Mathematics Education Research Journal* 14 (December 2002): 154–68.

Ladson-Billings, Gloria. "Toward a Theory of Culturally Relevant Pedagogy." *American Educational Research Journal* 32, no. 3 (1995): 465–91.

Maldonado, Luz, Erin Turner, Higinio Domínguez, and Susan Empson. "English-Language Learners Learning from and Contributing to Mathematical Discussion." In *Mathematics for Every Student: Responding to Diversity, Grades Pre-K–5*, edited by Dorothy Y. White and Julie Sliva Spitzer, pp. 7–22. Reston, Va.: NCTM, 2009.

Moschkovich, Judit. "Supporting the Participation of English Language Learners in Mathematical Discussions." *For the Learning of Mathematics* 19, no. 1 (1999): 11–19.

———. "A Situated and Sociocultural Perspective of Bilingual Mathematics Learning." *Mathematical Thinking and Learning* 4, nos. 2 and 3 (2002): 189–212.

National Center for Education Statistics (NCES). *Public Elementary and Secondary Students, Staff, Schools, and School Districts: School Year 2003–2004*. NCES 2006-307. Washington, D.C.: U.S. Department of Education, 2006. http://nces.ed.gov/fastfacts/display.asp?id=96.

National Council of Teachers of Mathematics (NCTM). *Principles and Standards for School Mathematics*. Reston, Va.: National Council of Teachers of Mathematics, 2000.

Oakes, Jeannie. *Multiplying Inequalities: The Effects of Race, Social Class, and Tracking on Opportunities to Learn Mathematics and Science*. Santa Monica, Calif.: Rand, 1990.

Stein, Mary K., Margaret S. Smith, Marjorie A. Henningsen, and Edward A. Silver. *Implementing Standards-Based Mathematics Instruction: A Casebook for Professional Development*. New York: Teachers College, 2000.

Turner, Erin, and Sylvia Celedón-Pattichis. "Problem Solving and Mathematical Discourse among Latino/a Kindergarten Students: An Analysis of Opportunities to Learn." *Journal of Latinos in Education* 10, no. 2 (2011): 146–69.

Turner, Erin, Sylvia Celedón-Pattichis, and Mary A. Marshall. "Opportunities to Learn Problem Solving and Mathematics Discourse among Latino/a Kindergarten Students." In *Promoting High Participation and Success in Mathematics by Hispanic Students: Examining Opportunities and Probing Promising Practices*, Research Monograph of TODOS: Mathematics for ALL, edited by Richard Kitchen and Edward Silver, pp. 19–42. Washington, D.C.: National Education Association Press, 2008.

Turner, Erin, Sylvia Celedón-Pattichis, Mary Marshall, and Alan Tennison. "'*Fíjense Amorcitos, Les Voy a Contar Una Historia*': The Power of Story to Support Solving and Discussing Mathematical Problems among Latino/a Kindergarten Students." In *Mathematics for Every Student: Responding to Diversity, Grades Pre-K–5*, edited by Dorothy Y. White and Julie Sliva Spitzer, pp. 23–43. Reston, Va.: NCTM, 2009.

Turner, Erin, Higinio Domínguez, Luz Maldonado, and Susan Empson. "English Learners' Participation in Mathematical Discussion: Shifting Positionings and Dynamic Identities." Special Equity Issue, *Journal for Research in Mathematics Education*, 2012, http://www.nctm.org/jrme/equity.

Turner, Erin, Corey Drake, Amy Roth McDuffie, Julia M. Aguirre, Tonya Bartell, and Mary Q. Foote. "Promoting Equity in Mathematics Teacher Preparation: A Framework for Advancing Teacher Learning of Children's Multiple Mathematics Knowledge Bases." *Journal of Mathematics Teacher Education* 15 (February 2012): 67–82.

Yamakawa, Yukari, Ellice Forman, and Ellen Ansell. "The Role of Positioning in Constructing an Identity in a Third Grade Mathematics Classroom." In *Investigating Classroom Interaction: Methodologies in Action*, edited by Kristiina Kumpulainen, Cindy Hmelo-Silver, and Margarida Cesar, 179–202. Rotterdam, The Netherlands: Sense Publishers, 2009.

Yoon, Bogum. "Uninvited Guests: The Influence of Teachers' Roles and Pedagogies on the Positioning of English Language Learners in the Regular Classroom." *American Educational Research Journal* 45, no. 2 (2008): 495–522.

Chapter 13

Professional Development Suggestions and Resources

by Nora G. Ramirez and Sylvia Celedón-Pattichis

- Lesson in Portuguese (video)
- Triangle Lesson (video)
- Reflections on Teaching Perimeter (first-person notes)
- Fractions on a Number Line (video)
- Arrays: A Collaboratively Planned Lesson (first-person account)
- TODOS LIVE! Presentations
- TODOS Teaching English Learners Mathematics (TELM) Resources:

     Introduction to TELM (PowerPoint presentation)

     TELM Participant Agenda (template)

     TELM Agenda for December 6, 2007 (sample)

     TELM Overall Goal and Plan (sample)
- Planning a Mathematics Lesson for ELLs (worksheet template)
- NCSM Position Paper on Teaching Math to ELLs
- Online Resources (list)

The intent of this chapter is to share ideas, lessons, and resources. Brief descriptions in the chapter have connected resources at www.nctm.org/more4u. We present two lessons that have been successfully used with both preservice and in-service teachers, one in written format and the other as a video clip. We share a video of a classroom lesson and suggest ideas for its use with teachers, and we include additional vignettes, reflections, and short clips from teachers and coaches of ELLs. In addition, we introduce here and have included at the More4U website some recordings of TODOS LIVE! online interactive professional development sessions that we think you will find useful in your work. Finally, we share a template for lesson planning that attends to the strategies that are essential for teaching mathematics to ELLs. We also invite you to explore additional resources and links that are provided at www.nctm.org/more4u.

We begin our presentation of resources with a mathematics lesson designed by Elsa Medina for the purpose of giving teachers an understanding of the experience of learning mathematics as language learners. In chapter 1, Elsa shared the story of her experiences as an ELL, and these experiences have been an impetus for her to give teachers a small glimpse of what some of their ELL students may be experiencing in the classroom.

by Elsa Medina

A Lesson in Spanish on Number Sequences

I often present a thirty- to forty-minute lesson in Spanish at summer workshops and some conferences to current or future mathematics teachers, and the lesson always ends with a rich discussion. The lesson is basic-level mathematics, so the content itself does not become an issue, and we can focus on the language issues. I start the lesson by reminding the participants of sequences of numbers that are very familiar to them, such as natural, even, or integer numbers. I then ask participants to provide an example of a sequence of numbers that they know. Someone, usually a Spanish-speaking person, is likely to suggest odd or prime numbers as an example. Up to this point, I have conducted the discussion without any handouts or writing of complete sentences on the board. After a couple of examples of sequences familiar to the participants, I introduce the sequence of triangular numbers and ask the group to find the next triangular number. I distribute a handout and ask them to answer the questions on it. An example of the questions on the handout appears in figure 13.1.

Podemos representar números entros mediante collecciones de puntos. Cada punto representa una unidad. El número uno es representado con un punto. El número dos es representado por dos puntos, etc.

Cada colleccion de puntos de los números uno, tres, seis, y diez se pueden organizar para formar un triángulo: es por eso que estos números son llamados números triangulares.

n	1	2	3	4	
T_n	1	3	6	10	son números triangulares

a) Observa como el siguiente número se forma a partir del anterior y escribe los tres siguientes números triangulares.

Fig. 13.1. Triangular numbers (handout 1)

I ask the participants to work in groups to answer the questions. After ten to fifteen minutes, I distribute a second handout, which has pictures, highlighted key words, and cardinal numbers written in both numerical and word form. Figure 13.2 shows an example of how the questions are presented in the second handout.

Podemos representar números entros mediante collecciones de puntos.
Cada punto representa una unidad. El número uno es representado con
un punto. El número dos es representado por dos puntos, etc.

Cada colleccion de puntos de los números uno, tres, seis, y diez se pueden
organizar para formar un triángulo: es por eso que estos números son
llamados números triangulares.

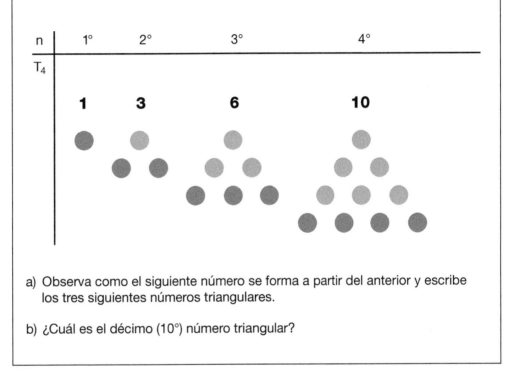

a) Observa como el siguiente número se forma a partir del anterior y escribe
   los tres siguientes números triangulares.

b) ¿Cuál es el décimo (10°) número triangular?

Fig. 13.2. Triangular numbers (handout 2)

After the participants have time to work on the second handout, volunteers present
their solution to the group. I ask participants who don't speak Spanish to write answers
on the board to show that even if they don't speak the language, they can still contribute
to the class. We then finish the mathematics lesson and have a discussion of the challenges that the participants experienced and how they dealt with them. This discussion is
framed around a set of questions given to the group:

Discussion Questions and Common Answers

1. What frustrations did you experience during this lesson?
    *   I was frustrated and wanted to leave the presentation at the beginning but
        decided to stay.
    *   I was so frustrated trying to follow you that I gave up on that.
    *   I tuned out since I could not keep up with your questions.

- I know how to do the math but was very frustrated because I could not contribute to the discussion and share my answers.
- I wanted time to think and figure things out, but I felt that there was too much going on for me to follow.
- I was overwhelmed by not knowing the language—now I know how my students feel.

2. How did you handle or deal with not knowing the language?
   - I tuned out.
   - I stopped trying to understand the instructions and gave up on the lesson.
   - I asked someone to help me translate.
   - I worked individually.
   - I did not want you to ask me any questions.
   - I waited for others to do the work.

3. What strategies did you use to help you carry out the task?
   - The handout was helpful with the pictures.
   - I tried to make sense of key words.
   - I asked people who spoke Spanish but felt bad bothering them when they were also trying to answer the questions.
   - Working in groups helped me to see what others were doing.
   - It would be nice to have an opportunity to work individually as well as in groups.

When I have presented this lesson, there are usually people who also speak Spanish (at different levels). These participants mention that they were happy to help but also felt some frustration because they wanted time to answer the questions without having to translate for others. This was especially true for those participants who speak Spanish but don't know the mathematical terms in Spanish.

Participants always share their feelings of frustration, their strong desire to simply give up (some do), and their discovery that they can now relate to some of the students who have given up in their classrooms. They also mention that they never realized how overwhelming it can be for someone who does not speak the language to have to learn both mathematics and English at the same time. Furthermore, they say how happy they are to be done with the Spanish lesson, and that they now realize that their students are in this situation an entire day at school. As an educator, I recognize that developing teachers' awareness of and sensitivity to students' issues in learning mathematics in a second language can benefit their English language learners.

A Mathematics Lesson Taught in Portuguese

contributed by Elmano Costa

Elmano Costa teaches at California State University, Stanislaus. He shares a video (see Lesson in Portuguese at www.nctm.org/more4u) of a mathematics lesson taught to pre-service teachers in Portuguese to help educators experience learning as ELLs. As you view the video, take note of what you understood and what Elmano Costa did to aid you in comprehending the mathematics, the instructions, and the dialogue.

A Fourth-Grade Lesson on Triangles

contributed by Jana Ward and Cathy Kinzer

Cathy Kinzer, a professor from New Mexico State University, collaborates with Jana Ward, who is in her second year of teaching, in presenting the Triangle Lesson video (see www.nctm.org/more4u). This video shows a lesson taught by Jana Ward at the end of the school year to twenty-five students in a monolingual (English) inclusion classroom in Hatch, New Mexico, a rural farming town in southern New Mexico. The school has a large population of English language learners and is designated a Title I school, with all students receiving free lunch. More than 50 percent of the students in the classroom are ELLs, two of whom have Individualized Education Plans (IEPs) that include accommo-dations for mathematics learning disabilities. The ELLs are at varying stages of English language acquisition, and all the students are strategically seated in groups determined by their English language proficiency level. Each group has at least one student who can serve as a strong English language model, as well as other ELLs who can provide first-language support if needed.

The following are some suggestions for using this video (see www.nctm.org/more4u for specific tools named below):

- Identify ELL teaching strategies individually or in a professional development setting (see chapter 2).
- Use the Language Demands in Mathematics Lessons Tool (see chapter 10).
- Use the Learning Lens, Power and Participation Lens, Teaching Lens, and Task Lens (see chapter 12).
- Use the Classroom Observation Protocol and the Lesson Reflection Template (see chapter 9).

Reflections on Teaching Perimeter

by Erin Salazar

Erin Salazar's fourth-grade classroom in south Phoenix, Arizona, consists of students who are all ELLs. In her first-person notes (see www.nctm.org/more4u), Erin shares her reflections on students' learning when she provided them with an opportunity to devel-op an understanding of a concept in a context that was accessible to the students before "teaching" them related vocabulary terms and formulas for finding perimeter and area.

by Victoria Enoch

Fractions on a Number Line

Victoria Enoch teaches third grade in a school in south Phoenix, Arizona. She shares a brief video clip (see Fractions on a Number Line at www.nctm.org/more4u) that shows her questioning an ELL to facilitate the student's recognition of an error when placing fractions on a number line. Positioning the student as a competent problem solver, Victoria asked guiding qustions that motivated the student to use her fingers on the number line to reason mathematically. In the moments following what occurred in the video clip, the student explained her strategy to the class, and many students began using their fingers as tools. Victoria shares the fact that she is now asking more questions and not telling as much. Consequently, she is finding that her students, many who are ELLs, can generate their own strategies and solutions.

by Andrew Hutchinson

Arrays: A Collaboratively Planned Lesson

Andrew Hutchinson, a district mathematics coach in Roger Sherman School, Meriden, Connecticut, shares a lesson (see Arrays: A Collaboratively Planned Lesson at www.nctm.org/more4u) planned by a group of mathematics coaches and classroom teachers. He describes and reflects on the multiplication lesson that he taught and the posters that the group used to give students visuals of new terminology related to arrays.

TODOS LIVE! Professional Development Sessions

In the 2010–11 school year, TODOS: Mathematics for ALL, a professional organization whose mission is to enhance the mathematics learning for all students—in particular, Hispanic and Latino students—offered some online interactive professional development sessions for its members. TODOS has generously given us permission to include some recordings and corresponding PowerPoint presentations in the online material for this book (see TODOS Live! Presentations at www.nctm.org/more4u). Brief descriptions of the included sessions follow (TODOS members can access other recordings at www.todos-math.org).

Kathryn Chval

TODOS LIVE!

In her presentation, "Achieving Excellence and Equity for Latino Students: A View through Their Eyes," Kathryn Chval, also an author of chapter 5, shares what she has learned from a study of Latino ELLs in which elementary students film their mathematics classrooms by using head-mounted video cameras.

Nora Ramirez and Bob McDonald

TODOS LIVE!

Nora G. Ramirez and Bob McDonald, TODOS vice president, describe and share materials for a professional development project at the middle school level, "Teaching

Mathematics to English Language Learners (TELM)," which included a professional learning community and culminated in a public research lesson. For a PowerPoint presentation and examples of materials used in the project, see TODOS Teaching English Learners Mathematics (TELM) Resources at www.nctm.org/more4u.

Melissa Hosten

TODOS LIVE!

"Supporting Proof for ELLs, Struggling Learners, and Others," presented by Melissa Hosten, a mathematics specialist in the Chandler Unified School District, Chandler, Arizona, describes a strategy for supporting high school students with disabilities, struggling learners, and ELLs in writing and understanding proofs.

Heather Navarro

TODOS LIVE!

In "Multiplication from Concrete to Abstract," the second part of a two-part session, Heather Navarro, a third grade teacher in the Chandler Unified School District, Chandler, Arizona, shares a lesson sequence focusing on big ideas in multiplication while guiding classroom discourse that involves problems in context to aid ELLs to move from concrete models to abstract understanding while reinforcing language proficiency.

Planning a Mathematics Lesson for ELLs

We provide a lesson template, Planning a Mathematics Lesson for ELLs (see www.nctm.org/more4u) for use as a guide in preparing mathematics lessons for ELLs. The questions in the template are intended to help teachers consider important aspects presented in chapter 2. Although addressing all of these questions simultaneously may be overwhelming to some, we suggest paying particular attention to areas that may need improvement in your classroom. It is also important to collect data to verify that you are implementing these strategies effectively.

NCSM Position Paper on Teaching Math to ELLs

The National Council of Supervisors of Mathematics (NCSM) publishes the NCSM Improving Student Achievement Series, a set of position papers that provide research-based practices for classroom teachers and other educators. One of those papers, "Improving Student Achievement in Mathematics by Addressing the Needs of English Language Learners," is available at www.nctm.org/more4u, by courtesy of NCSM.

Online Resources

Included in the resources for chapter 13 at www.nctm.org/more4u is a list of related materials that are on the NCTM website and other resources that we hope that you find useful.

Index